Theology and Philosophy
in Eastern Orthodoxy

Theology and Philosophy in Eastern Orthodoxy

Essays on Orthodox Christianity and Contemporary Thought

EDITED BY

CHRISTOPH SCHNEIDER

PICKWICK *Publications* · Eugene, Oregon

THEOLOGY AND PHILOSOPHY IN EASTERN ORTHODOXY
Essays on Orthodox Christianity and Contemporary Thought

Pickwick Publications
An Imprint of Wipf and Stock Publishers
199 W. 8th Ave., Suite 3
Eugene, OR 97401

www.wipfandstock.com

PAPERBACK ISBN: 978-1-60899-421-2
HARDCOVER ISBN: 978-1-4982-4309-4
EBOOK ISBN: 978-1-4982-4308-7

Cataloguing-in-Publication data:

Names: Schneider, Christoph, editor.

Title: Theology and philosophy in Eastern Orthodoxy : essays on Orthodox Christianity and contemporary thought / edited by Christoph Schneider.

Description: Eugene, OR: Pickwick Publications, 2019 | Includes bibliographical references.

Identifiers: ISBN 978-1-60899-421-2 (paperback) | ISBN 978-1-4982-4309-4 (hardcover) | ISBN 978-1-4982-4308-7 (ebook)

Subjects: LCSH: Orthodox Eastern Church—Doctrines | Philosophy, Modern | Philosophy, Ancient | Philosophical theology | Philosophy and religion.

Classification: BX323 S36 2019 (print) | BX323 (ebook)

Manufactured in the U.S.A.   OCTOBER 21, 2019

Contents

Contributors

Christina M. Gschwandtner, Professor of Philosophy at Fordham University, New York.

David Bentley Hart has taught at the University of Virginia, the University of St. Thomas (Minnesota), Duke Divinity School, Loyola University in Baltimore, has been a visiting chair at Providence College and Saint Louis University, and has of late been a Templeton Fellow and Director's Fellow at the University of Notre Dame Institute for Advanced Study.

Sergey S. Horujy, Head Researcher, Institute of Philosophy of the Russian Academy of Science; Director, Institute of Synergic Anthropology, Moscow.

Paweł Rojek, Assistant Professor at the Jagiellonian University in Krakow, Poland.

Christoph Schneider, Academic Director at the Institute for Orthodox Christian Studies, Cambridge, UK.

Kristina Stoeckl, Professor of Sociology and Principal Investigator of the project *Postsecular Conflicts* at the University of Innsbruck, Austria.

Dmitry Uzlaner, Director of the Center for the Study of Religion at the Russian Presidential Academy of National Economy and Public Administration (RANEPA) and Research Fellow at the University of Innsbruck, Austria and Moscow School of Social and Economic Sciences (MSSES).

Rico Vitz, Professor and Chair, Department of Philosophy, Azusa Pacific University, Los Angeles, California.

Evert van der Zweerde, Professor of Social and Political Philosophy at Radboud University, Nijmegen, Netherlands.

Introduction

The Quest for a Christian Philosophy

Christoph Schneider

Orthodoxy and Orthodox theology have long become "global projects," and are no longer confined to traditionally Orthodox countries. Furthermore, the number of non-Orthodox scholars who possess in-depth knowledge about Orthodox theology and Orthodox thought is increasing. The authors who have contributed to this volume live and work in Austria, the Netherlands, Poland, Russia, the UK, and the US. The aim of this collection of essays is to reflect on the relationship between Orthodox theology and contemporary philosophy. The contributors were invited to write specialized, but at the same time accessible, essays on key philosophical topics.

The first two contributions are dedicated to Orthodox theology and political philosophy. *Evert van der Zweerde* discusses the relationship between theocracy, *sobornost'*, and democracy in the works of Vladimir Solovyov, Nikolai Berdyaev, and Ivan Ilyin. According to these thinkers, there is no strict opposition between either theocracy and democracy, or between democracy and *sobornost'*. In order to understand their main ideas, one has to pay attention to the more fundamental difference between a theocractic and an "anthropocratic" understanding of politics. It is the "anthropocratic" approach that all three thinkers reject—although they hold different views about how to realize the theocratic ideal.

Kristina Stoeckl and *Dmitry Uzlaner* reflect on the notion of the *post-secular* in contemporary Russia, focusing on the descriptive as well as normative meaning of this concept. They raise the question of whether it is possible to discern a "third way" in Russian society that avoids both a reactionary return to pre-Soviet conditions *and* an uncritical embrace of modern secularism. Yet they come to the conclusion that a profound and creative reconfiguration of the religious-secular divide that goes beyond these two extreme positions is missing in contemporary Russia.

Christina Gschwandtner takes a little-known text on Eastern Orthodoxy by Max Scheler as the starting point of her reflections on Orthodox theology and phenomenology. Drawing on ascetic texts by Evagrius of Pontus and Symeon the New Theologian, as well as on the anonymous writing *The Way of Pilgrim*, she provides a phenomenological analysis of Orthodox consciousness, discernment, and spiritual experience. She argues that Scheler's view of the Orthodox ethos as a passive, otherworldly, and apolitical quietism that pays little attention to neighborly love and social responsibility, is insufficiently nuanced and disregards important aspects of Orthodox spiritual life.

David Bentley Hart argues for the inevitability of metaphysics in Orthodox theology. For him, the concept of a wholly "post-metaphysical theology" amounts to a contradiction in terms. Hart appreciates Jean-Luc Marion's subtle phenomenological analyses, but gives an account of a religious epistemology and ontology that is more consistently based on the christological and trinitarian doctrines as well as on a non-dualistic understanding of the relationship of nature and grace. Hart refuses to view the apocalyptic novelty of the event of revelation and the metaphysical conjectures of human reason in anticipation and response to this event as mutually exclusive.

Sergey Horujy presents a summary of his *Synergic Anthropology*, an original and complex Orthodox philosophy of the self that combines Zizioulas's personalism with the Palamite doctrine of the divine energies, and aspects of secular, postmodern conceptions of the self. His aim is to establish a constructive dialogue between religious and secular thought, and to widen the horizon of Orthodox discourse on the self that is often too narrowly defined in ecclesial and eucharistic terms.

Paweł Rojek reflects on the claim that Christian truth is antinomic—a view which either leads to a radical theological irrationalism, or a non-classical logic. More specifically, he explores whether Pavel Forensky's deabsolutization of the law of identity and non-contradiction is best interpreted in terms of a paraconsistent, L-consistent, or non-monotonic logic, or whether a rhetorical understanding of his discourse about antinomy is more plausible. Rojek argues that this question cannot be conclusively answered, and that all four options express aspects of Florenky's views.

Rico Vitz begins his considerations on Orthodoxy and ethics with a brief account of the three dominant approaches in philosophical ethics: virtue ethics, deontology, and utilitarianism. He sees a particular affinity between Orthodoxy and virtue ethics and explains how the church fathers adopted and modified the pre-Christian understanding of virtue, and how it helped them to conceive of the way to deification in Christ. Moreover, he points to some interesting parallels between Orthodox virtue ethics and Confucianism. Vitz also articulates a response to the "situationist challenge" that questions the plausibility of virtue ethics to explain human behavior.

The last contribution focuses on philosophy of language and looks at three dimensions of linguistic meaning in the works of Pavel Florensky and Sergii Bulgakov: meaning as reference, meaning as use, and meaning as sense. An attempt is made to give an outline of a triadic, trinitarian, philosophy of language that takes into account all three aspects of meaning, and that avoids the various reductionist fallacies of modern philosophy of language. For instance, an Orthodox philosophy of language must transcend both logical empiricism (ideal language philosophy) that sought to conceive of meaning in terms of verifiability, and ordinary language philosophy (and its Continental equivalents), which tended to overemphasize the pragmatic aspect of meaning.

Even in the twenty-first century, critical and creative engagement with modern and postmodern philosophy is still a rarity in Orthodox theological circles—although the situation is changing rapidly now. The reasons for this deficiency are manifold and complex, and not just the result of the suppression of free theological thinking in twentieth-century Eastern Europe. As John Panteleimon Manoussakis harshly but cogently remarks: "The Orthodox Church can be seen as a case-study of a church that undercuts her theological future by falling victim to a narcissistic nostalgia for a glorious past. Symptoms of this pathology are to be found in the way theology is done by the majority of Orthodox theologians in the last millennium . . . a merely philological collection and exegesis of patristic fragments."[1]

Even among contemporary Orthodox theologians, one often finds the attitude of a "first naiveté," i.e., the view that the intellectual risk of engaging with contemporary thought must be avoided, because no theological gain

---

1. Manoussakis, "Anarchic Principle of Christian Eschatology," 44.

is to be expected from such an endeavor. One of the aims of this book is to advance the transition from a first to a *second* naiveté. There is a fundamental difference between blindly and unreflectively *presupposing* that the patristic era is normative for Orthodox theology, and consciously and reflectively *knowing* why pre-Kantian and pre-Reformation thought still has something to contribute to contemporary debates. For even if Orthodox theology takes a critical stance on the emergence of modern secular thought and the divorce of theology and philosophy, it will nonetheless deepen its insights and gain intellectual credibility if it engages with the intellectual debates of its time.

This book is not meant to promote one particular approach to the relationship between Orthodox theology and philosophy. Rather, the idea is to give an overview of how scholars working on the intersection between Orthodox theology and philosophy understand the interrelationship between these two academic disciplines. Accordingly, the following, sketchy reflections on theology and philosophy express in the first place my own views and should not be read as an attempt at articulating a consensus among the authors who have contributed to this volume.

The Orthodox tradition must emphasize the need for a "Christian philosophy"[2]—against the general trend in contemporary philosophy.[3] Whereas the sciences isolate and theorize about a limited aspect of reality, philosophy "aims at an all-encompassing overview" and forms "a general theory of reality and a general theory of knowledge."[4] Every philosophical theory—whether pre-modern, modern, or post-modern—is, explicitly or implicitly, based on ontological and epistemological presuppositions.

To be sure, proponents of post-metaphysical philosophy in the wake of Kant, Wittgenstein and Heidegger argue that the task of philosophy is quite different and more modest compared to the pre-modern era.[5] According to the later Wittgenstein, philosophy no longer makes ontological statements. It merely fulfils a therapeutic function and helps us discern and overcome our metaphysical illusions about knowledge, truth, and how

2. Bulgakov, *Svet nevechernii*, 78; *Unfading Light*, 91.

3. See, e.g., Heidegger, "Phänomenologie und Theologie," 66. According to Heidegger, the idea of a Christian philosophy is a "square circle" (*ein hölzernes Eisen*).

4. Clouser, *Myth of Religious Neutrality*, 70.

5. Braver, *Groundless Grounds*, 223–39; Phillips, *Religion and the Hermeneutics of Contemplation*, 318–26.

language refers to the world: "All that philosophy can do is destroy idols. And that means not creating a new one—for instance as in 'absence of an idol.'"[6]

That this new paradigm of philosophy has been successful in eliminating certain problematic and implausible philosophical approaches is relatively uncontested. What is less clear, however, is what the destruction of "idolatry" has been replaced with, and whether the menace of new forms of idolatry has really been averted. Wittgenstein and Heidegger have—in very different ways—provided a more nuanced understanding of the contingent aspect of human language and existence under spatio-temporal conditions. But what post-metaphysical philosophy has repudiated is not metaphysics *per se*, but at best a *specific* type of metaphysics that privileges the univocal sense of being ("onto-theology"), or a problematic, atomistic correspondence theory of meaning. Furthermore, it is evident that this sensitivity for the temporal, contextual and finite aspect of human existence is inextricably intertwined with a *radical, dogmatic finitism*. Post-metaphysical philosophy establishes rigid rules as to what counts as intelligible discourse and what not.[7] As William Desmond explains:

> Postulatory finitism first supposes, then later presupposes, that the finite and nothing but the finite constitutes the ultimate horizon for human thinking, one greater than which none can be thought. Originally a postulate, this finitism now becomes the presupposition of all thinking. But that it is a postulate recedes into the background, falls asleep to its postulatory nature, even as it functions silently as a presuppositional censor of what is to be deemed as a significant and worthy question.[8]

Like post-metaphysical philosophy, the sophiological movement in Russian religious philosophy paid much attention to time, history, as well as to contextual and cultural differences. But unlike post-metaphysical philosophy, it combined "post-modern" with pre-modern thought insofar as it sought to establish a metaphysical model that conceives of finitude, historicity, synchronic difference and diachronic change as grounded in divine eternity and infinity.[9] It thus continued and advanced the theological and

6. Wittgenstein, *Philosophical Occasions*, 171.
7. Meillassoux, *Après la finitude*, 51–80.
8. Desmond, "On God and the Between," 102.
9. Bulgakov, *Bride of the Lamb*, 69; Florensky, *Pillar and Ground of the Truth*, 35.

philosophical project of the Byzantine era.[10] Furthermore, the sphiolo-
gists were aware that "philosophy, no matter how critical it might seem,
is at its base mythical or dogmatic." They realized that the notion of an
independent, neutral and pure philosophy is an illusion. There is always
a "metaphysical premise that represents only an expression of an intuitive
world-perception."[11]

For this reason, Orthodox theology can embrace neither an (uncritically) *instrumental* nor a *foundational* use of philosophy. The instrumental
use of philosophy rejects the view that Christian theology must have a non-
theological foundation but uses philosophy for the intellectual elucidation
of its beliefs. Theology uses the conceptual tools that are available in a
particular context and at a particular time: e.g., hermeneutics, phenomenology, existentialism, and so forth. The problem with this approach is
that—although Christian thought never becomes dependent on any *particular* philosophy—certain logical, epistemological and ontological presuppositions are (explicitly or implicitly) incorporated into the Christian
understanding of reality. It wrongly presumes that on the most fundamental level of philosophical reflection (logic, epistemology, ontology, etc.), the
Christian worldview is neutral, and that, paradoxically, its unique character
is only fully actualized if its basic beliefs are expressed within ever-new
conceptual frameworks. In fact, the instrumental use of philosophy tends
to undermine the transformative power of Christianity and results in ac-
commodation to secular thought.

Furthermore, even within a limited historical era, or a limited cultural
space, there is a wide variety of different, and often conflicting, philosophical movements. The instrumental use of philosophy cannot explain why a
particular philosophical model is privileged. For if *theological* reasons are
adduced for why a particular approach is selected rather than another, the
instrumental approach has already been abandoned. The more authority is
granted to theology to decide which philosophical model is appropriate to
express theological truths, the more the criteriological and methodological
primacy of theology is preserved. If one follows this rule, the instrumental
use of philosophy gives way to (the development of) a *Christian* philosophy. However, this is not to say that there is "*a single, absolute philosophical*

---

10. Tollefsen, *Christocentric Cosmology of St. Maximus*; Tollefsen, "Metaphysics of
Holomerism"; Mitralexis, *Ever-Moving Repose*.

11. Bulgakov, *Svet nevechernii*, 78; *Unfading Light*, 91.

system that would accommodate absolute truth."[12] A Christian philosophy is always in the making. It is a never-finished, eschatological project. Thus, it may well adopt insights and theories from various philosophical traditions and schools. Yet it must always retain its criteriological independence and uphold the normativity of the christological and trinitarian doctrines.

According to the foundational use of philosophy, for theological truth-claims to be intellectually meaningful and respectable, they require a philosophical, non-theological justification. This view makes theology dependent on philosophy and regards human reason as the ultimate, universal arbiter. This foundational use of philosophy is particularly characteristic of the Enlightenment era and philosophical theism. As John Locke points out, "revelation must be judged of by reason," for reason is "the last judge and guide in everything."[13] The main goal of philosophical theism is thus to provide reasons for why the belief in God's existence is rationally justified. Only that which can be proved, or made probable, on the basis of generally recognized standards of formal logic and argument, and which meets clearly defined epistemological criteria, can be regarded as knowledge.[14] The *rationalists* consider reason to be a source of indubitable and self-evident truths that are innate and common to all human beings. Following the paradigm of mathematics, it is possible to logically infer certain knowledge from these truths. The *empiricists*, by contrast, deny the existence of innate ideas and emphasize that all true knowledge is experiential knowledge. The function of reason is limited to processing this empirically acquired knowledge. Accordingly, the empiricists favor the inductive reasoning of the empirical sciences that generates insights and beliefs of different degrees of probability. With respect to philosophical theology, rationalists rely on the ontological argument and *a priori* versions of the cosmological argument (rational theology), whereas empiricists focus on *a posteriori* interpretations of the cosmological argument, and on the argument from design (natural theology).[15]

The way Enlightenment theism (and its continuation and development in analytic philosophy of religion) conceives of the relationship between theology and philosophy, makes it unsuitable for an Orthodox

12. Bulgakov, *Svet nevechernii*, 79; *Unfading Light*, 93.

13. Locke, *Essay Concerning Human Understanding* 4.19, 14.

14. Dalferth, *Theology and Philosophy*, 89.

15. Dalferth, *Theology and Philosophy*, 92. See also Dalferth, *Die Wirklichkeit des Möglichen*, 257–307.

Christian philosophy. Even more than the instrumental use of philosophy, the foundational use undermines the transformative power of the Incarnation and fails to envisage a christological and trinitarian reconfiguration of reason and rationality. In the Orthodox tradition, grace is always mediated by nature, and there is no such thing as "pure nature" to which grace is extrinsically added.[16] Accordingly, although it is possible to differentiate between theology and philosophy, the two disciplines cannot be separated.[17]

Both the notions of "pure reason" and "pure faith" (without the involvement and mediation of reason) are theologically problematic. However, theology does not have to conform to preconceived, non-theological notions of knowledge, reality and rationality. Rather, it is the discourses of faith and theology that should determine epistemology, ontology, and logic. This is not to say that Christian philosophy cannot critically and creatively appropriate new and innovative philosophical thought models and conceptual schemes—even if they do not have an explicitly theological origin. However, this exploratory experimenting will eventually give way to a consolidation of the Christian tradition. In the end, it must be possible to put forth a theological rationale for the innovation that was embraced.[18]

But what is unique about Christian philosophy? For instance, the way it conceives of the relationship between the universal and the particular. It avoids the Scylla of an abstract, indeterminate and impersonal universal, as well as the Charybdis of an equally indeterminate, solipsistic interiority. In William Desmond's terminology, it allows us to envisage an "intimate universal"[19]—a philosophical model derived from the doctrine of the Incarnation. Many essays in this volume seem to imply something like an intimate universal. For instance, the centrality of virtue ethics for traditional Christianity, lucidly set out by Rico Vitz (see chapter 7), can be explained by the fact that we can think together universal divine goodness and truth (universality) with the most intimate gift of "being good" that allows us to perform virtuous acts in changing contexts and situations (particularity). In Maximus the Confessor, for instance, it is the free and active reception

16. Lossky, *Mystical Theology of the Eastern Church*, 101.

17. Gregory, *Five Theological Orations*, 29.21 (260); Martzelos, "Vernunft und Offenbarung," 295; Kapriev, "Es sind zwei Augen der Seele."

18. See Meredith, *Christian Philosophy in the Early Church*, 155.

19. See Desmond, *Intimate Universal*, esp. 23–59.

of the divine *energeiai*, proceeding from the divine *ousia* that enable us to acquire a *hexis* (i.e., habitus) and lead a virtuous life.[20]

Similarly, Orthodox political theory endeavours to transcend both abstract universalism and individualism/atomism. With respect to the relationship between society and the individual, they seek to overcome both impersonal collectivism and individualism. "Social life is not a condition superadded to the individual life, but is contained in the very definition of personality."[21] Regarding international relations, we find a notion of the supernational that goes beyond nationalism and cosmopolitanism. A nation's activity should strive to be "national in its origin and means of expression, but wholly universal in its content and in its objective result."[22] Moreover, the brief outline of an Orthodox philosophy of language in chapter 8 on the one hand sees language as a determinate, objective, eternal and transpersonal *logos* (universality), and on the other hand as something intimate and subjective that enables the interlocutors to express what is most personal to them (particularity).

Bibliography

Braver, Lee. *Groundless Grounds: A Study of Wittgenstein and Heidegger.* Cambridge, MA: MIT Press, 2012.

Bulgakov, Sergei. *The Bride of the Lamb.* Translated by Boris Jakim. Grand Rapids: Eerdmans, 2002.

———. *Svet nevechernii. Sozertsaniia i umozreniia.* Moscow: Respublika, 1994.

———. *Unfading Light: Contemplations and Speculations.* Translated by Thomas Allan Smith. Grand Rapids: Eerdmans, 2012.

Clouser, Roy A. *The Myth of Religious Neutrality: An Essay on the Hidden Roles of Religious Belief in Theories.* Rev. ed. Notre Dame, IN: University of Notre Dame Press, 2005.

Dalferth, Ingolf U. *Die Wirklichkeit des Möglichen. Hermeneutische Religionsphilosophie.* Tübingen: Mohr Siebeck, 2003.

———. *Theology and Philosophy.* Oxford: Blackwell, 1988.

Desmond, William. *The Intimate Universal: The Hidden Porosity among Religion, Art, Philosophy, and Politics.* New York: Columbia University Press, 2016.

———. "On God and the Between." In *Between Philosophy and Theology: Contemporary Interpretations of Christianity*, edited by Lieven Boeve, et al., 99–125. Farnham: Ashgate, 2010.

Florensky, Pavel. *The Pillar and Ground of the Truth: An Essay in Orthodox Theodicy in Twelve Letters.* Translated by Boris Jakim. Princeton: Princeton University Press, 1997.

20. Renczes, *Agir de Dieu*, 329–36.

21. See, e.g., Solovyov, *Justification of the Good*, 175.

22. Solovyov, *Justification of the Good*, 256.

Gregory, Nazianzen. *Faith Gives Fullness to Reasoning: The Five Theological Orations of Gregory Nazianzen*. Translated by Lionel Wickham, et al. Leiden: Brill, 1990.

Heidegger, Martin. "Phänomenologie und Theologie." In *Wegmarken*, edited by Friedrich-Wilhelm von Herrmann, 45–77. GA 9. Frankfurt am Main: Vittorio Klostermann, 1976.

Kapriev, Georgi. "Es sind zwei Augen der Seele. Vernunft und Offenbarung gemäss der Hesychasten des 13. und 14. Jahrhunderts." In *Vernunft und Offenbarung. Die Wurzeln der Europäischen Rationalität in der Lateinischen und Byzantinischen Tradition*, edited by Georgi Kapriev, et al., 57–69. Sofia: East-West, 2006.

Locke, John. *An Essay Concerning Human Understanding*. Ware: Wordsworth, 2014.

Lossky, Vladimir. *The Mystical Theology of the Eastern Church*. Crestwood, NY: St. Vladimir's Seminary Press, 1976.

Manoussakis, John Panteleimon, "The Anarchic Principle of Christian Eschatology in the Eucharistic Tradition of the Eastern Church." *The Harvard Theological Review* 100.1 (2007) 29–46.

Martzelos, Georgios. "Vernunft und Offenbarung in der Theologie Luthers und in der Orthodoxen Überlieferung." In *The Function and the Limits of Reason in Dogmatic Theology*, edited by Ioan Tulcan, et al., 275–302. Thessaloniki: Astra Museum, 2012.

Meillassoux, Quentin. *Après la finitude. Essai sur la nécessité de la contingence*. Paris: Seuil, 2006.

Meredith, Anthony. *Christian Philosophy in the Early Church*. London: T & T Clark, 2012.

Mitralexis, Sotiris. *Ever-Moving Repose. A Contemporary Reading of Maximus the Confessor's Theory of Time*. Eugene, OR: Cascade, 2017.

Phillips, Dewi Z. *Religion and the Hermeneutics of Contemplation*. Cambridge: Cambridge University Press, 2001.

Renczes, Philipp Gabriel. *Agir de Dieu et liberté de l'homme: recherches sur l'anthropologie théologique de saint Maxime le Confesseur*. Paris: Cerf, 2003.

Solovyov, Vladimir Sergeyevich. *The Justification of the Good: an Essay on Moral Philosophy*. Edited by Boris Jakim. Translated by Natalie Duddington. Grand Rapids: Eerdmans, 2005.

Tollefsen, Torstein. *The Christocentric Cosmology of St. Maximus the Confessor*. New York; Oxford: Oxford University Press, 2008.

———. "A Metaphysics of Holomerism." In *Maximus the Confessor as a European Philosopher*, edited by Sotiris Mitralexis, et al., 24–34. Eugene, OR: Cascade, 2017.

Wittgenstein, Ludwig. *Philosophical Occasions: 1912–1951*. edited by James Carl Klagge, et al. Indianapolis: Hackett, 1993.

1

Theocracy, *Sobornost'*, and Democracy

Reflections on Vladimir Putin's Philosophers[1]

EVERT VAN DER ZWEERDE

"Russia's democracy means the power of the Russian people with their own traditions of self-rule and not the fulfillment of standards imposed on us from the outside."

VLADIMIR V. PUTIN, ADDRESS TO THE FEDERAL ASSEMBLY, DECEMBER 12, 2012[2]

"We are neither the West's disciples nor its teachers.
We are disciples to God and teachers to ourselves."

IVAN A. ILYIN, "ABOUT THE RUSSIAN IDEA," FEBRUARY 15, 1951[3]

A mere fifteen years ago, many people thought that Russia was on its way to becoming a "normal" country. This normalcy meant the kind of country that Western countries claimed to be: where people could freely move in and out, where government would be held accountable, where

---

1. My gratitude goes to Sofie Kemps for the editorial work that she did on a handwritten manuscript. All translations, unless otherwise stated, are mine.

2. See Eltchaninoff, *Dans la tête*, 86. English translation taken from Putin, "Address to the Federal Assembly."

3. Ilyin, *Nashi zadachi*, 2.1:427.

people would organize themselves politically or engage in the unpredictable variety of activities called "civil society," where critical journalism would have its place, where law would rule rather than being an instrument in the hands of a ruling elite, and where officials would be elected in free, fair, frequent, universal, secret and competitive elections. Nobody expected this new Russia to take shape overnight, but there was a perspective.

In the twenty-first century, Russian reality took a different direction: civil society became "managed [*upravliaemoe grazhdanskoe obshchestvo*]," INGO's were increasingly regarded as foreign agents, a "vertical of power [*vertikal' vlasti*]" reestablished a Kremlin-centrically organized polity, and the Russian Orthodox Church [ROC] became an integral part of the political machinery. Democracy was made "sovereign [*soverennaia demokratiia*]," which actually meant the uncontested predominance of a single "party of power [*partiia vlasti*]," aptly called *Edinaia Rossiia*, an expression that means both *single*, *unique*, and *united* Russia, protests were crushed, and even elections that could have been won easily were manipulated. Independent, critical journalism was limited to radio and television stations like *Ekho Mosvky* and *Dozhd'*, and the courageous newspaper *Novaia Gazeta*.

Many people today think that Russia, rather than trying to become a country that might be "normal" by some cosmopolitan standard, has returned to its *own* "normality": that of a relatively closed, mildly imperialist country with an authoritarian government, heavily controlled media, and a simultaneously state-supporting and state-supported religious and secular ideology. A country, also, with a substantial diaspora. Russia, having decided to do it *its own way*, would seem to be back to *its* normal condition.

Anybody who has recently visited Russia can testify that the country has changed dramatically in terms of wealth, services, reliability, and even habits, making it a much less "other" place than it was in the past. Also, there is incomparably more freedom than there was in Soviet times: in part, this is due to the cunning of those in power, who understand that "repressive toleration" is more effective, and also cheaper than omnipresent oppression. Finally, new generations of Russians must be seduced rather than fooled. Russians have become much less different from "us," just as "we" have become much less different from each other. Consumerism, including *political* consumerism, is the globally dominant form of subjectivity.

Russia has partly returned to pre-Soviet rather than Soviet patterns. In many respects, the Soviet period has functioned as a *refrigerator*, preserving ideas and developments at low temperature, not allowing them to sprout or take root, but keeping them alive for future times. The field of philosophy is no exception. The late 1980s and the 1990s saw massive republication of the works of thinkers who had been condemned by the Soviet ideological authorities as bourgeois subjectivists and/or religious idealists. This category includes three thinkers who were recently mentioned as being the current president's favorites: Vladimir Solovyov, Nikolai Berdyaev and Ivan Ilyin.

The objective of this paper is to explore the political philosophies of these three thinkers with a relative focus on their conception and critique of democracy, as a way to gain some insight into the ideas that "move" the part of Russia that claims to be in charge, politically and/or intellectually. I start with a brief discussion of "democracy." After that, I address the political philosophy of the three thinkers just mentioned, indicating both what separates them and what they have in common. With respect to Solovyov and Berdyaev, I will partly draw on earlier publications;[4] my relative emphasis will be on Ilyin, also because of the three he stands closest to present-day political reality in Russia. Thirdly, I will address the question of the relationship between theocracy, *sobornost'*, and democracy. In all this, I do *not* assume that ideas actually are what moves history; what I *do* assume is that ideas are "at work" in history, both as ideologemes (elements of legitimizing ideological constructs) and as ideals (parts of motivating practice-oriented theories).[5] In both capacities, they display a logic of their own, which both facilitates and limits their deployment.

The key idea of this paper is that the idea of a strong, sovereign state, and the idea of *sobornost'* represent two alternatives to the "Western" idea of liberal democracy, both elaborated by thinkers standing in, roughly, the broad tradition of Russian Religious Philosophy. Their positions vary with respect to the extent to which they try to incorporate elements of the "Western" model in their own conception, for example political parties and general elections. What they categorically reject, is the conception of the polity as made up of autonomous individuals on an equal footing. Their advocacy of freedom relates to *personal*, not *individual* freedom, which sets clear limits to perceiving them as "liberal" thinkers.[6]

---

4. Van der Zweerde, "Das Böse und das Politische"; "Rise of the People."

5. For the notion of a "working idea" see Van der Zweerde, "Ideas at Work!" The notion of *ideologeme* as the smallest identifiable unit of ideological discourse is derived from the works of Mikhail Bakthin, Fredric Jameson, and Gasan Guseinov.

6. The highly interesting question why scholars try to either glorify or vilify Solovyov as a liberal falls outside the scope of this essay.

Political Philosophy and Democracy

This is an exercise in *philosophy*, trying to combine political philosophy and history of philosophy: what I do is neither history of Russia (or analysis of current affairs), nor political science, nor, finally, history of political ideas, though it is on the last that it probably borders most. Moreover, as a *political* philosopher I do employ a specific philosophical conception of democracy, and since there is no generally accepted conception of democracy (the fact that contestation is a fundamental trait of democracy extends to its conception, too), it is appropriate to indicate this conception in a few points:

1. Democracy is neither a form of government or regime, nor a form of state, and even less a type of country, but a *possible quality* of all societal situations in which political power is exercised (including, therefore, forms of government and state, but also academia).

2. Democracy is the partial realization of three principles: equality (of all members of a given *dēmos*), dēmic sovereignty (meaning that the "will" of the given *dēmos* is decisive),[7] and majority rule.

3. Consequently, democracy is *one* of the possible qualities of regimes, power constellations, and other situations, and, as never realized fully or purely, it always is an aspiration and a claim, or a threat and a risk.

If we want to assess the relation between theocracy, *sobornost'*, and democracy, we need a suitable conception of democracy. Following theoreticians like Norberto Bobbio and Chantal Mouffe,[8] I theorize liberal democracy as a *contingent* combination of democratic principles (the three just mentioned), and *liberal* principles, i.e., human rights, individual rights and liberties (including the right to property), and the separation of powers into legislative, executive and judiciary. "Contingent combination" not only means that the combination is historically contingent in its genealogy, a point that even Jürgen Habermas would readily concede, but also that the combination itself remains logically and politically contingent: "liberal"

7. A *dēmos* is defined here as the *political people* of any given polity: this includes all those who are engaged/concerned in entities such as country or municipality, but also family. The notion of *dēmic* sovereignty means that those concerned have the decisive say in the decisions that concern them.

8. Others include Isaiah Berlin, Michael Oakeshott, Jacques Rancière, and Carl Schmitt: the point is not whether one favors this contingent combination (like Oakeshott or Mouffe) or criticizes it (like Rancière and Schmitt), but rather that all these thinkers reject the elevation of a historical contingency to a substantial achievement.

and "democratic" neither imply, nor presuppose each other. Indeed, the shortest description of the "Western" type of political system is that of a liberal-democratic rule of law state, in which both liberal, democratic, and rule of law are qualities of the polity.[9]

Interestingly, we find support for the non-identity of democracy and liberal constitution in the authors at hand. Berdyaev is most explicit on this point. In *Russia's Fate/Destiny* [*Sud'ba Rossii*] (1918) he writes that democracy can be just as detrimental to the human person and to freedom as monarchy or autocracy: "Power of the people [*narodovlastie*] can just as well deprive the person of his inalienable rights as single-handed power [*edinovlastie*]," further, "the formal absolutism of the democratic idea . . . must be restricted by other ideas,"[10] and he ends his short piece by stating in almost exactly the same words what Mouffe has labelled the "democratic paradox": "The power of democracy cannot be absolute, unlimited power; it is restricted by qualities that have been put forward by [this power, EvdZ] itself."[11] For Berdyaev, these qualities are two: the idea of a self-determining nation and the idea of inalienable individual freedom; Mouffe would bring in liberal principles, including the principle of a rule of law state [*pravovoe gosudarstvo* or *Rechtsstaat*].[12] Pace Mouffe, I keep rule of law out of this equation: although liberals generally support it, they are not alone in this, and there is nothing inherently liberal about rule of law, a principle also endorsed by conservative *étatists* such as Ilyin, Christian corporatists such as Solovyov, or advocates of *shari'a*. The common point is that democracy in itself does not imply these ideas and therefore will always have to be supplemented, limited or balanced by them. Also, as Mouffe and Berdyaev make clear, in the case of a democratic polity, this can only take the form of a *self-limitation* on the part of the sovereign *dēmos*.[13]

---

9. This implies that there can be illiberal democracies and liberal non-democracies, and both can vary in the extent to which they qualify as a rule of law state. For example, a *shari'a*-based polity is a rule of law state *par excellence*, and it can also be democratic in terms of equality, demic sovereignty, and majority rule, but it is unlikely to have a liberal constitution. Arguably, if pushed to their limit, each of the three—democracy, liberalism, rule of law—excludes the other two.

10. Berdyaev, *Sud'ba Rossii*, 231.

11. Berdyaev, *Sud'ba Rossii*, 237.

12. Mouffe, *Democratic Paradox*, 2–3.

13. Mouffe, *Democratic Paradox*, 4.

Putin's Favourite Philosophers

In early 2014, news spread that the Russian president, Vladimir Putin, had favorably referred to three Russian philosophers and had handed out copies of their works to high officials as a New Year's present.[14] The three were, first, Vladimir Solovyov (1853–1900), a pre-Soviet thinker who had, to say the least, a troubled relationship with the tsarist autocratic regime, and especially the Holy Synod of the ROC; second, Nikolay Berdyaev (1874–1948), a radical individualist, alternatively qualified as anarchist and as Christian socialist, who opposed both tsarist autocracy and Bolshevik regime, and who had to emigrate to Germany in 1922 with the Philosophy Steamer [*Filosofskii parokhod*],[15] only to start a brilliant career as an existentialist thinker in France; third, Ivan Ilyin (1883–1954), a monarchist, militarist, and Russian nationalist, who also left Russia in 1922 with the same philosophy steamer, but belonged to the opposite, White opposition. The obvious question is *why* Vladimir Putin started referring to Solovyov, Berdyaev and Ilyin, and *why* he handed out their *Opravdanie dobra* [The Justification of the Good], *Filosofiia neravenstva* [The Philosophy of Inequality] and *Nashi zadachi* [Our Tasks].

First of all, we should not make too much of this "philosophical turn." The incumbent Russian president is far too clever and pragmatic to be profoundly influenced by any of these three thinkers, whose ideas moreover go in many different directions. At the same time, we should not make too little of it either. Even if we doubt that politicians themselves are strongly influenced, let alone steered, by theories or ideas, we should acknowledge that ideas can give substance and direction, can provide—or at least suggest—unity of vision and, perhaps most importantly, create both opportunities *and* hindrances in politicians' communication with audiences home and abroad. Clearly, Putin's choice entails an *appeal* to a Russian audience: these three thinkers are indeed central to *Russia's* intellectual heritage, and their works have appeared in large editions ever since this became politically possible around 1986 (before that date, they were banned and hard to access, which adds to their appeal).

Secondly, one of the peculiarities of ideas and theories is that they exclude, logically and/or polemically, other ideas and theories. In this

---

14. See Eltchaninoff, "Dans la tête," 7. See also the original article, Schulz, "Der Präsident als Philosoph."

15. See Chamberlain, *Philosophy Steamer*.

case, two potentially competing ideological constructions, namely Russian [*rossiiskii*, not *russkii*] *nationalism*, and *eurasianism* [*evraziistvo*], jointly exclude several of the Kremlin's constitutive others: ethnic [*russkii*] nationalism, "(n)ostalgic" communism, and liberalism and Westernism [*zapadnichestvo*]. Ideology can give purpose and direction if it also tells what *not* to identify with and which direction *not* to take.

Finally, and perhaps most importantly, ideology helps to direct attention from burning issues like poverty, corruption, or the cost of war. Ideological space is both infinitely expanding and always completely filled: there is no such thing as an "ideological vacuum"—in fact, "ideological vacuum" is itself an ideologeme. At this point Russia is not different from other polities, but the content of the ideological constructions that are used and the ideologemes that are expected to "work" may strike as odd.

There is no reason, then, to be particularly surprised that Putin makes selective use of the visions of Solovyov, Berdyaev, and Ilyin, since suitable ideologemes can indeed be easily found there. We can place these three thinkers within the broad category of Russian Orthodox-Christian political philosophy. Religion, as Ilyin emphasizes, is connected to notions like "binding to" and "strengthening," and he defines it as "the living spiritual bond of man with God [*zhivoi dukhovnyi soiuz cheloveka s Bogom*]."[16] This definition implies three questions: first, *which* God? second, is it an individual bond or a collective one, or perhaps both? and third, what is the connection of this bond with the sphere of politics, to which democracy would belong? If we follow Ilyin, we do get a partial answer: a state is connected to a territory and a nation [*narod*], it is *self-reliant*, and its power is independent: "The state does not receive its power from any other authority or union; it always independently creates those legal norms, on the basis whereof it exercises its power and is ruled."[17]

Ilyin is a very different thinker from both Solovyov and Berdyaev: his conservatism and authoritarianism, as well as his emphasis on state and legal order, his "statism" as it is sometimes called, certainly give a very different flavor to his political philosophy. At the same time, however, we have good reasons to situate him in the same tradition of Russian religious philosophy. If we ask, for example, why Ilyin makes a distinction between *formal* [*formal'naia*] and *creative* [*tvorcheskaia*] democracy, the answer is that for Ilyin a political community (whether it is monarchic, aristocratic,

16. Ilyin, *Obshchee uchenie*, 80.
17. Ilyin, *Obshchee uchenie*, 151.

democratic or a mixture thereof), is only worthy of that name if it is a living organic whole in which a specific national spirit [*narodnyi dukh*, a direct translation of Hegel's *Volksgeist*] concretely manifests itself. In Hegel, Ilyin states, this national spirit, or *Volksgeist*, is an occurrence of the Divine Spirit.[18] For Ilyin, as for Hegel, the state, as moral community *and* legal order, and hence as *objective spirit*, ultimately is part of the concrete realization of absolute spirit, i.e., God. In other words, the "creative force" of a state, i.e., its capacity to create and sustain a just legal and moral order, is explicable only through its connection to the force of creation itself. This is a common theme in Russian religious philosophy.

Ilyin published his major work on Hegel in 1918, shortly after the 1917 revolutions (the first of which he applauded), and defended it at Moscow State University in the same year, which brought him in one stroke the titles of *magister* and *doctor*.[19] Later, he distanced himself from the idea that the state is "the very organic life of the national spirit."[20] According to Igor Evlampiev, after his escape from Germany in 1938, "the main principle . . . of Ilyin's philosophizing becomes the rigorous harmonization [*neukosnitel'noe soglasovanie*] of all his ideas with canonical orthodox dogmatics."[21] The effect is a reduction of the *role* and *status* of the state in the whole picture of man and world, but not a change in his conception of that state as such: "After all, the state is not an *institution*, rising *over* the citizens, but a *corporation* [*korporatsiia*], realized by them, in them, and *through them*."[22]

An apparent difference between Ilyin and Solovyov might be the idea of theocracy. Solovyov's ultimate universal socio-political ideal is "free theocracy," a free union of all of humankind under a single political and religious roof, while Ilyin, like Hegel and Hobbes before him, and Carl Schmitt at around the same time, sticks to the idea of a "pluriverse" of sovereign states—of different character—which can organize their mutual relations through pacts and treaties, but the condition of which is essentially one of "state of nature."[23]

However, we must bear in mind here the difference between *two types* of *ideal theory* in the case of Solovyov. In his later work, Solovyov returned

18. Ilyin, *Filosofiia Gegelia*, 413.

19. Evlampiev, "Ivan Il'in," 5.

20. Ilyin, *Obshchee uchenie*, 417.

21. Evlampiev, "Ivan Il'in," 11.

22. Ilyin, *Obshchee uchenie*, 162.

23. Ilyin, *Obshchee uchenie*, 150.

THEOCRACY, SOBORNOST', AND DEMOCRACY

from the utopian project of a global, all-encompassing, free theocracy, depicted in *Istoriia i budushchnost' teokratii* [The History and Future of Theocracy] (1887) and *l'Idée russe* [The Russian Idea] (1888), both of which have their roots in the utopian vision he outlined in his unpublished youth work *La Sophie* (1876),[24] to a more "realistic" conception of a just state in *Opravdanie dobra* [The Justification of the Good] (1897). I doubt if we should distinguish between two stages in Solovvyov's intellectual development; rather, I think we are looking at two levels of ideality, "utopian" and "realistic." If the first type of ideal theory can be qualified as the highest aim of human history, just one step short of the Kingdom of God on earth, then the second type of ideal theory can be placed more easily in the category of normative political philosophy, which is one reason why Solovyov's theocratic utopia is not generally known among political philosophers, while his later, more realistic, albeit still far-fetched conception of a just Christian polity, is taken into serious consideration.

This "second-best utopia" can be fruitfully compared with the vision of Ilyin: for both, the state must be a *nation*-state, it must be *organic*, and it must entail *rule of law*. In one of his more explicitly *liberal* writings, *Pravo i nravstvennost'* [Law and Morality] (1897) (liberal in the sense of defending personal human freedom, not in the sense of individual rights and liberties in the tradition from John Locke via John Stuart Mill to John Rawls), Solovyov clearly marks his position as seeking a *middle path* between two extremes. He writes: "Thus law (and the lawful state [*pravovoe gosudarstvo* = *Rechtsstaat*, EvdZ] in historical reality does not have a single empirical source but occurs as a fickle result of the complex interrelationship of two opposing and counteractive principles. It is easy to see that these are only modifications or early applications in the politico-juridical sphere of the two elementary principles lying at the foundation of all human existence, community and individualism."[25] And, he continues, "these two principles . . . manifest themselves in the political struggle between absolutism and liberalism, traditional aristocracy and revolutionary democracy, and so on. And both conflicting principles are alike unjust and unsound."[26] and so is, one may add, any type of external compromise between them.

As always, Solovyov seeks not a pragmatic position *between*, but a normative position *beyond* the two opposed principles: "Freedom, as the

24. See Van der Zweerde, "Between Mysticism and Politics."
25. Solovyov, *Justification of the Good*, 136.
26. Solovyov, *Justification of the Good*, 136–37

foundation of all *human* existence, and equality, as the essential form of all *societal* existence, in combination form *human society* as a *lawful order.*"[27] As elsewhere, Solovyov defends the idea of a *single* politico-juridical *whole*; if he oscillates, it is not with respect to that principle, but with respect to the question whether it should be situated at the level of the individual *nation*, leading to a plurality of legal orders, each of them a single whole, or at the level of humankind as a whole, leading to the ideal of free theocracy.

The affinity between Solovyov and Ilyin is illustrated by their treatment of a cornerstone of the modern, constitutional state: the *trias politica*. In Montesquieu, habitually treated as the main source of this principle, we find the following key sentence: "Here, therefore, is the fundamental constitution of the government of which we are speaking. As its legislative body is composed of two parts, the one will be chained to the other by their reciprocal faculty of vetoing. The two will be bound by the executive power, which will itself be bound by the legislative power. [Voici donc la constitution fondamentale du gouvernement dont nous parlons. Le corps législatif y étant composé de deux parties l'une enchaînera l'autre par la faculté mutuelle d'empêcher. Toutes les deux seront liées par la puissance exécutrice, qui le sera elle-même par la législative]."[28]

Interestingly, Montesquieu states his principle in his discussion of the *English* constitution, so the point here is not that of a *written* constitution: "constitution" is used by Montesquieu for the overall political form of a society, much like the ancient Greek notion of *politeia*. More interestingly, Montesquieu clearly indicates the possibility of *conflict*: the two chambers of the legislative body can *veto* each other's decision, thus blocking each other's power: "l'une enchaînera"—literally: to put in chains, i.e., to bind in a compulsory manner—"l'autre par sa faculté mutuelle d'empêcher"—i.e., to *hinder* or to keep from doing.[29] Legislative and executive power are, similarly, mutually bound by each other. For Montesquieu, a political double bind lies at the heart of the modern constitutional state. Most interestingly, however, is the fact that we do not necessarily find, in Montesquieu, a single supreme power or "a" sovereign: sovereign power is with the constitution as such, not with any of its constituent parts. If monarchy means that a single

---

27. Solovyov, *Justification of the Good*, 140.

28. Montesquieu, *De l'esprit des lois*, 302 [English: *Spirit of the Laws*, 164].

29. Montesquieu, *De l'esprit des lois*, 302 [English: *Spirit of the Laws*, 164].

monarch is sovereign, his rule must be "according to established laws" if it is not to be despotic.[30]

Later, judiciary power, earlier considered part of executive power, obtained independence vis-à-vis the other two (executive proper and legislative), leading to the classical separation of three powers: legislative, executive, and judiciary. It is this *trias politica* that Solovyov and Ilyin address in a similar way. In *Opravdanie dobra*, Solovyov shows in which sense he can and in which sense he cannot be qualified as a "liberal thinker": "It is clear that these three different powers—the legislative, the judicial and the executive, though necessarily *distinct* [*razdel'ny*], cannot be *separate* [*razobshcheny*], and ought on no account to conflict with one another: they all have one and the same purpose—to serve the common good in accordance with the law. Their unity finds its real expression in their being equally subordinate to one supreme authority, invested with all the positive rights of the social whole as such."[31] In Solovyov's theocratic utopia, this supreme authority is the trinity of King (Tsar), Priest (Pope) and Prophet (educated society), in his "second level ideal theory" it is the Christian monarch, but, significantly, the same triad of royal, priestly, and prophetic authority plays a key role, too.[32]

Ivan Ilyin addresses the same *trias politica* in his 1915 *Obshchee uchenie gosudarstva i prava* [General Theory of State and Law]: "It is clear from the preceding [discussion], that the organs of the state [NB: organs of a whole, not powers in a constellation as in Montesquieu, EvdZ] are called *legislative, executive* and *judiciary*, according to the *main* thing that is their province."[33] And, he continues, "By general rule, only *the head of state* (a monarch or the president of a republic) is the *highest* organ in *all three* domains [*napravleniia*]—legislation, governance and jurisdiction."

Solovyov and Ilyin (like Hegel) stick to the idea that there must be a single sovereign head of state, a *person*, an idea that Berdyaev connected to Russian cultural history: Russians hate the state, but they love to have a tsar at its top, who takes upon him the dirty job of power.[34] What, according to Berdyaev, Russians either misunderstand or reject, is that "sovereign" is not a single power or organ, but the very constellation of powers in mutual

---

30. Montesquieu, *De l'esprit des lois*, 302 [English: *Spirit of the Laws*, 21].

31. Solovyov, *Opravdanie dobra*, 460–61 [English: *Justification of the Good*, 329].

32. Solovyov, *Opravdanie dobra*, 542–43 [English: *Justification of the Good*, 402].

33. Ilyin, *Obshchee uchenie*, 156.

34. Berdyaev, *Russian Idea*, 163.

"potential conflict"—a constellation that both requires and enables "checks and balances." From a "Western" perspective, any discourse of a single "sovereign" (whether royal, presidential, or popular) is ideological: European absolutism, i.e., the idea of the presence of a single "sovereign," in both its monarchic and its democratic variant, was never a description, but an ideologeme haunting Western political reality. Similarly, but in an inverted manner, the idea of the *absence* of a single sovereign haunts Russian political reality as a dreadful, "negative ideologeme" frequently invoked to legitimize the powers that be.

In *Nashi zadachi* [Our Tasks] (1948–1954), Ilyin reflected on Russia's possible futures *after* World War II and the Soviet regime: "If anything can inflict new, very serious blows onto Russia after communism, then it is precisely obstinate attempts to establish in it a democratic structure after the totalitarian tyranny."[35] Ilyin distinguished two types of democracy, formal [*formal'naia*] and creative [*tvorcheskaia*], and opposed the idea that democracy would be a cure for all ills. According to him, a formal, quantitative approach to democracy, i.e., the idea of universal and equal suffrage, would not preclude any ills at all: "Such a 'democracy' does not protect from anything: neither from total corruption [*prodazhnost'*], nor from treacherous conspiracies, nor from exploitation by crooks [*plutami*] of the weak, the good, the blind and the stupid, neither from anarchy, nor from tyranny, nor from totalitarianism."[36]

The remark about "*prodazhnost'*" reminds one of the discourse about the "selling out [*prodazha*]" of Russia in the late 1980s and the 1990s. There is something peculiar to note here, namely the idea that a *country* can be sold or sold out. This not only suggests that the country is someone's property, or at least in someone's possession, but it also presupposes a one-to-one-to-one correspondence between three things: a *territory*, a *polity*, and a *nation* that populates the territory. This is precisely Ilyin's conception: according to him, the foundations of statehood are a people or a nation [*narod*], a territory [*territoriia*], and political power [*vlast'*].[37] Here is another point that links Ilyin, Berdyaev, and Solovyov: all are *theoretical nationalists*, despite the fact that they think differently about what this nation should be or do. They may differ as to *what* is Russia's destiny or historical task, but it is beyond dispute *that* there is a "Russian idea," and it also is clear that this

35. Ilyin, *Nashi zadachi*, 2.1:449.
36. Ilyin, *Nashi zadachi*, 2.1:449.
37. Ilyin, *Obshchee uchenie*, 141–57.

idea is *not* what freely deliberating Russians might arrive at, but, to use Solovyov's famous words from *l'Idée russe*, "what God thinks about Russia in eternity": "l'Idée d'une nation n'est pas ce qu'elle pense d'elle-même dans le temps, mais ce que Dieu pense sur elle dans l'éternité,"[38] This formulation almost literally returns 50 years later in Berdyaev's *Russkaia ideia*: "What will interest me in the following pages is the question: what was the thought of the Creator about Russia."[39] As for Ilyin, he wrote about "the Russian idea" in 1951: "This creative idea . . . formulates what is *already inherent* in the Russian people [*uzhe prisushche russkomu narodu*], what constitutes its *good power* [*blagaia sila*; NB: with the connotation of *blessing*], in which it is *right, in the face of God* [*prav pered litsom Bozhiim*] and *original* among all other peoples. At the same time, this idea shows us our historical *task* and our *spiritual way* [*dukhovnyi put'*]. . . . The Russian idea is something living, simple, and creative. . . . God's gifts—history and nature—have made Russian man the way he is [*sdelali russkogo cheloveka imenno takim*]."[40]

For Ilyin, part of Russia's destiny is a strong, authoritarian state. Interestingly, he does not reject democracy in general, but rather argues that its preferability or non-preferability is strongly context-dependent. He opposes democratic universalism, arguing that six conditions have to be met for democracy to be *creative* instead of *formal*: first, the people must understand the meaning of freedom, otherwise the result will be anarchy and despotism; second, there has to be a sufficiently high level of legal consciousness or awareness [*pravosoznanie*], i.e., people have to understand themselves as a "*free subject of rights*"; a third precondition is the economic independence of the citizen; fourth, there has to be a "minimal level of education and awareness"; fifth, an indispensable precondition is "political experience, of which in a future Russia both the *more* educated social strata and the *less* educated masses will be devoid"; sixth, finally, "genuine, creative democracy presupposes in man a whole series of properties and capacities," including character, patriotism, integrity, responsibility, and civic courage.[41]

These are highly recognizable points, not only to be found in Western political philosophy, but also in the discourse about whether or not particular parts of the world are "ready for democracy"—those parts include the

38. Solovyov, *l'Idée russe*, 83.

39. Berdyaev, *Russian Idea*, 19.

40. Ilyin, *Nashi zadachi*, 2.1:419, 424.

41. Ilyin, *Nashi zadachi*, 2.1:451–55.

Arab world, sub-Saharan Africa, and, obviously, the post-Soviet world. Ilyin's empathic claim, uttered in 1951, that "a country that lacks the necessary preconditions for a healthy, creative democracy, should not introduce that regime before those fundamental preconditions have been established,"[42] is not at all exotic. It remains, moreover, squarely within the right-Hegelian current of thought that he belongs to. For Hegel, as Ilyin paraphrases him, "every nation has the [political] system [*ustroistvo*], that is "commensurate [*sorazmerno*]" to and "corresponds [*sootvetstvuet*]" to its spirit [*dukh*, i.e., *Geist*]."[43]

Theocracy, Sobornost', and Democracy

The three thinkers under scrutiny all depart from a monotheistic political theology that implies a concept of theocracy: there ultimately is a single, sovereign God. There is not, however, any strict opposition of principle between theocracy and democracy, nor is there between democracy and *sobornost'*. The opposite of democracy is a whole range of forms of monarchic, oligarchic, aristocratic, kleptocratic and hierocratic rule, and even these are not absolute opposites: most empirically existing political systems combine monarchic, aristocratic, and democratic elements. Even a self-declared theocracy like the Islamic Republic of Iran entails monarchic (the Supreme Guardian ayatollah Khamenei), aristocratic (effectively hierocratic), and democratic elements (the elections that put Rohani in the position of president were limited, but genuine ones).

The true opposite of theocracy is "anthropocracy," and although this opposition is conceptually clear, it is, of course, not easily assessed in daily political life. If there is an omnipotent God, she or he will rule society anyway—the question merely becomes: directly or indirectly, and if the latter, by which means. If there is no such omnipotent God, or if she or he has abandoned the world once it was created, then all government is "anthropocratic," but some participants in it may still refer to a God. If, finally, we do not agree about the existence of a God and of her or his involvement in this—or: the—world, then either we have to accept a plurality of perspectives and interpretations, or we have to subscribe to one or to some while persecuting, oppressing, or tolerating the others. To the extent to which a given polity is democratic, it will have to deal with this plurality: a majority

42. Ilyin, *Nashi zadachi*, 2.1:457.
43. Ilyin, *Nashi zadachi*, 2.1:417; Hegel, *Rechtsphilosophie*, 360.

can still impose its own perception of these matters, i.e., its own political theology, but this hegemony will then be manifest. Many will point to Moses as a model case of *true* theocracy, but this depends on taking the Old Testament as *literally* true—theocracy as direct and manifest rule by God.[44] Reading the book Exodus symbolically solves this problem, but turns theocracy into something that is only "there" for the faithful, the believers, those who think that God rules even if not manifestly so.

Here is why there is no opposition of principle between theocracy and democracy: a *dēmos* that firmly believes in one and the same God, i.e., a *dēmos* that is "in God" together, can rule its affairs democratically, while considering itself a theocracy: if religious congregation and political community coincide, democracy and theocracy are identical. If "God" is more or less loosely defined and not connected dogmatically to any particular monotheistic religion or denomination, this model can even be expanded: Christians, Muslims, Jews, and even Native Americans can identify with the God of "God bless America" and put their trust in him, leaving it open what this "God" exactly means to them: Jahweh, Allah, Manitou, God, Gott, *theos*, or *Bog*. It also explains why the ROC, unlike for example the Roman Catholic Church, does not have a preference for our against democracy as such: as the official social doctrine of the ROC states, the actual "form and methods of government are conditioned in many ways by the spiritual and moral condition of society. Aware of this, the Church accepts the people's choice or does not resist it at least."[45]

There is no opposition between democracy and *sobornost'* either. If we define *sobornost'* in its socio-political meaning, as "internally differentiated organic whole of interconnected individuals," there is, again, no reason why this should be incompatible with democracy: relative opposition between the various parts of this whole, minor conflicts as it were, are perfectly imaginable, and they can be solved democratically, by majority vote, against the backdrop of shared membership of the same organic whole. This is, in principle, how the "liberal" or "progressive" representatives of Russian religious philosophy, thinkers like Frank, Bulgakov, and Berdyaev sought to give democratic representation a place.

---

44. See the official Social Doctrine of the ROC: "In Ancient Israel, before the Kingdom, there existed the only genuine theocracy, i.e., divine rule, in history" (Russian Orthodox Church, "Basis of the Social Concept" 3.1).

45. See Russian Orthodox Church, "Basis of the Social Concept" 3.7. For an elaboration, see Hoppe-Kondrikova et al., *Christian Social Doctrine*.

The opposite of *sobornost'* thus is *not* democracy, but dividedness, atomization, individualism, particularization or, as Solovyov puts it, *obosoblenie* or "being on one's own." Using a more present-day notion taken from Jean-Luc Nancy, I would suggest that the real opposition of *sobornost'* is not even particularity (which is still related to something general or universal of which it is the particularization), but *radical singularity*. Even there, however, a connection can be established: if we humans are radically singular, we can—and according to Nancy: should—create our own form of being-together or commonality, not as something pre-given or pre-ordered, as in Solovyov, but as a real life possibility, a kind of grassroots *sobornost'*.[46] Indeed, I think that connections with some theological positions outside Orthodox Christianity, for example in radical theology, are very well possible here. In any case, there does not exist a necessary opposition between democracy and *sobornost'*, either.

So, where *is* the opposition, or where are the oppositions? Ultimately, I think, they are to be found at the level of social ontology and the overall idea of society, whether at the level of a single nation (Ilyin) or that of humankind (Solovyov), as an *organic whole* (however internally differentiated it may be), and whether as a presupposed *fact*, a *normative ideal*, or a *regulative idea*. The (arch)enemy of the idea of *sobornost'* and of its defenders is formed by division, separation, opposition. Difference is only acceptable as differentiation *within* a single whole, separation and opposition are legitimate only if they are relative; in political terms, opposition is only legitimate if it is *loyal* opposition, i.e., opposition *in*, not *to*, the incumbent government.

If there is no strict opposition between theocracy and democracy, then we must allocate *sobornost'* in its *political* meaning [I do not deny other, especially ecclesiological meanings, they just are not my focal point] not in some "between," but in the interconnection of the two concepts. Here, I suggest, following Claude Lefort, that *modern*, liberal democracy, which above I have broken down into the three dimensions of democracy, liberal principles, and rule of law, is an "adequate" answer to a condition in which all "markers of certainty" have been dissolved.[47] As a result, modern, late-modern, or post-modern individuals no longer can relate to any somehow *given* points of reference. Of course, many do have certainties, in the existential, ideological, or religious sense, or a combination thereof, but those

46. Nancy, *Être singulier pluriel*.
47. Lefort, "La question," 29.

certainties appear as *individual* preferences, answers to the questions that humans face, and as long as any such answers are no threat to others, they are accepted as simply *different.*

This also is one key to understanding the qualification of our current condition as "post-secular." Post-secularity does not mean a return to religion or a goodbye to the secular state. It means that secularity *also* has stopped being a marker of certainty, and that secularism, like all other -isms (jihadism included), has become one out of many possible "positions." Post-secularity does not *imply* a return to religion, or to a religion-based polity, it rather implies the returned possibility of both.

Paradoxically, this *also* generates new "legitimate space" for a notion like *sobornost'.* Dogmatic, strongly "church-bound" conceptualizations are unlikely to gain wide support, but then the notion of *sobornost'* that we know from Russian religious philosophy also developed largely *outside* the official church.[48] Moreover, it took on very different forms: the *sobornost'* of Berdyaev is not the *sobornost'* of Frank or the *sobornost'* of Florenskii. People of Orthodox faith, itself today one "option" among many on the religious market, can voice and "propagate" the notion of *sobornost'* as a communal and political ideal.

Unexpected alliances are, moreover, possible, for instance between a conservative interpretation of *sobornost'* as tightly-knit community life based on a shared religious faith and certain interpretations of Islamic *ummah.* At the other end of the spectrum, unexpected alliances are possible between pluralistic interpretations of *sobornost',* pluralistic interpretations of Islam, and the type of communalism that we find in a left-Heideggerian like Nancy whose idea of *être ensemble* [being together] on the basis of a radical *être-avec* [being with] can be qualified as agnostic grass roots *sobornost'. Surely,* we are not talking about political coalitions or organizational associations, but rather about elective affinities [*Wahlverwandschaften*]. *Surely,* there are many different ways in which political philosophy and political theology can relate to this—the very blurring of the distinction between those two is *also* part of our current, "post-secular" condition. *Surely,* all this is not necessarily "good news": such affinities can also have aggressive or violent consequences, depending for example on more inclusive or more exclusive interpretations of a notion like, in this case, *sobornost'.*

However, if modern democracy is the proper political answer to a situation in which the markers of certainty have dissolved, including the

48. See Berdyaev, *Russian Idea*, 114.

marker of certainty that was provided by the very idea of the dissolution of all markers of certainty, then modern democracy is also the political form that embodies the *legitimacy of conflict*. The late modern liberal democratic rule of law state not simply allows, but even invites the articulation not only of a plurality of world views—including ones with *sobornost'* at their center—but also of interests, preferences, aims, projects, etc., that may, but need not peacefully coexist. Democracy can be seen, from this angle, and with the presupposed warrant of essential rights and liberties—speech, assembly, association, demonstration—as the proper *battle field* where conflicts are played out that might otherwise go underground. (To be sure, this is ideal theory: if the demands of young people in suburbs had been taken more seriously, if they had been facilitated to articulate themselves politically, we would have seen less *jihadis* today.)

Clearly, the idea of a constitution that renders conflict *legitimate*, is fundamentally at odds with the idea of society as an organic whole. It can, therefore, accommodate a notion like *sobornost'* that points to the *possibility* of community and commonality, but it conflicts with one that implies an organically structured society, differentiated only *internally,* and topped off with, to quote Solovyov, "one supreme authority, invested with all the positive rights of the social whole as such."[49] The paradox is that the idea(l) of society as an organic whole can have a place within the liberal-democratic rule of law state only because the latter is, precisely, *not* an organic whole, and must resist, on the basis of its own principles, any attempt to establish such an organic whole. The political visions of Solovyov, and especially Ilyin, are incompatible with the idea of a liberal-democratic rule of law state; the same may apply less to Berdyaev.

Conclusion

Any discussion of democracy, freedom, state, or law is, for Solovyov, Berdyaev and Ilyin, intimately connected with the Russian idea, which is not a human, but a divine idea. What unites these three Russian religious philosophers is their resistance against the replacement of a theocentric by an anthropocentric perception of world and man, and of a theocratic by an anthropocratic view of politics. The idea(l)s of a Christian monarchic state and of *sobornost'* are two "theocratic" alternatives to the idea of a *merely* worldly polity consisting of autonomous individuals. The rejection of a "Western"

49. Solovyov, *Justification of the Good*, 329.

model by these thinkers, and by the current regime in Russia, depends on the opposition not of authoritarianism (or: strong state) and democracy (or: republic), but on that between theocracy and anthropocracy. For this current in Russian political philosophy, theology is never far away, just as it is a short walk from the Kremlin to the Khram Khrista Spasitelia.

What singles out the political philosophies of the three thinkers who were recently referred to favorably by the incumbent president of Russia, is the idea of the polity, or, more specifically, the state, as an *organic whole* that organizes a particular nation which is somehow part of "God's plan with humanity." This organicism comes to the fore, among others, in the subordination of the *trias politica* to a single "head of state." The idea of society as an organic, internally differentiated, but not divided whole, excludes giving societal conflict, and its political articulations, a legitimate place: opposition can only be loyal opposition *within* the organic whole.

Vladimir Putin's recent invocation of Solovyov, Berdyaev, and Ilyin is less superficial than it may seem. If it is instrumental, we should acknowledge that it does help Russians in making sense of their historical situation. These thinkers can provide ideas that, as ideologemes, are not mere window dressing, but appeal to a broad Russian audience and match the "spirit" that has gained prominence in Russia today. Moreover, the ideas of a strong, sovereign state and of a *sobornost'*-based community do not only mutually exclude each other, they also, jointly, oppose the "Western" model of a liberal-democratic rule of law state based on free individuality. At the same time, the idea(l) of *sobornost'* can unexpectedly gain new legitimacy and can align itself with other ideas about grass roots commonality, e.g., those of Nancy. Paradoxically, *sobornost'* can be accommodated in post-modern, post-secular society precisely because the latter is *not* an organic whole.

We can thus can flesh out two alternative models: a "Russian" model that, based on a Divine Russian Idea, comes in two variants, the strong state and the *sobornost'*-based community, and a "Western" model that, based on a post-secular human idea, answers the situation after the dissolution of all markers of certainty and excludes the idea of society as an organic whole, but does offer space for the idea of *sobornost'*. The question if and how either Russia or Western societies correspond to these models is, however, quite a different one.

Bibliography

Berdyaev, Nikolai. *Russaia ideia*. Moscow: Folio, 2004 [English: *The Russian Idea*. Hudson, NY: Lindisfarne, 1992].

———. *Sud'ba Rossii*. Moscow: Reabilitatsiia, 2004.

Chamberlain, Lesley. *The Philosophy Steamer*. London: Atlantic, 2006.

Eltchaninoff, Michel. *Dans la tête de Vladimir Poutine*. Arles: Actes Sud, 2015 [English: *Inside the Mind of Vladimir Putin*. London: C. Hurst & Co., 2018].

Evlampiev, Igor. "Ivan Il'in i ego kniga o Gegele." In *Filosofiia Gegelia kak uchenie o konkretnosti Boga i cheloveka*, by Ivan Ilyin, 5–12. St. Petersburg: Nauka, 1994.

Hoppe-Kondrikova, Olga, et al. "Christian Social Doctrine East and West: the Russian Orthodox Social Concept and the Roman Catholic Compendium Compared." *Religion, State, and Society* 41 (2013) 199–224.

Ilyin, Ivan A. *Filosofiia Gegelia kak uchenie o konkretnosti Boga i cheloveka*. St. Petersburg: Nauka, 1994.

———. *Nashi zadachi; stat'i 1948–1954 gg*. Vol. 2.1–2 of *Sobranie sochinenii v 10-i tt*. Moscow: Russaia kniga, 1993.

———. *Obshchee uchenie o prave i gosudarstve*. Moscow: Khranitel', 2006.

Kaehne, Axel. *Political and Social Thought in Post-Communist Russia*. Abingdon: Routledge, 2007

Lefort, Claude. "La question de la démocratie." In *Essais sur le politique; XIXe-XXe siècles*, by Claude Lefort, 17–30. Paris: Seuil, 1986.

Montesquieu. *De l'esprit des lois*. Paris: Garnier-Flammarian, 1979 [English: *The Spirit of the Laws*. Cambridge: Cambridge University Press, 1989].

Mouffe, Chantal. *The Democratic Paradox*. London: Verso, 2000.

Nancy, Jean-Luc. *Être singulier pluriel*. Paris: Galilée, 1996 [English: *Being Singular Plural*. Stanford, CA: Stanford University Press, 2000].

Putin, Vladimir. "Address to the Federal Assembly." *President of Russia*, December 12, 2012. http://en.kremlin.ru/events/president/news/17118.

Russian Orthodox Church. "The Basis of the Social Concept: III. Church and State." *Department for External Church Relations*. https://mospat.ru/en/documents/social-concepts/iii.

Schulz, Luisa Maria. "Der Präsident als Philosoph: Putins Flüsterer." *Frankfurter Allgemeine Zeitung*, May 29, 2014. http://www.faz.net/aktuell/feuilleton/der-praesident-als-philosoph-putins-fluesterer-12961159.html.

Solovyov, Vladimir S. "Law and Morality: Essays in Applied Ethics." In *Politics, Law, and Morality: Essays by V. S. Soloviev*, edited by Vladimir Wozniuk, 131–212. New Haven: Yale University Press, 2000.

———. "L'idée russe." In *La Sophia et les autres écrits français*, edited by François Rouleau, 83–102. Lausanne: L'Age d'Homme, 1978.

———. *Opravdanie dobra*. Vol. 1 of *Sochineniia v dvukh tomakh*. Moscow: Mysl', 1988 [English: *The Justification of the Good*. Grand Rapids: Eerdmans, 2005].

Van der Zweerde, Evert. "Das Böse und das Politische. Zur anti-politischen politischen Philosophie Vladimir Solov'evs." In *Das Böse in der russischen Kultur*, edited by Bodo Zelinsky and Jessica Kravets, 60–75. Köln: Böhlau, 2008.

———. "Ideas at Work!" In *Sushchnost' i slovo; sbornik nauchnykh statei k iubileiu professor N. V. Motroshilovoi*, edited by M. A. Solopova and M. F. Bykova, 61–80. Moscow: Fenomenologiia–Germenevtika, 2009.

————. "The Rise of the People: the Political Philosophy of the Vekhovtsy." In *Landmarks Revisited: The Vekhi Symposium One Hundred Years On*, edited by Ruth Coates and Robin Aizlewood, 104–127. Boston: Academic, 2013.

————. "Between Mysticism and Politics: The Continuous Pattern of Vladimir Solov'ev's Thought." *Journal for Religion and Transformation in Contemporary Society* 8.1 (forthcoming).

2

The Russian Postsecular[1]

Kristina Stoeckl & Dmitry Uzlaner

Introduction

The place of religion in public sphere and the validity of religious arguments under conditions of political modernity are important topics
in political philosophy. Comprehensive visions of the "good life" endorsed
by religious traditions are almost always bound to clash with the modern,
thin, secular and procedural conceptions of what holds a pluralistic political community together. Orthodox Christianity, as any other religious
tradition, has been challenged to define its relationship with political modernity.[2] For the most part of modern history, the work of definition of the
religious-secular relationship has been conceptualized as a one-way street:
it was the religious traditions that had to come to terms with secularization as a social process, and with secularism as increasingly predominant
worldview. In the twentieth century, this has meant downright repression
for the churches in communist Eastern Europe, but even in the Western
world, religious traditions could either reject the secular world all together,
in which case the secular side considered them "fundamentalist," or they
could try to arrange themselves with the secular order, in which case they
were considered as "modernizing."[3]

1. This chapter has received funding from the European Research Council (ERC) under the European Union's Horizon 2020 research and innovation programme (POSEC,
ERC-STG-2015-676804).

2. Stoeckl et al., *Political Theologies in Orthodox Christianity*.

3. Stoeckl, "Political Theologies and Modernity."

Whichever road they chose, it remained a unilateral move; it was all about religion coming to terms with political modernity. In recent years, however, this one-way street model of the religious-secular relation has lost persuasiveness, and has given way to a model that sees the relationship between political modernity and religion in a more reciprocal way. Two factors have been decisive for this shift. First, there is the sociological observation that religions continue to occupy an important role in the modern world, despite all predictions of their imminent decline.[4] Second, we can observe a philosophical and conceptual shift, which disputes the normative validity and democratic legitimacy of secularism as the quintessence of modern politics.[5] As a consequence, today's debates over the secular-religious relationship have lost the character of a one-way street and start to resemble a two-way road; it is the secular and the religious side defining *with and vis-à-vis each other* the terms of their coexistence. The term that catches both the sociological and normative novelty of this moment is *postsecularity*.

Arguably, Orthodox Christianity is being challenged by postsecularity more profoundly than Western Churches: sociologically, because after the fall of communism, Orthodox Churches in Eastern Europe are experiencing a resurgence, whereas Western Churches have had continuity; and normatively, because in the context of political transition, matters like state-church relations, largely settled in the West, are open to discussion and new institutionalization.

In this chapter, we examine how *postsecularity* is engaged both as an empirical condition and as a philosophical concept in the Orthodox context. Our focus lies on Russian Orthodoxy, because Russian Orthodox theologians and philosophers have been active in discussing postsecularity, and have created a new and original "Russian postsecular." This Russian postsecular, we will demonstrate, is characterized by the desire to define a middle ground between anti-modernism and modernization, or—sticking to our road metaphor—to map a two-way road in a maze of one-way streets. However, the Russian postsecular is, as we show in the last section of this chapter, not immune to ideological instrumentalization, and has been used to justify Russia's recent anti-liberal turn to "traditional values." This

---

4. Casanova, *Public Religions in the Modern World*; Berger, *Desecularization of the World*.

5. Poignantly expressed in the title of Veit Bader's book, *Secularism or Democracy?*

anti-liberal instrumentalization of postsecular theory is partly connected to the lack of normative reflections in Russian debates on postsecularity.

Postsecularity and Orthodox Theology

Postsecularity as a concept is rooted in empirical claims regarding the demise of the secularization thesis, and the widely shared agreement that modern societies are experiencing a "return of religion." Several Western sociologists have disputed the validity of this last claim, arguing that the world "is as furiously religious as it always was."[6] However, whether sociologists have taken a critical[7] or an affirmative stance on postsecularity as a new empirical reality,[8] contemporary scholars, philosophers and theologians tend to agree that something has changed in the way secular public discourse, academic political philosophy, and social theory approach religion. The epitomizing moment of this new relationship between secular philosophy and theology was the face to face discussion between the German philosopher Jürgen Habermas and the future Pope Benedict, Cardinal Ratzinger, in 2004.[9] In the wake of this event, Christian theologians of different denominational backgrounds have started to discuss the place of religion in a political modernity that appears to be shedding off its anti-religious reflexes in terms of postsecularity.[10]

Orthodox theologians have made no exception to this trend. Contemporary Orthodox theologians have affirmed that we live in a post-secular age, from Pantelis Kalaitzidis in his summary of the proceedings of the international conference "Academic Theology in a Post-Secular Age"[11] and Davor Dzalto in "Religion and Realism,"[12] to Sergej Horujy[13] and Alexander Kyrlezhev, about whom we will write in detail below. Even church leaders

6. Berger, *Desecularization of the World*.

7. Turner, "Religion in a Post-Secular Society"; Gorski et al., *Post-Secular in Question*.

8. Rosati and Stoeckl, *Multiple Modernities and Postsecular Societies*; Molendijk et al., *Exploring the Postsecular*; Rosati, *Making of a Postsecular Society*.

9. Habermas and Ratzinger, "Vorpolitische moralische Grundlagen."

10. Reder and Schmidt, *Ein Bewußtsein*; Eggermeier, "Post-Secular Modernity?"; Yudin, "Dialektika postsekuliarizatsii."

11. Kalaïtzidis, "Orthodox Theology."

12. Dzalto, *Religion and Realism*.

13. Horujy, "Postsekuliarizm i antropologiia"; "Anthropological Dimensions"; "Postsekuliarizm i situatsiia cheloveka."

use the term freely in their speeches—for example, Ecumenical Patriarch Bartholomew[14] or Patriarch of Moscow Kirill.[15] But what does this reference to postsecularity actually entail from an Orthodox theological perspective? What do Orthodox thinkers mean when they use this term? In this chapter, we look into the Russian debate for an exemplary answer to these questions. However, before we turn to the Russian texts, let us clarify what postsecularity stands for.

What is Postsecularity?[16]

In Western academia, the most influential interpretation of postsecularity was given by the political liberal agenda formulated in particular by John Rawls and Jürgen Habermas.[17] The Habermasian interpretation of postsecularity holds that an ideology of secularism is not an integral part of liberalism, and that liberalism should instead be qualified by "reflexive" forms of secularism.[18] Secularism as a political ideology, the argument goes, discriminates against religious citizens. All citizens must in principle be free to enter into public debates from within the framework of their "comprehensive doctrines," provided that they are ready to deliberate over political norms in a reasonable fashion, and in the view of a consensus that can become valid for all (the "overlapping consensus"). Habermas himself describes this kind of reasoning as "post-metaphysical," because it affirms the validity of moral and political principles not by indication of some transcendental point of reference, but through an immanent deliberation process. The equality of public deliberation is threatened, however, when the secular public discourse renders it difficult for religious citizens to voice their arguments. Habermas responds to this particular problem with the assertion that not only should religious citizens be asked to translate their claims into the language of secular public discourse, but also the non-religious citizens are asked to play their part, namely, to scale down their secularist aspirations. Such a reciprocal work of translation should give rise to what he calls "the complementary learning process," Habermas's concepts

---

14. Bartholomew I, "Religions and Peace."

15. Kirill, "Tserkovnaia zhizn.'"

16. For more on this, see Stoeckl and Uzlaner, "Four Genealogies of Postsecularity."

17. Rawls, *Political Liberalism*; Habermas, "Religion in the Public Sphere."

18. Calhoun et al., *Rethinking Secularism*; Ferrara et al., *Philosophy and Social Criticism*; Gorski et al., *Post-Secular in Question*.

of translation and of complementary learning are premised on the idea that religions undergo a process of modernization in response to the challenges of religious pluralism, modern science, and positive law and profane morality. This notion of "modernization of religious consciousness" has been accused of a secularist and ethnocentric bias by some commentators, who see in it merely a softened version of the old one-way street model of religious-secular relationships, where religious traditions just react to secular developments and ideas.[19]

The Habermasian version of postsecularity can be said to be the most influential tradition of understanding postsecularity. Apart from Habermas's powerful interpretation, there exist alternative accounts of postsecularity. One can find examples of these alternative understandings of postsecularity in works of John Caputo, in particular his "On Religion" (2001), or in John Milbank's "Beyond Secular Reason" (1990) and the movement of "Radical Orthodoxy" that he initiated (1998). These non-Habermasian interpretations are different from each other,[20] but they basicaly agree with the double shift connected to the postsecular turn: the sociological shift in the sense that religions are increasing their social significance; and the philosophical shift in the sense of rethinking the modern antireligous bias and a new readiness to consider religious arguments seriously.

But there is a very important difference between the Habermasian and these alternative accounts of postsecularity: the non-Habermasian interpretations aim at a more direct critique and rethinking of modern secular reason. For Habermas, the postsecular is "a sociological predicate," it refers to "modern societies that have to reckon with the continuing existence of religious groups and the continuing relevance of the different religious traditions," as well as to "an altered self-understanding of the largely secularized societies."[21] But this, in Habermas's view, is not "a genealogical predicate" as it has nothing to do with "the paths of a genealogy of modern thought." Reason still "remains secular even in a situation depicted as 'postsecular.'"[22] Habermas protests against blurring distinctions between faith and reason, theology and philosophy, the religous and the secular. According to him,

19. Habermas, "Dialogue"; Leezenberg, "How Ethnocentric is the Postsecular?"; Maclure and Taylor, *Secularism and Freedom of Conscience.*

20. It is important to note that Caputo and Milbank provide very different alternatives to Habermasian postsecularity: Caputo follows deconstruction, whereas Milbank relies on a theology of analogy and participation.

21. Habermas and Mendieta, "Post-Secular World Society," 4.

22. Habermas and Mendieta, "Post-Secular World Society," 3.

the postsecular "altered self-understanding" does not imply the necessity to rethink or even question the basic foundations of modern secularity. Habermas, in short, offers a very balanced vision of postsecularity. On the one hand, he recognizes the fact that religion is not a "configuration of the past," and that religious traditions should be fruitfully engaged with; but on the other hand, Habermas wants to leave the modern foundations of the distinction between the religious and the secular intact.

The non-Habermasian interpretations of postsecularity, by contrast, go right to the foundations of modern secular reason. They interpret postsecularity as an important turning point in the genealogy of modern thought. Postsecularity, in this view, becomes a constitutive element of a postmodern turn, which marks a rethinking of key tenets of modernity, the rejection of religion being the most important of them.[23] Rethinking the key tenets of secular modernity implies reconsideration of the very distinctions that Habermas would prefer to leave intact—between faith and reason, the religious and the secular, philosophy and theology.

The blurring of the boundary between theology and philosophy leads to the emergence of new, we could say "hybrid" forms of theological-philosophical reflection. Philosophers look to religion as "a key 'site of resistance' against the alienations of what is perceived as a singularly Western modernity."[24] Some observers even call this trend "contamination of philosophy with theological thinking," or "theologisation of philosophy."[25] At a moment in time when secular philosophy reflects upon its secularist bias and opens itself towards religion, theology also reacts to this turn, and perceives it as a chance to re-enter into philosophy and social theory on its own grounds.[26] The postsecular turn is perceived as a kind of emancipatory moment for Christian theology, which is now free to speak with its own language, without constantly looking back at secular epistemology and ontology.[27] Radical Orthodoxy, as proposed by John Milbank and his colleagues, is a good example of this kind of postsecular theology.[28]

The postmodern dimension of postsecularity is closely connected to genealogical studies about the modern construction of "religion," the

23. Caputo, *On Religion*, 37.

24. Žižek and Milbank, *Monstrosity of Christ*, 255–56.

25. Whistler and Smith, *After the Postsecular*, 2.

26. Blond, *Post-Secular Philosophy*.

27. Smith, *Introducing Radical Orthodoxy*.

28. For example, Pabst, *Metaphysics*; Milbank and Pabst, *Politics of Virtue*.

"secular," and the "religious-secular binary." These studies show that the perception of modern religion and the modern secular as two incompatible dimensions is contingent, i.e., a construct resulting from theoretical and political efforts dating back at least to the fifteenth century.[29] Postsecularity becomes, in this genealogy of argumentation, the study of religion and society after the rejection of the strong assumptions of the secularization thesis, and after the deconstruction of conceptualizations of religion in the Western social sciences.

We need to stress that the field of theological-philosophical postsecularity is far from unanimous—this is a pluralistic, burgeoning conflict field ranging from Milbank's "Radical Orthodoxy"[30] to Caputo's spiritual deconstruction,[31] to Michel Henry and Jean-Luc Marion's theological turn in phenomenology,[32] to Žižek's "theology of the death of God."[33]

Most non-Habermasian interpretations of postsecularity consider postsecularity not merely as a rethinking of the antireligious bias of modern secular thought, but as reconsideration of secular reason itself, to the point of considering the possibility of going beyond secular modernity to some alternative versions of it. Such a "strong" version of postsecularity, which implies not just an adjustment of directions (from one-way to two-way) inside the fixed structure of the religious-secular divide, but a more radical rethinking of not just the directions of influence, but of the very foundations of this structure, is attractive from an Orthodox, conventionally modernity-critical perspective. Little wonder, therefore, that it is this non-Habermasian version of postsecularity that was appropriated and developed in the Russian philosophical and theological context.

Orthodox theologians question the fact that liberal secular modernity is something that must be taken for granted, and that postsecularity is what happens inside this configuration. There is a strong temptation to go beyond modernity and secularity, at least in the sphere of philosophical and theological reflection. For this reason, the Russian debate on postsecularity has remained peculiarly non-Habermasian; in fact, the postsecular theory

---

29. Asad, *Genealogies of Religion*; Nongbri, *Before Religion*; Cavanaugh, *Myth of Religious Violence*; Fitzgerald, *Discourse on Civility and Barbarity*.

30. Milbank, *Theology and Social Theory*.

31. Caputo and Vattimo, *After the Death of God*.

32. Staudigl and Alvis, "Phenomenology and the Post-Secular Turn."

33. Žižek and Milbank, *Monstrosity of Christ*, 110–233.

offered by Habermas finds only very limited reception and support,[34] and the initial Russian debates on postsecular society were almost completely devoid of any references to Habermas.

The Russian Postsecular

The first scholarly article to introduce the term "postsecular" into Russian in a systematic way was "A Postsecular Age" by Alexander Kyrlezhev, published in 2004.[35] It took another couple of years before the term gained wider prominence and a more systematic reception set in, mostly with the works of Dmitry Uzlaner,[36] Kyrlezhev[37] and few others.[38] The authors, who actively introduced the term into the Russian language were theologians, philosophers, and sociologists of religion. The prevailing use was that of postsecular as an adjective (*postsekuliarnyi*), such as in "postsecular society," "postsecular world," or "postsecular philosophy," but also postsecularism (*postsekuliarizm*) and postsecularity (*postsekuliarnost'*) was used. The popularity of postsecularity as a theory and concept among Russian Orthodox scholars rested on two factors: First of all, theological and philosophical debates on religion, secularism, modernity and politics were, just like almost all other philosophical trends in the West, new food for thought in a post-Soviet context that had been cut off from the Western humanities for decades. Postsecularity, intellectually, was the topic to study. Secondly, the term postsecularity had an immediate sociological appeal in twenty-first-century Russia, characterized by religious revival and a renewed public role of the Russian Orthodox Church.

In order to illustrate the way postsecularity has been conceptualized in Russia, we are going to consider the ideas of Alexander Kyrlezhev (b. 1957), a contemporary Orthodox theologian and philosopher, who, as we

34. Uzlaner, "Dialog nauki i religii."

35. Kyrlezhev, "Postsekuliarnaia epokha." See English version, Kyrlezhev, "Postsecular Age."

36. Uzlaner, "V kakom smysle sovremennyi"; "Vvedenie v postsekuliarnuiu filosofiiu"; "Kartografiia postsekuliarnogo."

37. Kyrlezhev, "Postsekuliarnoe"; "Postsekuliarnaia kontseptualizatsiia religii"; "Sekuliarizm i postsekuliarizm."

38. Morozov, "Has the Postsecular Age Begun?"; Shishkov, "Osmyslenie poniatiia 'postsekuliarnoe'"; Horujy, "Postsekuliarizm i antropologiia"; Antonov, "'Secularization' and 'Post-Secular.'" Horujy and Antonov identify the Russian religious philosophy of the Silver Age as a prologue to present-day postsecularity.

mentioned above, initiated discussions on postsecularity in Russia, and offered his own original interpretation of this concept. This interpretation is non-Habermasian (but definitely not anti-Habermasian) in the sense that ideas of Habermas play a very small role in his conceptualization of postsecularity. The Habermasian postsecular is much more normative than descriptive, while the Russian interpretation turns out to be much more descriptive and less normative.

The Russian reception of postsecularity is not interested in Habermas's "postmetaphysical postsecularism," as Bengtson calls it.[39] Instead, it emphasizes the link between postsecularity and postmodernity. "The start of the postsecular age coincides with the start of the postmodern age," Kyrlezhev writes, because "postmodernism gives freedom to religion, religiosity."[40] In many regards, Kyrlezhev's vision echoes the one of the theology of Radical Orthodoxy: "The theoretical foundations for the secular have been systematically dismantled. So if we are witnessing the advent of the postmodern . . . then we should also be seeing the advent of the post-secular. And insofar as twentieth-century Christian theology . . . allied itself with the Enlightenment project, resigning itself to an "apologetic" project of correlation with secular thought, the demise of modernity must also spell the demise of such theology."[41] It is little wonder that Alexander Kyrlezhev, together with other interpreters of postsecularity, was one of the key popularizers of Radical Orthodoxy's project in Russia.[42]

Postsecularity in this interpretation is first of all a *descriptive* concept. It describes the end of secularization, which in the Russian context refers to the end of the Soviet atheistic project, and the beginning of post-Soviet religious revival or desecularization. At the same time, postsecularity goes deeper and describes fundamental changes concerning the religious-secular divide. The contemporary situation, according to Kyrlezhev, should be scrutinized against the background of paradigm changes, which he describe as three consecutive shifts or stages: the religious, the secular, and the postsecular.[43] It is important to stress that Kyrlezhev does not intend this narrative to express a Hegelian triad of thesis-antithesis-synthesis. The postsecular in his view is *not* a synthesis, which unites crucial elements of

39. Bengtson, *Explorations in Post-Secular Metaphysics*.
40. Kyrlezhev, "Postsekuliarnaia epokha."
41. Smith, *Introducing Radical Orthodoxy*, 33.
42. See Kyrlezhev, "Dzhon Milbank."
43. Kyrlezhev, "Postsekuliarnoe," 100.

both the religious (thesis) and the secular (antithesis). Secondly, his is not a historicizing account, according to which at one time religion prevailed, which was then suppressed by the secular, only to be overtaken again by religion (as proponents of the de-secularization thesis would argue).

Kyrlezhev's original theory of postsecularity rests on the observation that all three stages (the religious, the secular, the postsecular) define in different ways the religious-secular divide; so the sequence can also be conceived of as a pre-modern religious-secular divide, a modern religious-secular divide, and, finally, a postmodern religious-secular divide. The key event in this series of shifts is the emergence of modern secularity. For this reason, the sequence could also be divided into the pre-secular, the secular, and the postsecular stages.

1. At the pre-secular (pre-modern or religious) stage, the world is thought of as God's creation. In this configuration, "everything secular is religious in the sense that it is thought of from inside the religious view of the world."[44] The secular here is just a pole of human existence that exists along the religious pole inside a world created by God. Historically, Kyrlezhev associates this configuration with the Middle Ages. In this configuration it is not possible to differentiate between the religious and secular, as religion is everywhere, "here religion is diffusive—even though there still is, so to say, a proper sphere of religion (for example, liturgy)."[45]

2. A proper religious-secular divide emerges only at the second, modern or secular stage; this is the emergence of modern secularity. In this modern configuration "the secular is not a specific aspect of theory/practice, it is not one of the poles of the world outlook, but a fundamental, ontological characteristic of the world, which is revealed by "the light of natural reason." The secular, in this new meaning, emerged as a construct of human thought, which describes the cosmic (natural) and the social as existing independently from the religious pole. From now on Nature (the natural) is not a distorted, but intrinsically good Creation of God, but a neutral givenness of the world, self-sufficient, and for that reason an ultimate reality with which human being and humanity in general are in contact."[46] Modern secularity

44. Kyrlezhev, "Postsekuliarnoe," 100.

45. Kyrlezhev, "Postsekuliarnaia kontseptualizatsiia religii," 56.

46. Kyrlezhev, "Postsekuliarnoe," 101.

emerges when the universe and society are conceptualized as natural, as existing without any reference to God or to something transcendental. This natural universe and society could be cognized without any references to transcendent sources, be it faith or revelation. The light of natural reason is enough to get all necessary theoretical and pragmatic knowledge about this secular order. This could be called a secular epistemology alongside a secular ontology.

In this secular configuration, religion turns into "that-which-enchants," and consequently must be "disenchanted."[47] In that sense, "it is important that the sociocultural whole is secular in its essence, whereas the religious is just a specific zone (along with art, ethics, law, economics, state, sport etc.). In other words, we are witnessing an immanentization of the religious, as all its claims to transcendence, to exit (theoretical and practical) beyond the boundaries of natural givenness to an other-worldly foundation of the natural world contradict the new basic vision that it is Nature, this-worldy by definition, that is the ultimate reality." In this new secular age, some place is still left for religion. But from now on this is a "sphere of the subjective and personal, a space of individual worldviews and corresponding psychology."[48]

3. The third, postmodern or postsecular stage sets in with a critique of secularism. Kyrlezhev writes: "The postsecular age starts at the moment when the true nature of secular knowledge as quasireligious is revealed; when it becomes clear that the universalist ambitions of secularism are in no way different from the universalist ambitions of religion." Kyrlezhev echoes postmodern theoreticians when he writes: "The scientific, objective Reason of Modernity—in its ultimate foundations—is a myth and nothing more."[49] Postsecularity shares with postmodern theory the fact that it is, in its first impulse, critical or negative: "The first and basic definition of the postsecular age is principally negative. This is a situation that reveals itself after the historical negation of the axiomaticity and firmness of basic meanings, ambitions and zeal of the modern secular paradigm. We are witnessing the death of the secular God, we are witnessing the secularization

---

47. Kyrlezhev, "Postsekuliarnoe," 102.

48. Kyrlezhev, "Postsekuliarnoe," 103.

49. Kyrlezhev, "Postsekuliarnoe," 106.

of secularism."[50] As a result, Kyrlezhev argues, the world is entering situation of "principle undecidedness concerning the eternal, ultimate and absolute foundation of the world which was established by the secular paradigm (of disenchantment)."[51]

To summarize, with postsecularity, the world is entering a post-secular *and* a postreligious stage, in the sense of moving beyond both the pre-modern and the modern religious-secular configuration. Kyrlezhev offers several examples of such post-religious and post-secular configurations: "spirituality," in the sense of forms of belief that mix various bits and pieces of traditional and new age religion and secular reason; and "Orthodox atheism," a form of belief in Orthodoxy as a cultural tradition without faith. Both are examples of people uniting irreconcilable elements—religious and secular—under one identity. All this gives us the basic definition of postsecularity according to Kyrlezhev: "Postsecularity is a (new) uncertainty concerning the religious-secular configuration."[52]

At the end of this three-stage narrative, Kyrlezhev goes on to argue for a positive understanding of postsecularity, seeing it not just as a moment of critique, but also as a situation of creativity: "There is only one solution for this situation: the creation of a new concept or a new model of religion which, on the basis of the above mentioned, would be postsecular."[53]

Up until this point, Kyrlezhev's argument has closely followed the non-Habermasian line of reasoning about postsecularity that we described in the first section; in particular Milbank's, "Beyond Secular Reason," but also Charles Taylor's "A Secular Age." Likewise, his scheme of the religious-secular-postsecular reminds of Caputo's "On Religion." Eventually, however, Kyrlezhev's attempt to develop not only a critical, but also a positive formulation of postsecularity goes beyond these sources. He sharply differs from Taylor's liberal communitarianism inasmuch as he rejects the Western religious-secular configuration as viable; but he also differs from reactionary antimodernism inasmuch as he criticizes any attempt to "recreate pre-modern religion."[54]

50. Kyrlezhev, "Postsekuliarnoe," 106.
51. Kyrlezhev, "Postsekuliarnoe," 105.
52. Kyrlezhev, "Postsekuliarnoe," 101.
53. Kyrlezhev, "Postsekuliarnaia kontseptualizatsiia religii," 57.
54. Kyrlezhev, "Sekuliarizm i postsekuliarizm," 173.

Kyrlezhev develops the normative dimension of his theory in the light of the post-Soviet experience. Soviet communism was for him a radical version of the secular configuration, which introduced a self-sufficient natural and social order, and considered religion obsolete. The failure of the Soviet project is interpreted by Kyrlezhev as the failure of modern secularism as such. Soviet communism has come to an end, and in a similar vein the age of secularization, from a Russian Orthodox perspective, has also come to an end. Western secularism—even though it unfolded in much less violently anti-religious ways than Soviet atheism—is seen as equally outdated and in need of reconsideration. At the same time, Kyrlezhev resists any attempt to glorify the religious past, or to embrace an all-saving Orthodox "tradition" that should reasserts itself in twenty-first-century Russia. Instead, he speaks of a "postsecular model of religion," by which he means a religious stance of engagement with the world that overcomes, on the one side, the pre-secular desire to give shape to the world as such, and, on the other side, the anti-secular desire to fight the world.

Kyrlezhev's interpretation of postsecularity as a kind of "third way" actually echoes the sociologist Kim Knott, who also speaks of the advent of a "third camp" in the field formerly defined by the binary between secular versus religion.[55] However, Kyrlezhev remains rather vague as to how exactly we should imagine this "postsecular model of religion." This vagueness, this lack of an elaborate normative vision—which is the strongest side of the Habermasian approach—is becoming a real theoretical and practical challenge to the Russian interpretation of postsecularity. This is especially true in the light of recent attempts to instrumentalize the theory of postsecular for the sake of particular ideological projects—a phenomenon we turn to in the next section.

Instrumentalization of Postsecularity and its Criticism

The concept of postsecularity emerged in the context of the academic study of the contemporary religious situation. In this sense, the Russian interpretation of postsecularity must be placed in one context with similar efforts by scholars in the West. It is, first of all, a value-free description of what is going on with religion in the twenty-first century. However, concepts travel beyond academic debates, and descriptions can turn in the eyes of some interpreters into prescriptions. Postsecularity is not an exception to this; in

55. Knott, "Cutting through the Postsecular City."

fact, it has acquired a popularity and political significance that few other philosophical terms presently enjoy.

In the Russian context, vague appeals to postsecularity have become an important argument in favor of strengthening relations between traditional religious organizations and Russian state institutions. Any criticism of this rapprochement is interpreted as attempt to hold on to outdated forms of secularism, which are untenable in the new postsecular context. The postsecular criticism of secular ontology and epistemology is also used as argument in the context of debates about the place of religion in the Russian educational system, for example theology in universities and lessons of religion in schools. Important church leaders such as Metropolitan Hilarion have referred to postsecular society in order to justify the inclusion of religious subjects into public school curricula.[56] Patriarch Kirill refers to the postsecular in the sense of a "new postsecular age," which means that "rigid and aggressive secularism is losing dominant positions in social and cultural life";[57] and Alexander Shipkov, the vice-chair of the Russian Orthodox Church's Synodal Department of Relations between the Church and Society and Mass Media, supported his ideas about the necessity of increasing the presence of the Orthodox Church in the life of the Russian state with reference to postsecularity.[58] To a certain extent, one can say that speaking about the postsecular has become part of official rhetoric of the Russian Orthodox Church.

It is little wonder that in this context postsecular theory faces harsh criticism from those who do not welcome Russian "desecularization from above."[59] As one author claimed: "a theologically informed vision about the coming of a postsecular age is based on unjustified sociological data: the postsecular world turns out to be a dream of a small group of believers, who aspire to hasten the time of spiritual revival."[60] Opponents criticize the theory of postsecularity as an ideological tool, which shakes the very weak foundations of the Russian secular state. In the logic of this criticism, the postsecular genealogical, philosophical and theological deconstruction of secularism does not lead to anything new. Instead of bringing greater

---

56. Metropolitan Hilarion, "Theology in Contemporary Russian Academia"; Shmonin, "Toledo Principles."

57. Kirill, "Teologiia v vuzakh."

58. Shipkov, "My dolzhny vziat' vse luchshee."

59. Karpov, "Social Dynamics of Russia's Desecularization."

60. Quoted in Dannenberg, "Tupiki 'Postsekuliarnogo.'"

democratic equality, or new legitimacy, it results or can result in destruction of important achievements of secular modernity—science, secular state, "civilized" religion, liberalism. Postsecular theory, the critics warn, is just a strategy for reinstalling a pre-secular order.

This dynamic of conflict leaves us, as scholars engaged in the elaboration of postsecular theory, with more questions than answers. As an analytical concept, postsecularity meant that scholars should look impartially at the social significance of religion, to the point of rethinking the very configuration of the religious-secular divide. It implied the search for new forms and models of the secular-religious relation that would not repeat the old ones. Postsecularity is interpreted by most theorists, from Habermas to Caputo to Kyrlezhev, as an opportunity for change, creativity and comprehensive learning. But the reality of most Russian Orthodox debates about postsecular society, which turn the theoretical concept into an ideological weapon, clearly shows that the novel term can easily be used to justify old and very well-known binaries. The postsecular research field is a site of conflict.

Kyrlezhev is well aware about the danger of such an instrumentalization. He admits that the novelty of the postsecular constellation is not really appreciated, nor positively exploited in the Russian Orthodox context. Referring to the possibility of a postsecular political theology, that is, a theology that positively and creatively reckons with secularization, he writes: "We are forced to assert that . . . the Orthodox ecclesial milieu, clergy and laity alike, rejects any *new* political theology as a theological reaction to historical and current developments."[61] Kyrlezhev is aware that in his present Russian Orthodox context, where theological antimodernism prevails, postsecular theory is only too often interpreted "as a foundation for religious revenge in the sociopolitical sphere," and could "serve as an obstacle to the development of a political theology . . . responsive to the processes of secularization."[62]

Conclusion

The concept of the postsecular and corresponding theories were introduced into the Russian context in order to make sense of the post-Soviet experience. Initially, this was a predominantly academic and sociological

61. Kyrlezhev, "On the Possibility or Impossibility," 187 (italics added).

62. Kyrlezhev, "On the Possibility or Impossibility," 187.

endeavor to address the end of Soviet secularization, and the increasing social significance of religion in the Russian context. Postsecularity provided
a theory according to which Russia was facing not just a simple "religious
revival," or a return to pre-communist forms of religiosity and church-state
relations, but a more profound reconfiguration of the religious-secular divide. The normative dimension of this theory implied the emergence of
new creative spaces of postsecularity, where new forms of religion, of political theology, and of church-state relations would appear, and would allow
to move beyond habitual pre-Soviet or Soviet forms. These forms would
be postsecular and postreligious with regard to the outdated pre-modern
and modern conceptualizations of religion and secular. In short, postsecular theory contained a promise of religious flourishing. It also contained
the promise of a flourishing of alternative worldviews and of pluralism in
general, but this last point was willfully overlooked when the theoretical
concept got appropriated by the official Orthodox discourse.

The concept of postsecularity was gladly taken on by Russian Orthodox Church representatives, who perceived the post-Soviet situation as un-
fair to the increasing social significance of Orthodox Christianity in Russia.
This led to an oversimplification of this concept, to the point that it has
become a justificatory tool for just any expansion of the Church's presence
in Russian society. In the last five years, a series of measures have considerably expanded the power of Russian Orthodox Church and have marked
Russia's turn to "traditional values."[63] As a consequence, antireligious and
anticlerical sentiments among secular groups who perceive this expansion
not as something new, but as a simple return to pre-Soviet forms, have also
increased. In order to oppose Russia's conservative turn the critics refer to
arguments which more and more remind of traditions of Soviet "scientific
atheism." As a result, the Russian public sphere is divided between two
incompatible camps—one hyper-religious, which argues for tradition and
perceives any criticism of Church and Orthodoxy as intrigues of enemies of
the Church and of the state, the other—hyper-secularist, which argues for
science, progress, liberalism, secularism, and which perceives any conces-
sion to religion as a betrayal of the fight for the future of civilized forms of
life in Russia. Postsecularity as the theory that would unpack the modern
secular-religious divide and create space and imagination for new forms
of interaction, is just a faint echo in these debates. There is no longer any

---

63. Stepanova, "Spiritual and Moral Foundations of Civilization"; Agadjanian, "Tradition, Morality, and Community"; Tsygankov, "Crafting the State-Civilization."

trace of the postsecular imperative, described hopefully by Horujy as "both conflicting sides, secular consciousness and religious consciousness, must stop their confrontation and go over to dialogue and partnership."[64]

So where to will the Russian postsecular lead? As a descriptive social theory, it provides a useful approach to the study of the very conflicts that spring up around it, but as a normative theory, the postsecular search for a middle ground between two extremes becomes more and more problematic, if not obsolete. It almost seems as if the fateful logic of Russian culture, which implies constant oscillation between two extremes, masterfully analyzed by Lotman and Uspenskij,[65] has once more triumphed over idealistic aspirations for some middle position that would bring both camps into "a complementary learning process."

Bibliography

Agadjanian, Alexander. "Tradition, Morality, and Community: Elaborating Orthodox Identity in Putin's Russia." *Religion, State, and Society* 23.1 (2017) 39–60.

Antonov, Konstantin. "'Secularization' and 'Post-Secular' in Russian Religious Thought." In *Beyond Modernity: Russian Religious Philosophy and Post-Secularism*, edited by Artur Mrowczynski-Van Allen, et al., 25–38. Eugene, OR: Wipf and Stock, 2016.

Asad, Talal. *Genealogies of Religion*. Baltimore, MD: Johns Hopkins University Press, 1993.

Bader, Veit. *Secularism or Democracy? Associational Governance of Religious Diversity*. Amsterdam: Amsterdam University Press, 2007.

Bartholomew I. "Religions and Peace." *Public Orthodoxy*, April 30, 2017. https://publicorthodoxy.org/2017/04/30/religions-and-peace.

Bengtson, Josef. *Explorations in Post-Secular Metaphysics*. London: Palgrave Macmillan, 2016.

Berger, Peter L., ed. *The Desecularization of the World: Resurgent Religion and World Politics*. Washington, DC: Ethics and Public Policy Center, 1999.

Blond, Philip, ed. *Post-Secular Philosophy: Between Philosophy and Theology*. London: Routledge, 1997.

Calhoun, Craig, et al., eds. *Rethinking Secularism*. Oxford: Oxford University Press, 2011.

Caputo, John D. *On Religion*. London: Routledge, 2001.

Caputo, John D., and Gianni Vattimo. *After the Death of God*. Edited by Jeffrey W. Robbins New York: Columbia University Press, 2009.

Casanova, José. *Public Religions in the Modern World*. Chicago: University of Chicago Press, 1994.

Cavanaugh, William T. *The Myth of Religious Violence: Secular Ideology and the Roots of Modern Conflict*. Oxford University Press, 2009.

64. Horujy, "Anthropological dimensions," 1.

65. Lotman and Uspenskii, "Binary Models." See also Epstein, "Religiia posle ateizma [Religion after Atheism]," 159–221.

Dannenberg, Anton N. "Tupiki 'Postsekuliarnogo.' Noveishie filosofsko-teologicheskie kontseptsii kak vyrazhenie krizisa zapadnogo khristianstva [Deadlocks of the 'Postsecular.' The Latest Philosophical and Theological Concepts as an Expression of the Crisis of Western Christianity]." http://portal-credo.ru/site/?act=monitor&id=20488.

Dzalto, Davor. *Religion and Realism*. Cambridge: Cambridge Scholars, 2016.

Eggermeier, Matthew T. "A Post-Secular Modernity? Jürgen Habermas, Joseph Ratzinger, and Johann Baptist Metz on Religion, Reason, and Politics." *The Heythrop Journal* 53 (2012) 453–66.

Epstein, Mikhail N. *Religiia posle ateizma. Novye vozmozhnosti teologii [Religion After Atheism. New Possibilities for Theology]*. Moscow: AST, 2013.

Ferrara, Alessandro, et al., eds. "Special Issue: Postsecularism and Multicultural Jurisdictions." *Philosophy and Social Criticism* 36.3–4 (2010).

Fitzgerald, Timothy. *Discourse on Civility and Barbarity: A Critical History of Religion and Related Categories*. Oxford: Oxford University Press, 2007.

Gorski, Philip, et al., eds. *The Post-Secular in Question: Religion in Contemporary Societies*. New York: New York University Press, 2012.

Habermas, Jürgen. "Dialogue: Jürgen Habermas and Charles Taylor." In *The Power of Religion in the Public Sphere*, edited by Judith Butler, et al., 60–69. Columbia: Columbia University Press, 2011.

———. "Religion in the Public Sphere." *European Journal of Philosophy* 14.1 (2006) 1–25.

Habermas, Jürgen, and Eduardo Mendieta. "A Postsecular World Society? On the Philosophical Significance of Postsecular Consciousness and the Multicultural World Society." *Immanent Frame*, February 3, 2010. https://tif.ssrc.org/2010/02/03/a-postsecular-world-society.

Habermas, Jürgen, and Joseph Ratzinger. "Vorpolitische Moralische Grundlagen Eines Freiheitlichen Staates." *Zur Debatte* 34.1 (2004) 1–12.

Horujy, Sergej S. "Anthropological Dimensions of the Postsecular Paradigm." Paper presented at Workshop, Faenza, May 12–14, 2011. http://synergia-isa.ru/wp-content/uploads/2011/05/hor_faenza_2011.pdf

———. "Postsekuliarizm i Antropologiia [Postsecularism and Anthropology]." *Chelovek.ru* 8 (2012) 15–34.

———. "Postsekuliarizm i situatsiia cheloveka [Postsecularism and the Situation of Man]." *Institute of Synergetic Anthropology*, August 2012. Online. http://synergia-isa.ru/wp-content/uploads/2012/08/hor_postec_i_sit_chel.pdf.

Kalaïtzidis, Pantelis. "Orthodox Theology and the Challenges of a Post-Secular Age: Questioning the Public Relevance of the Current Orthodox Theological 'Paradigm.'" In *Proceedings of the International Conference "Academic Theology in a Post-Secular Age,"* edited by Roman Fihas, 4–26. Lviv: Institute of Ecumenical Studies; Moscow: St. Andrew's Biblical Theological Institute, 2013.

Karpov, Vyacheslav. "The Social Dynamics of Russia's Desecularisation: a Comparative and Theoretical Perspective." *Religion, State, and Society* 41.3 (2013) 276.

Kirill. "Teologiia v vuzakh [Theology at the Universities]." *Tserkov' i vremia* 4.61 (2012). https://mospat.ru/church-and-time/1376.

———. "Tserkovnaia zhizn' dolzhna by' sluzheniem [The Church Life Should Be a Service]." *Izvestiia*, May 12, 2009. http://www.patriarchia.ru/db/text/642516.html.

Knott, Kim. "Cutting through the Postsecular City: A Spatial Interrogation." In *Exploring the Postsecular*, edited by Arie L. Molendijk, et al., 19–38. Bristol: Policy, 2012.

Kyrlezhev, Aleksandr. "Dzhon Milbank: razum po tu storonu sekuliarnogo [John Milbank: Reason Beyond Secular]." *Logos* 4.67 (2008) 28–32. http://ecsocman.hse.ru/data/2010/07/14/1216091545/1_pdfsam_26_pdfsam_3_pdfsam_Logos_4_2008.pdf.

———. "On the Possibility or Impossibility of an Eastern Orthodox Political Theology." In *Political Theologies in Orthodox Christianity*, edited by Kristina Stoeckl, et al., 181–87. London: Bloomsbury, 2017.

———. "The Postsecular Age: Religion and Culture Today." *Religion, State, and Society* 36.1 (2008) 21–31.

———. "Postsekuliarnaia epokha [The Postsecular Age]." *Kontinent* 120 (2004). http://magazines.russ.ru/continent/2004/120/kyr16.html.

———. "Postsekuliarnaia kontseptualizatsiia religii: k postanovke problemy [Postsecular Conceptualization of Religion: Towards a Formulation of the Problem]." *Gosudarstvo, religiia, tserkov' v Rossii i za rubezhom* 2.30 (2012) 53–68. http://www.religion.ranepa.ru/?q=ru/node/119 [English: "A Post-Secular Conceptualization of Religion: Defining the Question." *State, Religion, and Church* 1.1 (2014) 7–72. http://srch.ranepa.ru/node/442].

———. "Postsekuliarnoe: kratkaia interpretatsiia [The Postsecular: A Brief Interpretation]." *Logos* 3.28 (2011) 100–106. http://www.logosjournal.ru/arch/28/82_4.pdf.

———. "Sekuliarizm i postsekuliarizm v Rossii i v mire [Secularism and Post-Secularism in Russia and in the World]." *Otechestvennye zapiski* 52.1 (2013) 175–92. http://www.strana-oz.ru/2013/1/sekulyarizm-i-postsekulyarizm-v-rossii-i-v-mire.

Leezenberg, Michiel. "How Ethnocentric Is the Concept of the Postsecular?" In *Exploring the Post-Secular: The Religious, the Political, and the Urban*, edited by Arie L. Molendijk, et al., 91–112. Leiden: Brill, 2010.

Lotman, Iurii, and Boris Uspenskii. "Binary Models in the Dynamics of Russian Culture (to the End of the Eighteenth Century)." In *The Semiotics of Russian Cultural History*, edited by B. Gasparov and A. D. Nakhimovsky, 30–66. Ithaca, NY: Cornell University Press, 1985.

Maclure, Jocelyn, and Charles Taylor. *Secularism and Freedom of Conscience.* Cambridge, MA: Harvard University Press, 2011.

Metropolitan Hilarion (Alfeyev). "Theology in Contemporary Russian Academia." *Gosudarstvo, religiia, tserkov' v Rossii i za rubezhom* 34.3 (2016) 224–39.

Milbank, John. *Theology and Social Theory: Beyond Secular Reason.* Oxford: Blackwell, 1993.

Milbank, John, and Adrian Pabst. *The Politics of Virtue. Post-Liberalism and the Human Future.* London: Rowman & Littlefield, 2016.

Milbank, John, et al., eds. *Radical Orthodoxy. A New Theology: Suspending the Material.* London: Routledge, 1998.

Molendijk, Arie, et al., eds. *Exploring the Postsecular: The Religious, the Political, and the Urban.* Leiden: Brill, 2010.

Morozov, Aleksandr. "Has the Postsecular Age Begun?" *Religion, State, and Society* 36.1 (2008) 39–44.

Nongbri, Brent. *Before Religion: A History of a Modern Concept.* New Haven: Yale University Press, 2015.

Pabst, Adrian. *Metaphysics: The Creation of Hierarchy.* Grand Rapids: Eerdmans 2012.

Rawls, John. *Political Liberalism.* New York: Columbia University Press, 1993.

Reder, Michael, and Josef Schmidt, eds. *Ein Bewußtsein von dem, was fehlt. Eine Diskussion mit Jürgen Habermas.* Frankfurt am Main: Suhrkamp, 2008.

Rosati, Massimo. *The Making of a Postsecular Society: A Durkheimian Approach to Memory, Pluralism, and Religion in Turkey.* Edited with a foreword by Alessandro Ferrara. Farnham: Ashgate, 2015.

Rosati, Massimo, and Kristina Stoeckl. *Multiple Modernities and Postsecular Societies.* Farnham: Ashgate, 2012.

Shchipkov, Aleksandr V. "My dolzhny vziat' vse luchshee ot traditsionalizma i ot moderna [We Must Take the Best from Traditionalism and from Modernity]." *Russkaia ideia,* January 29, 2016. https://politconservatism.ru/interview/my-dolzhny-vzyat-vse-luchshee-ot-traditsionalizma-i-ot-moderna.

Shishkov, Andrey V. "Osmyslenie poniatiia 'postsekuliarnoe' v russkoiazychnoi periodike za poslednee desiatiletie [Making Sense of the 'Postsecular' in Russian Language Publications for the Last Ten Years]." *Religare,* April 28, 2010. Online. http://www.religare.ru/2_75172.html.

Shmonin, Dmitry. "Toledo Principles and Theology in School." *Gosudarstvo, religiia, tserkov' v Rossii i za rubezhom* 35.4 (2017) 72–88.

Smith, James K. A. *Introducing Radical Orthodoxy: Mapping a Post-Secular Theology.* Grand Rapids: Baker Academic, 2004.

Staudigl, Michael, and Jason W. Alvis. "Phenomenology and the Post-Secular Turn: Reconsidering the 'Return of the Religious.'" *International Journal of Philosophical Studies* 24.5 (2016) 589–99.

Stepanova, Elena. "'The Spiritual and Moral Foundation of Civilization in Every Nation for Thousands of Years': The Traditional Values Discourse in Russia." *Politics, Religion, and Ideology* 16.2–3 (2015) 119–36.

Stoeckl, Kristina. "Political Theologies and Modernity." In *Political Theologies in Orthodox Christianity,* edited by Kristina Stoeckl, et al., 15–24. London: Bloomsbury, 2017.

Stoeckl, Kristina, et al., eds. *Political Theologies in Orthodox Christianity.* London: Bloomsbury, 2017.

Stoeckl, Kristina, and Dmitry Uzlaner. "Four Genealogies of Postsecularity." In *The Routledge Handbook of Postsecularity,* edited by Justin Beaumont, 269–79. London: Routledge, 2018.

Taylor, Charles. *A Secular Age.* Harvard: Harvard University Press, 2007.

Tsygankov, Andrei. "Crafting the State-Civilization: Vladimir Putin's Turn to Distinct Values." *Problems of Post-Communism* 63.3 (2016) 146–58.

Turner, Bryan S. "Religion in a Post-Secular Society." In *The New Blackwell Companion to the Sociology of Religion,* edited by Bryan S. Turner, 649–67. Oxford: Wiley-Blackwell, 2010.

Uzlaner, Dmitry A. "Dialog nauki i religii: vzgliad s pozitsii sovremennykh teorii demokratii [The Dialogue of Science and Religion from the Perspective of Contemporary Theories of Democracy]." *Gosudarstvo, religiia, tserkov' v Rossii i za rubezhom* 1 (2015) 136–63.

———. "Kartografiia postsekuliarnogo [Cartography of the Postsecular]." *Otechestvennye zapiski* 1 (2013) 17.

———. "V kakom smysle sovremennyi mir mozhet byt' nazvan postsekuliarnym [In Which Sense Can the Contemporary World Be Called Postsecular]." *Kontinent* 136 (2008) 16.

————. "Vvedenie v postsekuliarnuiu filosofiiu [Introduction to Postsecular Philosophy]." *Logos* 3.83 (2011) 2–32.

Whistler, Daniel, and Anthony Paul Smith. *After the Postsecular and the Postmodern: New Essays in Continental Philosophy of Religion*. Cambridge: Cambridge Scholars, 2010.

Yudin, Alexey V. "Dialektika postsekuliarizatsii [Dialectics of Postsecularization]." *Kontinent* 139 (2009). http://magazines.russ.ru/continent/2009/139/ud23.html.

Žižek, Slavoj, and John Milbank. *The Monstrosity of Christ*. Edited by Creston Davis. Cambridge, Massachusetts: MIT Press, 2009.

3

Orthodoxy and Phenomenology

Religious Experience in the Eastern Christian Tradition

Christina M. Gschwandtner

Phenomenology traditionally examines the experiences and acts of consciousness. It takes a step back from our immediate and direct experience of the world to reflect on that experience itself by looking at it more closely, and examining it carefully in order to understand it more fully. A focus on experience is central to Eastern Orthodox spirituality and has, in fact, often been cited as one of its most distinctive characteristics.[1] Yet, how might one examine that experience more closely and understand more fully how it impacts consciousness? Is there a uniquely "Orthodox" consciousness and what would that mean?

Introduction

Max Scheler, an early phenomenologist contemporaneous with Edmund Husserl, examines the difference between Eastern and Western Christian consciousness in an essay entitled "Über östliches und westliches Christentum [Concerning Eastern and Western Christendom]."[2] Scheler suggests that what upholds "czarism" is not something intrinsic to the Russian soul, which he thinks is a fairly recent invention by pan-Slavists, but instead the

---

1. Florensky, Lossky, Meyendorff, and others insist on the focus on "experience" as a distinctively Orthodox emphasis. See Gschwandtner, "Category of Experience."

2. Scheler, *Liebe und Erkenntnis*, 73–90. This essay was originally published in 1916, i.e., before the revolution.

peculiar consciousness of Eastern Orthodoxy.[3] He contends that the Eastern tradition is characterized by a groveling humility, the idea that leadership is always tainted with shame,[4] and a quasi-masochistic quiescence to suffering, which it regards as a good in itself, a hallowed means of redemption. Relying heavily on an essay by Adolf von Harnack that compares Eastern and Western soteriological thinking and ecclesial structures, he argues that they display a fundamentally different spirit.[5]

He notes several differences. While the West stresses redemption from sin, the East is focused on redemption from death and corruptibility. A good life can never be possible here, because mortality and corporeality are themselves associated with evil.[6] While the Western Christian focuses on Christ's redemptive acts culminating in the sacrifice on the cross and hopes for redemption from sin, the Eastern Christian is most concerned with the idea of incarnation, with God's kenotic humbling into an earthly condition, and focuses on contemplating this divine condescension. He suggests that this is demonstrated by the Eastern liturgy, which "elevates the soul into another sphere of existence, into a higher world."[7] Furthermore, East and West have different ideals of life: While Western Christianity focuses on love of neighbor and concrete acts of charity, Eastern Christianity "kills . . . the Christian thought of love" and values passive virtues, like humility

3. He concludes from this that the Western reduction of religion to economic, social, or political factors is nonsense; in Russia, it is at the very root of things and cannot be reduced to an "ideology" justifying other tendencies. The reverse would be much more justified, namely that the desire for a black sea harbor, pan-Slavism, and nationalism are "ideologies for this manner of deep organic Christianness and its drive to mission" (Scheler, *Liebe und Erkenntnis*, 74). Dostoevsky, whom he suggests serves as the source for most Western ideas about Russian Christianity, is already tainted by this nationalism imported from the West, ill-fitting in the East. One should not ask Dostoevksy "what a good Russian Christian is" (Scheler, *Liebe und Erkenntnis*, 75).

4. Scheler, *Liebe und Erkenntnis*, 73. Later he says that any notion of a good or holy government on earth would have to be rejected as "a false, Satanic compromise with the earth" (Scheler, *Liebe und Erkenntnis*, 84).

5. Scheler, *Liebe und Erkenntnis*, 76. Harnack's essay, originally delivered as a report to the Prussian Academy (February 6, 1913), is considerably more negative in its evaluation of Eastern Christendom and focuses primarily on the Balkan rather than Russia, as Scheler does. Harnack does not mention Dostoevsky.

6. He cites Harnack's claim that for Western Christians, death is the punishment or result of sin, while for Eastern Christians sin is the result of death. For the East, forgiveness of sins can only be envisioned within the redemption from death. Scheler relies heavily on the distinctions outlined by Harnack.

7. Scheler, *Liebe und Erkenntnis*, 78.

and patience, above active ones. Any concern for social or political justice is prohibited by the conviction that all earthly institutions are by definition already tainted with evil. Instead, the Eastern soul is most distinguished by sympathy for those suffering. Orthodoxy hence has a pronounced tendency to quietism.

Much of this is about an examination of a distinctive consciousness. For example, Scheler contends that humility functions differently in East and West: Western Christians measure themselves only against God and hence the humility such comparison engenders is perfectly compatible with pride and self-confidence vis-à-vis other people or the state, while the Eastern concept of humility extends to everything, and entails a groveling self-abasement that tends to masochism. The primary experience of Eastern consciousness hence is one of abject humility. Russians love to throw themselves before even the worst sinners to affirm a shared solidarity of wretchedness. Self-humiliation becomes a goal in itself rather than a means for the production of virtue. The Eastern Christian approaches God primarily in fear or awe, while the Western Christian's relation to God can entail confidence and love. The ascetic ideal and its dissemination in the larger culture lead to self-hatred, spiritual solitude, and elevation of self-sacrifice. Suffering as such has a fundamentally redemptive character in the East; it is not just a necessary byproduct of virtuous living, but something actively sought as valuable for its own sake.[8]

Scheler's analysis culminates in a comparison of Origen and Augustine, whom he takes as the representative church fathers for each tradition respectively. He claims with Harnack that Orthodoxy remains stuck in a Plotinian dualistic version of the third century, while Augustine encapsulates the core of "creaturely love" that leads the West to hold love for God and love for neighbor together and to express it in acts of mercy.[9] Eastern consciousness is marked by passivity, while Western Christian consciousness allows for activity.

8. Scheler points out that for Dostevsky, the promotion of happiness and love of neighbor are characteristics of the *evils* of Western Christendom (Scheler, *Liebe und Erkenntnis*, 84). Even the desire for sleep or bread is understood as catering to our animal nature and hence a kind of betrayal (Scheler, *Liebe und Erkenntnis*, 84).

9. He deduces from this that the czarist regime in Russia is rooted in a "holy irony," in which even the most oppressed and poor pity the ruler, who is so much more wrapped up in the earthly evils of government, authority, and domination (Scheler, *Liebe und Erkenntnis*, 87). The ruler always rules with a bad conscience, thus arbitrarily, and the ruled remain "free" in spirit (Scheler, *Liebe und Erkenntnis*, 88). Ultimately, the Eastern tradition is judged fundamentally incapable of change.

Obviously sweeping claims like this about the "Russian soul" or the "Greek psyche" lack nuance and disregard many aspects of individual and cultural diversity. They also tend to romanticized (or condescending) generalizations of national character that are hardly sustainable and ignore the many social, political, and economic factors that shape how groups of people respond to particular historical circumstances. Furthermore, it is patently untrue that all Orthodox adherents share a common predisposition across national or cultural boundaries; Orthodoxy's tendency to phyletism and fierce ethnic strife demonstrate otherwise. Yet, maybe the impetus of Scheler's project should not be rejected out of hand. It might still be worthwhile to examine features of religious consciousness as they are manifested in various aspects of Orthodox spirituality, and to seek to understand them more closely. Rather than making broad generalizations, a better approach might be to focus on specific examples, subjecting them to phenomenological analysis for insight into the sort of "lived experiences of consciousness" they display. This essay will explore three such examples: the writings of the desert ascetic Evagrius of Pontus, the *Discourses* of Symeon the new theologian, and the anonymous text *The Way of a Pilgrim*.

These texts come from vastly different time periods (the fourth, tenth, and nineteenth centuries, respectively), are written or set in different locations (Egypt, Constantinople, Russia), and addressed to correspondingly different audiences. Yet, they all have been influential in shaping Orthodox spiritual life in various ways and can hence be taken to some extent as representative for an Eastern spiritual approach. While three examples certainly do not constitute an exhaustive survey of the tradition, these texts have come to function in an exemplary fashion.[10] Evagrius, although maybe not representative of what came before him,[11] profoundly influenced the ascetic tradition that succeeded him. Although Symeon's description of his experiences and some of his ideas about spiritual direction were mostly unprecedented in the prior tradition, calling him the "new theologian" (after John the Evangelist and Gregory Nazianzen) attests to the exemplary

10. They are obviously not the only texts that could be taken as exemplary, but in their vivid descriptions of experience they lend themselves to a phenomenological analysis.

11. Louth suggests that "while no one could think that Evagrius was typical of anything—he is evidently a towering genius in his explanation of the metaphysical underpinning of the ascetic life" (Louth, "Christian in Late Antiquity," 86). In a different text he acknowledges him as "an influential figure among the monks of Byzantium (and even more so further afield)" in Syria and Armenia (Louth, "Orthodox Mystical Theology," 514).

stature accorded his writings after his death.[12] The *Way of a Pilgrim* became hugely popular soon after its publication and played a singular role in spreading the practice of reciting the Jesus Prayer.[13] They can hence serve as three significant lenses for an examination of Orthodox consciousness and religious experiences.

Evagrius of Pontus: Practicing Apatheia

Evagrius's texts are maybe the most detailed of the early writings on how to acquire habits of prayer and practice asceticism with profound insights into the thoughts and feelings shaping the inner life. He gives instructions about actions with various criteria of discernment that help distinguish one experience from another, correct practice from incorrect one. Yet, this is not just about actions, but actually much of the guidance concerns what happens in the ascetic's consciousness (often identified with the soul or heart). Religious experience, as he depicts it, has clear structures that can be identified and evaluated: "He who through experience makes known the error of the thoughts will not be recognized by all, except for those with experience, for experience constitutes the path towards the gnostic life."[14]

Evagrius counsels Eulogios and other students to "strip off the weight of the flesh" and to pursue virtue by "collecting your thoughts."[15] Patterns of thought (*logismoi*) are seen as an especial obstacle to the ascetic life. What happens in consciousness is at the root of what becomes expressed in actions later. Ascetic labors are meant to "restrain" and train the flesh, so that it cannot interfere with the mind's focus on prayer or lead it astray. Ascetic labor calls for strenuous training and total devotion. Thoughts can trick us to believe that we have come much further than we think by concealing our sins "with forgetfulness."[16]

12. Maloney, in the introduction to Symeon's *Discourses*, claims that "he exemplified the best in true Eastern Christian theology" (Maloney, "Introduction," 5).

13. Louth points in his introduction to the text's "extraordinary influence," which "has caused the Jesus prayer to evolve from a somewhat esoteric monastic devotion, popular among Orthodox hermits and solitaries, to a widespread practice in the modern world, not only among the Orthodox" (*Way of a Pilgrim*, xii). Although the account itself is probably fictional, it belongs to a set of tales that "are bearers of knowledge or wisdom," conveying "genuine spiritual truths, often of great profundity" (*Way of a Pilgrim*, xiv).

14. Evagrius, *Greek Ascetic Corpus*, 50.

15. Evagrius, *Greek Ascetic Corpus*, 29.

16. Evagrius, *Greek Ascetic Corpus*, 40.

There are types of thoughts to be avoided, controlled, or explicitly conjured. For example, Evagrius encourages them to hold their failings in active consciousness: "Do not forget that you have fallen, even if you have repented, but hold onto the memory of your sin as an occasion of compunction that leads to your humility."[17] Other thoughts are to be calmed or erased: "The person stung by the insults of others . . . rouses the mob of his own thoughts against himself."[18] Such thoughts are grounded in the self as the product of the disposition of the soul or mind: "Coals give off sparks of fire and so resentful souls give off evil thoughts."[19] One of Evagrius's most famous treatises focuses "on the eight thoughts" that give rise to their corresponding vices. It is crucial that they are recognized to be first thoughts or even patterns of thought, something that occurs in consciousness, before they become expressed in actions. The eight thoughts discussed are gluttony, fornication, avarice, anger, sadness, acedia, vainglory, and pride. In each case, Evagrius examines the ways in which the ascetic's consciousness might be troubled by imaginations and temptations, might dwell on them and hence engage them consciously.

Thoughts are then closely connected to vices. Entertaining thoughts leads to cultivation of desire, which results in action, creating habits or dispositions that become inscribed on character permanently.[20] Evagrius provides extensive descriptions of various virtues and vices. In fact, much of his writing is concerned with distinguishing them from each other and identifying the characteristics of certain vices. Many of these precisely concern the impact they have on consciousness and ultimately on behavior. They usually begin in imagination, continue by dwelling on such imagination and hence cultivating a desire for the imagined, finally giving way to acting on the desire, thus giving in to the temptation.[21] In the analysis of the vices, he shows how "good" and "bad" sadness might be distinguished from

17. Evagrius, *Greek Ascetic Corpus*, 40.

18. Evagrius, *Greek Ascetic Corpus*, 47.

19. Evagrius, *Greek Ascetic Corpus*, 48.

20. When thoughts take over, one may come close to madness: "So then, when the heart resounds with the glory of the thoughts and there is no resistance, he will not escape madness in the secret of his mental faculties, for his ruling faculty risks being shaken loose from its senses, either through dreams which are given credence, or through forms that take shape during vigils, or through visions seen in a change of light" (Evagrius, *Greek Ascetic Corpus*, 58). Here such visions are clearly not a sign of progress in the spiritual life.

21. See Evagrius, *Greek Ascetic Corpus*, 61–65.

each other, how certain errors are to be countered by certain practices, and how particular virtues can counter corresponding vices. Experience is again crucial in all this, not just the undergoing of experience, but acquiring it. Combatting vices and acquiring virtues is a strenuous and progressive exercise that extends over a lifetime. There are degrees of prayer; various emotions or thoughts might function differently at different levels.[22] Virtue is not accomplished in a moment or in a day, but involves acquiring dispositions through continuous practices and the formation of habits that sustain such dispositions. Abstinence and perseverance are required and virtue is never acquired without "warfare."[23]

Evagrius also gives concrete advice on how actions might influence our consciousness. We are to avoid loud noises and strenuous exercise, but at the same time continue to be attentive and aware of what goes on in consciousness: "Do not delay in paying the debt of prayer when you hear a thought (that arises) by reason of the approach of work and do not make loud noises, troubling your body, during manual labour, lest you trouble as well the eye of the soul."[24] In order to focus on prayer one should avoid cities, with their many distractions and loud noises, friends and especially quarrelsome people, fine food or an "indulgent lifestyle."[25] Fasting "sanctifies your way of thinking," while eating too much will trouble it.[26] "For the thoughts bring to the soul their opposing activity whenever they catch it unoccupied with godly considerations."[27] Discernment is crucial for analyzing the thoughts of consciousness and for distinguishing which experiences are indicative of progress in prayer and which are actually evidence of pride or various other attitudes.

Much of the focus on one's conscious thoughts and the feelings and acts to which they give rise is concerned with distinguishing whether they are authentic or inauthentic, i.e., to what extent they might be caused by demonic influence. Paying attention to the effect of particular feelings on consciousness allows one to discern them. E.g., he distinguishes between

22. "The elders approve highly of an anachoresis that is undertaken by degrees" (Evagrius, *Greek Ascetic Corpus*, 56).

23. Evagrius, *Greek Ascetic Corpus*, 31.

24. Evagrius, *Greek Ascetic Corpus*, 36.

25. Evagrius, *Greek Ascetic Corpus*, 7–8.

26. Evagrius, *Greek Ascetic Corpus*, 10. In all this, body and soul go together and are intimately related. Evagrius often comments on how one influences the other.

27. Evagrius, *Greek Ascetic Corpus*, 36.

"two types of sadness arising from evil," based on whether it arises on its own accord or has a clear cause, giving rise to different kinds of anxiety.[28] Various tricks of the demons can be recognized by the way they affect consciousness.[29] Disciples are therefore told to pay close attention to their thoughts and feelings. They must be analyzed and certain thoughts must be excluded or fought against. Indeed, "he who applies great ascetic effort to seeking which thought is countered by which ascetic labour finds himself an expert in the struggle against error."[30]

Consciousness must be constantly examined so that one is aware what thoughts attempt to enter. In order to make possible such discernment, Evagrius depicts common failings, such as the pursuit of honor or praise and provides guidelines for discerning them.[31] He also acknowledges that one might feel divided: "One of the brothers, having endured injustice and insult from a pious person, went away divided between joy and sadness: in the case of the former, because he experienced injustice and insult and returned not opposition; in the case of the latter, because the pious person was deceived and in causing his deceit he felt joy at his expense."[32] Some feelings of consciousness can fight against others.[33] The passions "yoke" consciousness in a particular way, thus enslaving it.[34]

The battle waged in the desert is a battle waged for the ascetic's consciousness. The goal is to move this consciousness away from being tossed about by various external influences to being in complete control of itself, in a state of stillness (*apatheia*). Only such a state of full self-transparency will be able to open consciousness to the divine and to discern between an experience of God and a demonic temptation or other external distraction. Apatheia is not apathy, but a form of consciousness in which the mind and the emotions have been stilled and no longer distract consciousness, so that it can focus entirely on the divine. It is a particular state of consciousness, a

---

28. Evagrius, *Greek Ascetic Corpus*, 34.

29. "For in the former situation there were insults, sorrows, and troubles, but here there is peace, tranquillity, and joy" (Evagrius, *Greek Ascetic Corpus*, 53). Here, ironically, peace and joy are actually an indication that the ascetic is on the *wrong* path, namely by not listening to his spiritual guide.

30. Evagrius, *Greek Ascetic Corpus*, 42.

31. Evagrius, *Greek Ascetic Corpus*, 31.

32. Evagrius, *Greek Ascetic Corpus*, 32.

33. Evagrius, *Greek Ascetic Corpus*, 33.

34. Evagrius, *Greek Ascetic Corpus*, 43.

distinctive experience that focuses all energies in a single point and opens itself to something other.

But such opening is selective; the elimination of passions from the experience is geared at closing down certain experiences in order to be open to others. The two are hence conceived as incompatible with each other and as displaying opposed characteristics, although one can masquerade as the other. Such false imitations can be detected precisely in the effects they have on consciousness, in the particular intentionality they display. Evagrius is quite explicit about how to acquire such stillness: "Seated in your cell, gather together your mind, give heed to the day of your death, and then look at the dying of your body."[35] Such focus will shape the ascetic's consciousness. The goal of stillness, then, is a perfectly controlled consciousness, entirely untroubled by passions, singularly focused on the good.

Symeon the New Theologian: Practicing Penitence

Symeon the New Theologian (949–1022) addresses the *Discourses* as instructions to his community of monks at the Studite monastery of St. Mamas in Constantinople, which he led as abbot from 980 to 998. They dispense advice on how to enter more deeply into the spiritual life and exhortations to pursue this calling as authentically as possible. Usually delivered in the context of the matins service, they are to some extent colored by their liturgical context, such as a focus on fasting and penitence during lent or celebration during the Pentecost season. Throughout they provide a rich account of the sorts of experiences that characterize a spiritual life and which Symeon seeks to evoke in his listeners.

The central theme for Symeon is heart-felt penitence: "For penitence is the gateway that leads out of darkness into light."[36] Humility and contrition are paramount. Symeon describes the experience of penitence in great detail. It is increased by conscious reflection upon it: "He endures every tribulation and bears every trial and in addition numbers himself among the lowliest of all; he thinks over his actions and his faults and daily blames himself and sees himself as a sinner."[37] It must be pursued dili-

---

35. Evagrius, *Greek Ascetic Corpus*, 9.

36. Symeon, *Discourses*, 298.

37. Symeon, *Discourses*, 80.

gently.[38] Repentance is engendered by a disposition of consciousness: "pay constant attention to yourself and keep death before your eyes."[39] In fact, the monks must "accurately examine [themselves] and carefully observe [their] souls."[40] This requires training, concentration, and a right attitude: "By piety we must train the soul to think as it ought to think and constantly meditate on the things that belong to eternal life, to be humble, meek, and contrite, filled with compunction, to mourn daily and by prayer invoke on itself the light of the Spirit."[41] Symeon counsels constant self-examination: "The monk must know not only the changes and transformations that take place in the soul but also their causes: the nature of these causes, and their origins."[42] This requires focus and recollection.[43]

This is not a merely passive humility. He constantly exhorts his monks to more strenuous effort and upbraids them for their laxity.[44] He describes this in terms of warfare: "Hour by hour, day by day, let us by penitence work at being renewed, so that we may learn to fight and wrestle with the devils, our enemies who are always at war with us."[45] While usual warfare has times of rest when the fighting stops, spiritual warfare is ongoing. While the sense of contrition seems to be the primary state of consciousness, he seeks to inculcate in his monks, this is not a purely passive state, but requires various activities of penitence. These include not just the soul but the body: "By bodily exercise we must exercise the body for the labors of virtue so that it may be vigorous and accustomed to the painful things that are pleasing to God and nobly bear the bitterness of fasting, the violence of abstinence, the necessity of vigil, all suffering of hardship."[46] Bodily exercises induce and shape the right sorts of dispositions.

38. Symeon, *Discourses*, 81.

39. Symeon, *Discourses*, 233.

40. Symeon, *Discourses*, 54.

41. Symeon, *Discourses*, 159.

42. Symeon, *Discourses*, 267.

43. Symeon, *Discourses*, 275, 282.

44. His description of a day in the life of a monk contains quite the list of activities (Symeon, *Discourses*, 274–83, 315). See also Symeon, *Discourses*, 74–79, which contains several depictions (and censure) of lack of effort.

45. Symeon, *Discourses*, 68.

46. Symeon, *Discourses*, 159.

For Symeon, an attitude of repentance is best expressed by copious weeping, a theme to which he returns frequently.[47] He exhorts the monks to mourn and to feel great grief over their sins and lack of penitence. Only if the soul is "watered and made fruitful by tears" does it "bring forth the fruit of the other virtues."[48] He exclaims: "But if they think it wholly impossible day by day to partake of the awesome Mysteries with tears, what ignorance on their part, what lack of feeling!"[49] Such failure is merely evidence of its own lack: "Those, then, who claim that it is impossible to mourn or weep every night and day are witnesses to their own lack of all virtue."[50] Weeping and penitence are inextricably connected with each other for Symeon. Only such constant tears lead to purity of heart. Weeping, suffering and humility are in fact connected,[51] as are humility and humiliation: "Humiliation brings about affliction, but affliction feeds the humility that is its source and makes it grow."[52]

This does not constitute an exaltation of suffering for its own sake. Rather, such tearful contrition always serves the purpose of purification from sin or worldly attachment and ultimately is the condition for being able to experience the divine: "You know that fervent penitence accompanied by tears that spring from the depth of the heart will melt and burn up the filth of sin like a fire and make pure the soul that has been defiled. In addition, penitence through the visitation of the Spirit generously imparts an abundant flow of light to the soul, whereby it is filled with mercy and good fruits."[53] Penitence must result in "absence of passion, humility attained together with gentleness, knowledge together with wisdom of the Spirit."[54] This is depicted as a happy and joyful experience, marvelous beyond words. Although happiness itself is not the goal per se, the goal of encounter with God is certainly conceived and experienced as blissful. Suffering is the means (or a means), but not the goal. And Symeon is clear that even tears

47. E.g., Symeon, *Discourses*, 45, 54, 63, 92, 159–60, 254–55, 320, 330–31. He devotes a whole homily to the topic, "On Tears of Penitence" (Symeon, *Discourses*, 70–89). At times one has the impression that he positively relishes the tears (see the depiction in Symeon, *Discourses*, 245).

48. Symeon, *Discourses*, 53.

49. Symeon, *Discourses*, 71.

50. Symeon, *Discourses*, 82.

51. Symeon, *Discourses*, 85.

52. Symeon, *Discourses*, 188.

53. Symeon, *Discourses*, 174.

54. Symeon, *Discourses*, 79.

ultimately produce joy: "When . . . this unceasing penitence is pursued with pain and tribulation unto death, it gradually causes us to shed bitter tears and by these wipes away and cleanses the filth and defilement of the soul. Afterwards it produces in us pure penitence and turns the bitter tears into sweet ones. It engenders increasing joy in our hearts and enables us to see the radiance that never sets."[55] The joy far outweighs the previous sadness or what has been left behind in the world.[56]

This joy and light are described in exorbitant terms. He describes what happens when someone is united to Christ: "His mind sees strange visions and is wholly illuminated and becomes like light, yet he is unable to conceive of them or describe them. His mind is itself light and sees all things as light, and the light has life and imparts light to him who sees it. He sees himself wholly united to the light, and as he sees he concentrates on the vision and is as he was. He perceives the light in his soul and is in ecstasy."[57] Although Symeon assures us that he is at a "loss for words" to describe the vision, he gives a quite detailed account of its effects on consciousness.[58] To provide one example: "At once I perceived a divine warmth. Then a small radiance that shone forth. Then a divine breath from his words. Then a fire kindled in my heart, which caused constant streams of tears to flow. After that a fine beam went through my mind more quickly than lightening. Then there appeared to me as it were a light in the light and a small cloud resting on his head, while I lay on my face and made supplication. Afterwards it moved away and shortly after appeared to me as being in heaven."[59]

Light is the central theme to which he returns over and over again, a sign of being completely filled and illuminated by God.[60] Tears and joy become one as God and the monk unite: "He was wholly in the presence of immaterial light and seemed to himself to have turned into light. Oblivious of all the world he was filled with tears and with ineffable joy and gladness."[61] The carefully cultivated affective states of contrition and penitence actively

55. Symeon, *Discourses*, 88.

56. Symeon, *Discourses*, 257.

57. Symeon, *Discourses*, 56.

58. The most detailed account is given in homily XVI, "Ecstasy in the Light" (Symeon, *Discourses*, 198–203).

59. Symeon, *Discourses*, 363.

60. Symeon, *Discourses*, 189, 191, 245

61. Symeon, *Discourses*, 246.

lead to abundant experiences of joy and illumination. A similar account of joy pervades the account of the Russian pilgrim.

Way of a Pilgrim: Practicing Perpetual Prayer

The Way of a Pilgrim is an anonymous treatise that purports to be the report of a traveling pilgrim, moderately educated but poor, with a handicap that makes physical labor impossible. The pilgrim desires to know how to keep the command to pray without ceasing. After finding the response near the beginning of the story—namely the constant invocation of the name of Jesus with the help of a prayer rope—the rest of the book narrates the various events that befall him in his travels and his conversations about the Jesus prayer with others, some of whom are converted to the practice through his account. This immensely popular text serves as a rich source of observations about the effect of prayer on consciousness. It contains extended guidance on how to learn to pray "ceaselessly," observations about how such prayer transforms a person, and encouragement to share the experience.

Prayer is regarded as the highest spiritual work that aligns the will with God. Like Evagrius and Symeon, the pilgrim counsels focus on internal insights: I "began to listen intently to my heart speaking."[62] He describes how such careful attention is possible, and how it ought to be conducted: "I closed my eyes and looked into my heart with my mind, that is to say with my imagination, trying to visualize it on the left side of my chest, and I listened attentively to its beating. It did this for half an hour, several times a day. At first all I saw was darkness, but quite soon I began to visualize my heart and became conscious of its movements."[63] The initial guide's description of the prayer serves as a good summary of what the rest of the book will demonstrate: "Anyone who makes a habit of this appeal will experience great consolation and need to repeat it always to the point when he cannot live without it and the prayer will, of its own accord, flow in him."[64] This proves true in the pilgrim's own experience as he reports it and also that of other people he encounters. The rest of the story serves to confirm these positive effects of consolation repeatedly in multiple narratives.

Such constant praying does require hard work and increasing focus. The pilgrim describes how the beginning is difficult; he "felt a great burden,

62. *Way of a Pilgrim*, 19.
63. *Way of a Pilgrim*, 32–33.
64. *Way of a Pilgrim*, 8.

laziness, listlessness, and an overwhelming drowsiness; my mind became clouded with all kinds of thoughts."[65] After reporting this state, the guide tells him to persist and say the prayer 3,000 times a day (this is increased to 6,000, then 12,000, then "as often as you can"). This initial report of fatigue and a slightly later description of a very brief period of light pain in the wrist (presumably from the handling of the rope) are really the only negative emotions reported in the book. Although the pilgrim experiences some external adversity and on occasion some anxiety regarding food or shelter, the text depicts almost exclusively positive emotions and experiences. He comes to feel a constant need for the prayer almost immediately,[66] is "filled with joy,"[67] and "glad the whole day long."[68] He feels "warmth" and "pleasure,"[69] often "happiness."[70] The prayer helps him to forget cold, hunger, rheumatism, or other pain.[71] He is "very happy" although he suggests that it is "to do with feelings," "something natural or the result of habit."[72] He worries that he "might fall into delusion, or might mistake natural effects for the action of grace."[73] Yet, most of the time he reports warmth and happiness.

This affects everything around him: "As I began to pray in my heart everything around me seemed entrancing to me: trees, grass, birds, the earth, the air, light. . . . All creation was praying and praising God."[74] The pilgrim learns "what inner prayer was about, how to reach it, what its fruits were and how it filled the heart and soul with joy, and how to recognize if this came from God or was due to natural causes or delusion."[75] His thoughts are filled with the prayer and the result is "a great happiness."[76] There is a "pleasant warmth of the heart" and "the body is full of delight"

65. *Way of a Pilgrim*, 10.

66. *Way of a Pilgrim*, 11.

67. *Way of a Pilgrim*, 11.

68. *Way of a Pilgrim*, 12.

69. *Way of a Pilgrim*, 13.

70. *Way of a Pilgrim*, 34, 38.

71. *Way of a Pilgrim*, 14.

72. *Way of a Pilgrim*, 14.

73. *Way of a Pilgrim*, 20.

74. *Way of a Pilgrim*, 27.

75. *Way of a Pilgrim*, 32.

76. *Way of a Pilgrim*, 33.

and "unceasing joy."[77] He feels light and comforted, "so that sometimes my heart would burn with infinite love for Jesus Christ and consoling streams seemed to flow through my whole body from this sweet welling. . . . I was moved to tears of joy and felt such gladness in my heart at times that I do not have the words to describe it."[78] He teaches the prayer to someone else who similarly feels "intense warmth and indescribable joy in his heart."[79] This sweetness and delight is unmatched by anything "material" and is described in superlative terms like "floating through the air."[80] Joy and delight are given explicitly as criteria: "if you wish your prayer to be pure, true and a source of joy, you need to choose some short, simple but powerful words to form your prayer and then repeat it frequently over a long time, and then you will develop a taste for it."[81]

The Way of a Pilgrim, then, teaches how to pray by counseling not just particular practices that are described in their structure, but also by observing the effect such prayer has on consciousness. These positive effects—consisting primarily in warmth, joy, happiness, and peace—partly recommend the prayer. The pilgrim counsels others to pursue such prayer practices not primarily because a particular dogma says so, or because it will save them from hell, or even because it will unite them to God or cause holiness, but generally recommends these positive benefits of happiness and peace. Feeling is explicitly claimed as a result of the prayer: "Experiencing these and similar consolations, I noticed that the effects of the prayer of the heart manifested themselves in three ways: in the spirit, in the emotions and through revelations. In the spirit, for example, you experience the sweetness of God's love, inner peace, gladness of mind, purity of thought, and delight in the awareness of God. Through the emotions, you feel a pleasant warmth of the heart, the body is full of delight, there is a joyful elation in the heart, lightness and courage, the pleasure of being alive, and indifference towards illness and sorrows. Revelations bring enlightenment of the mind, a grasp of Holy Scripture, the knowledge of the language of created things, renunciation of vanities and an acquaintance with the sweetness of inner life, and confidence in the nearness of God

77. *Way of a Pilgrim*, 34.
78. *Way of a Pilgrim*, 49.
79. *Way of a Pilgrim*, 79.
80. *Way of a Pilgrim*, 81.
81. *Way of a Pilgrim*, 85.

and his love for us."[82] Such feeling is almost exclusively positive: "prayer consoled my heart and made me oblivious to everything else."[83] Yet, they are not just "benefits"; they are its distinguishing characteristics: one knows one is doing the prayer correctly or at least on the right path to it, if one's consciousness displays these elements. The experience described follows a pattern and has a consistency and such consistency is expected in proper practice of the prayer. While the joy or the peace might be disturbed at times and indeed such disturbance is to be expected in fallible humans, if one does not ultimately experience such characteristics of warmth and joy, the activity would not be authentic, and one would know that one has not practiced it correctly or not yet learned it sufficiently.

Orthodox Consciousness?

What, then, are we to make of Scheler's claims about Orthodox consciousness in light of this? Does a coherent picture emerge? Scheler is certainly right that kenosis is a strong theme in the Eastern tradition and does lead to an emphasis on humility and self-abasement. This is evident in all three accounts. The pilgrim opens his account: "By the mercy of God I am a Christian, by my deeds a great sinner, by calling a homeless wanderer of the lowliest origins, roaming from place to place."[84] Evagrius condemns pride in the strongest terms. Symeon links humility explicitly to Christ's kenosis: "How shall we be accounted as showing mercy toward Him, who for our sakes became like us, while we show mercy toward ourselves?"[85] In fact, it is probably Symeon who most closely exemplifies the focus on suffering and even humiliation Scheler perceives in the East: "Do you then, brother, refuse to be humbled and submissive, afflicted and dishonored, despised and reproached? Or to become one of those who are obscure, foolish, insignificant, and have gone astray? Or to be the object of contempt on the part of everybody?"[86] Yet, Symeon does not remain there. Humiliation leads to exaltation: "The higher they ascend the more they abase themselves; the more they humble themselves the higher they are lifted up."[87]

82. *Way of a Pilgrim*, 33–34.
83. *Way of a Pilgrim*, 42.
84. *Way of a Pilgrim*, 3.
85. Symeon, *Discourses*, 153.
86. Symeon, *Discourses*, 127.
87. Symeon, *Discourses*, 207; "But if we are ashamed to imitate His sufferings, which

And although death is certainly a theme, Symeon emphasizes sin far more strongly. Contrition and penitence are not simply about finitude, but clearly about repentance from sinful action. It might be more accurate to say that sin is not conceived primarily in specific individual acts, but in a more general state of impurity. It is indeed pictured in superlative terms: Symeon often refers to himself as the worst of sinners and expects his monks to think of themselves similarly. One knows only one's own sinful state intimately and hence one's own sin is always experienced not only as exorbitant, but as exceeding anyone else's.[88] A strong emphasis on humility and self-abasement is then not incompatible with an acute consciousness of sin. Evagrius's lists of vices similarly assume that sin (and not just death) is an important factor in the state of one's soul and that such sins can be actively combatted. He never counsels the ascetics to pursue suffering for its own sake. In fact, *apatheia* is precisely about the stilling or even erasure of pathos, i.e., suffering or passion. The pilgrim's primary state of consciousness is joy rather than despair or depression. This can even be combined with recognizing one's own insufficiency: "Sometimes it was as though something were bubbling up in my heart, and I felt such lightness, freedom and consolation that I was completely transformed and enraptured. Sometimes I felt a burning love for Jesus Christ and all of God's creation. Sometimes I would shed involuntary tears, thanking God for his mercy towards me, a wretched sinner."[89] Similarly, Symeon's account ends in exorbitant delight.

It is thus not true that the Orthodox consciousness is uniformly depressed, always passive, or deliberately in search of suffering. Instead, a more careful examination shows that this care for the soul is quite active, requires immense effort and discipline, and is portrayed in predominantly positive terms. Although it is true that there is a desire for purification, that disintegration or corruptibility along with the passions that mark them are seen as something to be overcome, and that the goal is a state no longer characterized by these transitory markers of finitude, this is not entirely an abandonment of this earthly existence.[90] The pilgrim is conscious of the

He endured for us, and to suffer as He suffered, it is obvious that we shall not become partakers with Him in His glory" (Symeon, *Discourses*, 128).

88. E.g., Symeon, *Discourses*, 94–96, 118, 206.

89. *Way of the Pilgrim*, 33.

90. This may not be sufficient for determining whether the East maintains the same tension as the West between the "here" and the "hereafter," the affirmation that creation is good and beautiful, as well as hallowed by the incarnation, and a more ambivalent relation

beauty of nature. He prefers to dwell in solitude among the trees rather than in the noise of the cities. He appreciates the song of birds and even claims that practicing the prayer allows "to communicate with God's creation."[91] His prayer requires attention to his body: his breathing, the beating of his heart, etc. There are several accounts of healing and he clearly mourns the loss of the use of his hand or legs. Similarly, Evagrius's instructions assume that body and soul are closely connected and mutually influence each other: "Let the accounting of the heart take the measure of the body, lest when the latter is struck the former too may grow weary."[92] Symeon does think of soul and mind as imperishable, but concludes from this that they have a will that can become wicked, while the body which is mutable, irrational, and perishable is for precisely that reason "nonsinful and without condemnation before God."[93] He concludes: "Let nobody therefore think that he is being driven to these things and compelled by his own body! It is not true."[94]

The blanket assessment that there is no evidence of "neighborly love" in the Eastern tradition also has to be qualified. The pilgrim is clearly concerned about the well-being of others and tries to guide or even heal them. He also comments on their love for him: "the name of Jesus Christ constantly on my lips cheered me on my way, and all men were good to me; it seemed as though everyone had come to love me."[95] Similarly, the desert ascetics often counseled charity and there are several stories that suggest

---

to it as transitory and distracting. More work would have to be done here. Symeon, for example, does say: "Let us run, let us pursue, until we have laid hold of something that is permanent and does not flow away, for all things perish and pass away like a dream, and nothing is lasting or certain among things that are seen" (Symeon, *Discourses*, 57). But in other places he refers to "the spiritual regeneration and resurrection of the dead souls that takes place in a spiritual manner every day" (Symeon, *Discourses*, 129). He also affirms that some people have become holy "while they are living this present life" (Symeon, *Discourses*, 163).

91. *Way of the Pilgrim*, 27.

92. Evagrius, *Greek Ascetic Corpus*, 45. Rather, as in Diadochus and other ascetics, personal sin is regarded as a kind of illness that must be healed. Strenuous repentance is the medicine that effects the cure. Ascetic exercises are the athletic disciplines that bring the body and soul to health. The goal here is a state of full and glowing health, where body and soul are in harmony with each other. It is not an erasure of finitude, but a reconciling of it. This is not an abandonment of the earth or the body, as Scheler and Harnack seem to think, but rather their unification, a healing of soul and body.

93. Symeon, *Discourses*, 269.

94. Symeon, *Discourses*, 269.

95. *Way of the Pilgrim*, 14.

that even the most strenuous asceticism can be inferior to certain charitable actions in the world, such as feeding the poor or healing the sick. Symeon frequently exhorts his monks to works of charity, once going so far as to claim that not feeding the poor if one is able to do so is tantamount to murder: "He is exposed as one who has murdered as many victims as he was then able to feed."[96] Love goes out to others: "It is you [love] who surround me and inflame me, you who by the labor of my heart enkindle me with boundless desire for God and for my brethren and fathers."[97] Yet, Symeon also repeatedly—and more frequently—tells them that acts of charity do not make up for the personal pursuit of holiness and that one should not sacrifice one's own soul for the good of others.[98] The overwhelming attention is certainly focused on the individual pursuit of holiness, which must be as free from worldly distraction as possible.[99] This emphasis on the individual is really quite striking. Foucault may well be right that practices of confession to a spiritual father, focus on one's sins and the ways in which one is personally swayed by passions, or preoccupation with the secrecies of one's soul, lead increasingly to the construction of a certain kind of self.[100] This is clearly not (yet) in conflict with notions of community, or even with the strong conviction that sin, death and salvation are generally human affairs in which we all share together, not merely personal issues. Yet, a personal pursuit of salvation and personal consciousness of sin clearly develops here that may well be a first step to a more individualist approach.

96. Symeon, *Discourses*, 156.

97. Symeon, *Discourses*, 44.

98. Symeon, *Discourses*, 154, 157. All the charitable acts in the world do not outweigh the loss of one's own soul. Such acts are hence evaluated primarily in terms of their benefit for the one doing them rather than the ones receiving them. It is also telling that his prime example for charity is Mary of Egypt, who dwells in the desert for 40 years in complete solitude, occupied only with penitence for her sins (Symeon, *Discourses*, 105, 151–52). Once he refers to love for others as a mere means toward serving God (Symeon, *Discourses*, 45). See also his Homily VIII (Symeon, *Discourses*, 143–49).

99. The emphasis on compassion Scheler rightly recognizes need not exclude neighborly love. Yet, while compassion is always present and often actively counseled, it does not necessarily grow into a substantive defense of neighborly love. Certainly, monasteries often practiced charitable works, but just as often they insulated themselves from the outside world.

100. Foucault claims that they lead to "the apparition of a new kind of self" and "the development of a much more complex technology of the self," which "became victorious" in the West and "is nowadays dominating" (Foucault, "Hermeneutics of the Self," 221–22).

This is evident in all three sets of texts. Although Evagrius outlines common faults and provides general guidelines, these are clearly to be pursued and applied by particular individuals as they examine themselves. The desert saints are individually recognizable characters and they give advice (a "word") to particular individuals who come to them for help.[101] Similarly, processes of discernment are always concerned with applying general rules or guidelines to specific and particular situations. It is the state of this particular soul, the passion in this specific moment of consciousness that must be evaluated or combatted. Symeon speaks quite openly about his personal experiences, even more evident in his poetry, and assumes his monks to be closely and personally tied to him as spiritual father, as well as to expect and actively pursue such personal experiences themselves. The pilgrim, although anonymous and often recounting others' experiences, is a particular individual with a specific history that he is willing to divulge when asked and who is pursuing a particular path that personally brings him consolation. Experience is seen as falling into a pattern, is identified and discerned along broader generalizations, and posited as exemplary, but it is at the same time clearly *personal* experience.

Conclusion

Although we may not discern one unified "Orthodox consciousness" here, especially not one diametrically opposed to or fundamentally different from a unified "Western" consciousness, a phenomenological investigation could be pursued further in multiple ways. First, all three accounts offer rich reflections on affective states of consciousness and consider how they are connected to concrete actions, and how they might be evaluated. There is deep insight here—in a way that might even already be called proto-phenomenological—into how emotive states are linked to patterns of thought and to desires, how they lead to certain actions or shape predispositions

101. In this respect, it is plainly untrue that there is no care for souls in the Eastern tradition. All three speak of the importance of spiritual guidance. Evagrius often refers to such guides; receiving a "word" from an older ascetic is one of the prime features of desert spirituality. Symeon explains the importance of spiritual guidance in several of his homilies, including censuring unworthy ones (Homily XVIII [Symeon, *Discourses*, 209–225]; Homily XX [231–37]). He claims that "he who sees spiritually and hears in the same way sees the soul of him whom he sees and encounters and with whom he frequently converses . . . he sees its condition, its qualities, and its dispositions" (Symeon, *Discourses*, 304). The pilgrim often refers to his staretz and the wisdom he taught him.

to patterns of behavior, and how such affects may be both self-generated and experienced as overwhelming the self. One need not posit demonic influence to appreciate Evagrius's insights that anger or desire can become so overpowering that they are experienced as controlling the self without therefore implying that one is no longer responsible for their destructive effects. Similarly, the pilgrim's and Symeon's description of joy and its effect on body and mind lend themselves to further phenomenological analyses of the ways in which such emotions are manifested in human experience on corporeal and affective levels.

Second, these texts might give us further insight into human subjectivity and the constitution of the self, a topic that has preoccupied phenomenology maybe more than any other and that is particularly germane to religious experience. All three sets of texts are deeply preoccupied with the person's pursuit of a spiritual life and this strong focus on the self simultaneously involves a kind of loss of the self, or at least the loss of a certain kind of self. In Evagrius, the self, dominated by pathos and swayed by desires, is to be replaced with a self open to an other-than-self. Symeon counsels the monks to shed their old self via self-humbling contrition to become receptive to the divine gift of light and joy. The pilgrim's desire for prayer and single-minded focus on his breath and heart lead to surprising levels of contentment of self. These texts also provide resources for considering the concrete practices (such as the repetition of a prayer or mantra, focusing one's thoughts, or careful self-examination) that might lead to divestment of a certain kind of self and cultivation of a different subjectivity. Despite sometimes fairly strong language, this does not constitute a destruction of the self, but a transformation and even a freedom in which the self is released from the bondage of harmful passions or predispositions. This might give us further phenomenological insight into the ways in which addictions or destructive habits enslave people, and how a new self can emerge through the cultivation of predispositions that involve a struggle with certain aspects of the self, rather than simple self-affirmation. It might also help us to consider more fully the various ways in which subjectivity is experienced as hampered in—not necessarily self-inflicted—ways, such as experiences of illness, and the manner in which bodily activities are linked to affective or mental states, i.e., the fashion in which consciousness is concretely embodied.

Third, a recurrent theme in these texts is the importance of discernment in the investigation of consciousness. Careful distinctions are drawn between what thoughts or experiences are self-generated, and which manifest as coming from elsewhere. Previous phenomenological explorations of religious experience have often focused heavily on identifying the (divine) source of such experience (e.g., Scheler, Stein, Walther, Marion, Steinbock, etc.), i.e., to argue that the experience manifests as *given* rather than produced or imagined, or that this might make it possible to say something about how God manifests in human experience. Yet, maybe philosophically more interestingly, these descriptions of practices of discernment might elucidate more fully the role hermeneutics plays in the phenomenological investigation of experience, or—more accurately—the ways in which experience itself manifests as already hermeneutic to some extent. The "discernment of spirits" practiced by many ascetic and mystical writings is not simply an interpretation imposed on the experience afterwards, or a desire to judge the authenticity of the experience. It is also a phenomenological measure of depicting the experience itself more accurately, and hence revealing the ways in which any description of experience is already hermeneutic to the core, requires a hermeneutic circling back-and-forth between the immediacy of a particular experience and its larger context, including imaginative variation or comparison to other concrete experiences in order to discern underlying structures and the "essence" of the phenomenon.

Obviously, many other avenues of phenomenological exploration are possible, but it is clear that there are rich resources here for a deeper understanding of the religious or spiritual dimensions of the human condition and maybe even for more profound insight into human experience as such.

Bibliography

Evagrius of Pontus. *The Greek Ascetic Corpus*. Translated by Robert E. Sinkewicz. Oxford: Oxford University Press, 2003.

Foucault, Michel. "About the Beginning of the Hermeneutics of the Self." *Political Theory* 21.2 (1993) 198–227.

Gschwandtner, Crina. "The Category of Experience: Orthodox Theology and Contemporary Philosophy." *Journal of Eastern Christian Studies* 69.1–2 (2017) 181–221.

Harnack, Adolf von. "Der Geist der morgenländischen Kirche im Unterschied von der abendländischen." In *Ausgewählte Reden und Aufsätze*, edited by Agnes von Zahn-Harnack and Axel von Harnack, 80–112. Berlin: Walter de Gruyter, 1951.

Louth, Andrew. "On Being a Christian in Late Antiquity: St. Basil the Great between the Desert and the City." In *Christians Shaping Identity from the Roman Empire to Byzantium*, edited by Geoffrey D. Dunn and Wendy Mayer, 85–99. Leiden: Brill, 2015.

Louth, Andrew. "Orthodox Mystical Theology and its Intellectual Roots." In *The Cambridge Intellectual History of Byzantium*, edited by Anthony Kaldellis, 509–523. Cambridge: Cambridge University Press, 2017.

Maloney, George. "Introduction." In *The Discourses*, by Symeon the New Theologian, 1–36. New York: Paulist, 1980.

Scheler, Max. *Liebe und Erkenntnis*. Bern: Francke Verlag, 1955.

Symeon the New Theologian. *The Discourses*. Translated by C. J. Catanzaro. New York: Paulist, 1980.

The Way of a Pilgrim: Candid Tales of a Wanderer to His Spiritual Father. Translated by Anna Zaranko. London: Penguin Books, 2017.

4

Orthodox Theology and the Inevitability of Metaphysics

David Bentley Hart

I

I suspect that the task most incumbent upon theology today is that of overcoming the overcoming of metaphysics. For roughly five centuries, theological reason has been assailed from within by the tedious demand that it strip itself of philosophical tradition's glittering but cumbersome panoply of categories and concepts, and rush with lightness of limb—chastened, humbled, naked, but free—into the embrace of the God who reveals himself only to the eyes of faith. The injunction never changes, though it comes in varying forms: the Reformation era's disdain for "the God of the philosophers" and the "Schoolmen," "Kantianesque" prohibition on conjectures exceeding reason's transcendental limits, Heideggerean warnings against "onto-theology's" oblivion of the ontological difference, popular Barthianism's turgid dialectics, the dour linguistic mysticism of Protestants corrupted by Wittgenstein, postmodern alarm at the colonializing "violence" of all totalizing essentialisms (and so on).

Granted, not entirely without cause: There are any number of metaphysical regimes inimical to what Christians believe God revealed in Christ. And it would be impious to deny that metaphysics is not sufficient for knowledge of God, or that any philosophy that presumes to decide in advance what God *may* or *may not* reveal is an artifact of human self-delusion. Were that the entire issue, the call to go "beyond" metaphysics would be no more than the old imperative of apophatic reserve, humility before divine transcendence, a resolve to kick away the ladder of speculative reason when it becomes a hindrance to the soul's journey to God. For, as Augustine repeatedly affirms, any vision of God in himself is impossible for creatures,[1] none can know him as he is,[2] nothing the mind can comprehend or conceive is God,[3] God is known only to himself,[4] and we speak of God properly only through negation.[5] We truly *know* God not as an object of cognition, intuition, or speculative reason, but only in that incomprehensible intimacy beyond words into which the Spirit alone leads us. As Gregory of Nyssa says, creaturely intellect is incapable of a *theoria* of the divine essence, and can reach God only by stretching out in a spiritual ecstasy exceeding conceptual categories, so that the soul somehow sees God[6] and attains to a vision of the invisible,[7] without being able to account for what it has seen.[8] Or, as Maximus the Confessor insists, only an apophatic language is appropriate to the intimacy—the overwhelming super-conceptual immediacy—of the soul's knowledge when it ascends to its ultimate rest in the ineffable reality of God.[9] At that point, the mind passes beyond cognition, reflection, cogitation, and imagination, and knows God through union, the embrace in which God gives himself to the creature,[10] wherein no separation can be introduced between the mind and its first cause in God.[11] But this is not really the issue.

We can stipulate that God's mystery transcends our speculative schemes, but should nevertheless remain suspicious of the suggestion that theology should purge itself of all principles drawn from "natural revelation." The very concept of a wholly "post-metaphysical theology" is preposterous, rather on the order of "post-atmospheric air." A fully

---

1. See, e.g., Augustine, *De Trinitate* 2.16.27; *In Ioannis Evangelium* 3.17; *Contra Maximinum Arianorum Episcopum* 2.12.2.

2. Augustine, *Enarrationes in Psalmos* 74.9.

3. Augustine, *Sermon* 52.6; *Sermon* 117.5.

4. Augustine, *Epistle* 232.6; *Sermon* 117.5.

5. Augustine, *Enarrationes in Psalmos* 80.12.

6. Gregory of Nyssa, *De Vita Moysis* 2.87.

7. Gregory of Nyssa, *In Canticum Canticorum* 11.326.

8. Gregory of Nyssa, *In Canticum Canticorum* 11.307–311.

9. Maximus, *Ambigua*, 1240C–1241A.

10. Maximus, *Ambigua*, 1220BC.

11. Maximus, *Ambigua*, 1260D.

non-metaphysical theology would not open a return to a purer faith; it would merely inaugurate faith's eclipse. Metaphysics may be a ladder that should be dispensed with when it has discharged its function, but certainly not before then. After all, the most traditional forms of Christian metaphysics are simple conceptual hygienes, regulative negations meant to disabuse us of false pictures of divine transcendence. Taken in its barest acceptation, the word "metaphysics" merely indicates the mind's awareness of a region of thought implicit in every act of understanding, both as a necessary terminus or waystation of the mind's journey toward truth, and as a boundary that the mind cannot overstep. Taken specifically as a dimension within theology, it names a requisite grammar for thinking of God as truly transcendent, and a necessary modality for receiving revelation as an object of rational assent, helping the mind surrender to a God who is not an idol of sentiment or fantasy.

Yes, all concepts vanish in the soul's ecstatic union with God. But it is precisely the minimal but inviolable grammar of classical metaphysics that makes apophatic theology possible, and teaches the intellect to detach itself from mythological pictures of God as a discrete being among other beings, or as a finite psychological personality, or as an external object with which the soul forms a mere extrinsic moral association. By forbidding the mind the illusion that there exists a set of predicates that can be applied univocally both to creatures and to the God who is the source of all reality, it thwarts any reduction of faith to the cult of some local deity, embraced alongside ourselves within a single sphere of existence that exceeds him no less than it does us. Far, then, from constituting a presumptuous trespass upon God's transcendence, "metaphysics" in this purely regulative sense guards a proper awareness of that transcendence against inadequate and destructive conceptualizations, and prepares the soul to receive revelation without presupposition.

This should all be familiar for Orthodox thinkers. The formulations of "classical theism" are lavishly preserved in the tradition. Gregory of Nazianzus provides a stirring distillate in one of his sermons: God is, firstly, eternal "Being," both the sum of all Being and the one who contains all beings in himself; he is like "a great ocean of Being," limitless, transcending time and nature; he is eternal not by possessing mere endless duration, endless *chronos*, but by possessing the timeless fullness of the heavenly *aiōn* that comprehends and transcends the successive time of creatures.[12] As the

---

12. Gregory of Nazianzus, *Oration* 38.6–7.

Pseudo-Dionysius and Maximus say, God is perfect unity, utterly simple, the very simplicity of the simple,[13] who is all in all, present in the totality of beings and in each particular being, indwelling all things as their source without ever abandoning that simplicity.[14] The most compendious and magisterial exposition of the tradition, of course, is provided by John of Damascus: God is beginningless and endless, timelessly eternal, immutable, non-composite, incorporeal, invisible, impalpable, uncircumscribed, indeed infinite, beyond cognition, definition, or comprehension;[15] superessential, changeless, in his absolute simplicity and infinity beyond combination and dissolution;[16] absolute plenitude, impassible, having no contrary, both filling and transcending all essences, not deriving his Being from anything, but himself the fountainhead of all being,[17] in whom there is only one essence, one divinity, one power, one will, one entirely simple energy; the Good operating in all things, setting them to work;[18] though his nature is spoken of through multiple ascriptions, he is beyond any diversity of attributes, the infinite ocean of being in whose incomprehensible essence all divine "attributes"—such as Being and Goodness—coincide in undifferentiated identity.[19] And so on.

In the end, all these descriptions are variants upon a single logical, modal, and metaphysical definition (one almost always prefixed by an alpha-privative). One might reduce them to the simple claim that God is "pure actuality": unchangeable, beyond addition, modification, and qualification, not a being but Being in its fullness, possessing no intrinsic unrealized potentiality, but also having no truly extrinsic relations, as all things have their fullest actuality in him. Thus, even the free act of creation does not constitute the actualization of some divine potential, as though he were a demiurge situated in a landscape of possible worlds, drawing upon some source of being greater than himself. Rather, he donates being to the entire order of finite possibility and actuality out of his infinite actuality. As John of Damascus says, in neither the eternal begetting of the Son nor the creation of the world does God's act involve any *pathos* or change—that is, any

---

13. Pseudo-Dionysius, *De nominibus divinis* 1.3; Maximus, *Ambigua*, 1232BC.

14. Maximus, *Ambigua*, 1256B.

15. John of Damascus, *De fide orthodoxa* 1.2, 8.

16. John of Damascus, *De fide orthodoxa* 1.4, 8, 11.

17. John of Damascus, *De fide orthodoxa* 1.8.

18. John of Damascus, *De fide orthodoxa* 1.8, 10.

19. John of Damascus, *De fide orthodoxa* 1.9.

movement from potency to act—on his part.[20] In fact, one might equally well reduce all divine attributes to this very impassibility—so long as one recalls that a *pathos* or *passio* in the classical sense is merely the modification of a patient substance by an agent force within any instance of finite change. God is never extrinsically related to realities somehow beyond himself, which communicate themselves to him through an adventitious qualification of his "substance" actualizing a hitherto unrealized potency. This would entail that God is a finite being, in whom possibility exceeds actuality. There would be an infinity not only of possible worlds, but also of possible Gods.

Above all, this is a metaphysics of "being." Admittedly, that single English word is scarcely adequate to the full spectrum of terms it is often forced to represent: *on, ōn, ousia, einai, ens, esse, essentia, existentia, actus essendi*, and so forth. When the Greek Fathers spoke of God as Being—*to ontōs on*, or *ho ōn* (etc.)—or when later Latin theologians spoke of God as *actus essendi subsistens* or *esse* (etc.), they were speaking of the transcendent source and end of all things, whose being is not merely the opposite of nonbeing. At the same time, in precisely this sense God is also *epekeina tēs ousias*: "superessential," "supersubstantial," "beyond being." He transcends "beings," and discrete "substances," the "totality of substances," and the created common existence of beings. Hence, says Maximus, both names, "Being" and "not-being," simultaneously apply and do not apply to God: The one denotes that he is the cause of all beings and the latter that he is infinitely beyond all caused being; but neither should be mistaken for a "description" of what he is.[21] Or, as the Pseudo-Dionysius says, "Being" is a proper divine name since God is "He Who Is," the source of all things, present within them, around and within whose perfect unity all things abide, participate, and have their eternal exemplars; but he is not *a* being: He is not contained by—but rather contains—being, and with regard to his own essence should properly be called not-being.[22] In Augustine's terms, God is the plenitude of Being, without which nothing is,[23] but such is his transcendence as the One Who Is that, by comparison to him, things that are *are* not.[24] Again, none of this should sound strange to Orthodox theologians.

20. John of Damascus, *De fide orthodoxa* 1.8.

21. Maximus, *Mystagogia*, 664AC.

22. Ps.-Dionysius, *De divinis nominibus* 5.1–8.

23. Augustine, *Soliloquiae* 1.1.3–4.

24. Augustine, *Enarrationes in Psalmos* 134.4.

II

It is not really this minimal regulative grammar, though, except occasionally by association, that is at issue when contemporary theologians eschew "metaphysics." Instead, it is a perceived impasse peculiar to modern continental philosophy. Explicitly or implicitly, such theologians tend to be responding to Heidegger's great narrative of Western "metaphysics" as a succession of fated epochs, each at once disclosing and veiling the "ontico-ontological difference," and each, by virtue of its inevitable forgetfulness of the true nature of that difference, incubating its own downfall within itself. It is a very special kind of philosophical disenchantment, a fatigue with the futility of synthetic speculations, but also a moral indictment of a tradition that supposedly, in its will to power, seeks to seize hold of beings under a regime of inert categories, and thus to conquer the silent, indomitable mystery of Being. And this style of post-metaphysical suspicion, at least on the surface, may genuinely make some demand upon Orthodox thought, both because its arraignment of the "metaphysical" oblivion of Being is a challenge to Christian tradition, and because it poses a hermeneutical challenge to the whole tradition of Western philosophy that, if taken seriously, leaves not even the most fundamental ontological and logical presuppositions intact. That, though, is the question: How seriously should one take that tale? And what avenues remain open for Christian thought if it is granted the legitimacy it claims for itself? For a few theologians who give it credence, but who still aspire to orthodoxy (or Orthodoxy), one of the more inviting paths through the debris of metaphysics' aftermath is a language of radical phenomenological reduction, of the sort proposed by Jean-Luc Marion. This supposedly allows a return to a truly "apocalyptic" encounter with God, because it interprets the surfeit of divine transcendence over the moment of immanent experience principally as an extravagant excess of intuition over intentionality, not as yet captured and diluted in conceptual categories, and not dependent upon a concomitant metaphysical reduction.

This is an excellent strategy to follow if one's aim is to collapse all Christian thinking into very bad poetry, of a variety that flourishes only in the damp, cloyingly fragrant soil of that narrow alluvial plain where clastic sediments from the lower elevations of Victorian late Romanticism and French Symbolism intermingle. But I cannot credit the notion that any proper *general* definition of "metaphysics" names an entire dimension of discourse that proleptically precludes or distorts the apocalyptic novelty of God's self-manifestation to us. Nor can I imagine a more disastrous course

than confining theology within the limitations of phenomenological reasoning—most especially a phenomenology of saturation and intuitional
excess that would condemn it to the false profundity of paradox, or the
shrill register of perpetual surprise. All the evidence tells us that, once the
methodological *epochē* has discharged its entirely preliminary and pro-
legomenal role, any phenomenology that will not surrender to, or secure
itself within, a metaphysical deduction, must inevitably dissolve into inter-
minable, ever more impressionistic rhapsodies of pure description, which
can at most beguile us with their enchanting vacuity: ever more precise and
so ever more trivial, ever more exacting, and so ever more vague, constantly
dissipating in the inconclusiveness of a willful refusal to think deeply. Every
attempt at "pure phenomenology" is a mystification, the willful suppression of the memory of a prior metaphysical deduction, one that assures us
that the correlation between the phenomena's givenness and the perceiver's
intentionality is more than a happy chance or bizarrely persistent occasion-
alism. There is an inseparable liaison between the objective and subjective
poles within any experience, and hence an indissoluble nuptial intimacy
between being and mind that urges reason, willy-nilly, toward some more
eminent source of unity, where being and knowing are *one*. Every finite
intention is contingent upon a more primordial intentionality of the mind
toward Truth as a final, transcendental object of rational desire, and so ex-
hibits a metaphysical horizon in its very grasp of any discrete *noēma*. And
that more primordial intentionality can be described only as going "beyond
nature"—as, that is, "metaphysical" in the purest sense.

Even the rejection of a metaphysical deduction entails a metaphysical decision regarding the relation between being and knowing; even the
distinction between phenomenology and metaphysics is a metaphysical
distinction, made from some presumed higher vantage where it is possible to survey the exact boundary between intentional experience and
speculative reason. The phenomenological and metaphysical dimensions of
theological discourse cannot constitute opposed approaches to revelation,
since neither enjoys any warrant apart from its complementary relation to
the other; and this complementarity merely reflects the necessarily inverse
relation between the *taxis tēs gnōseōs* or *ordo cognoscendi*, and the *taxis
tēs huparxeōs* or *ordo essendi*—the order of knowing and order of being—
which can never be alienated from one another in theological reflection
without producing gibberish. "Does God reveal himself in order to make
himself known and take a place within our rationality?" asks Jean-Luc

Marion in his recent Gifford Lectures, "Or does he instead reveal himself in order to allow himself to be loved, and to love us?"[25] To which the only coherent answer is "Yes."

Not that I want to be too dismissive of the anxieties prompting these questions. "Metaphysics" in the sense Marion and others presume, means chiefly what Heidegger called "onto-theology," which grants to thought only the "God" of the "double founding"—the grounding of beings in Being and of Being in a supreme being—and so reduces all of reality (including divine reality) to a closed totality of ontic causal forces from which the mystery of Being has been fully exorcised. This is the "God" of the *causa sui*, that merely "supreme" principle before which a human being can "weder aus Scheu ins Knie fallen, noch . . . musizieren und tanzen."[26] And, indeed, if we are talking only about early modern philosophical systems—Suarezian, manualist Thomist, Cartesian, Leibnizian-Wolffian—and their sequelae, then why quibble? But for Heidegger these philosophical enormities do not represent a departure from classical thought, but rather a speculative pathology discernible as far back as Plato's "apostasy of the gaze," that turn away from beings in their "presencing" toward a realm of lifeless ideas, whose static impalpability affords the philosopher rational mastery. Heidegger's epochal story of this ontological "forgetfulness," and of its termination in the "age of the world-picture" and the technological "*Ge-Stell*," embraces the whole of Western intellectual history, including patristic and mediaeval metaphysics.

And, frankly, Heidegger's treatment of ancient, late antique, and mediaeval philosophy is so defective, and so soaked in ignorance of classical thought, that it seems not only idiosyncratic, but positively perverse, to allow his fabulous narrative to dictate how theologians should use the word "metaphysics," or understand the labor of reason in light of God's revelation. Heidegger wanted to tell a monolithic story about the history of Western thought (so that in this the moment of highest risk, when the nihilistic destiny of metaphysics has become explicit, a possibility of healing might appear, calling the "thinker" to retrieve and reflect upon that story, to avoid repeating the primordial error, to let the world *be* in its worlding while awaiting another dawn . . .) but the story is largely nonsense. Whenever we pronounce the word "metaphysics" with Heideggerean inflections, we artificially cast the shadow of the *causa sui* backward over ages of thought

25. Marion, *Givenness and Revelation*, 29.
26. Heidegger, "Die onto-theo-logische Verfassung der Metaphysik," 77.

that, in fact, possessed the best resources for resisting any such picture of the divine.

We also risk falling prey to an intolerably dialectical picture of revelation. In those same lectures, Marion rightly observes that the concept of "revelation" as a special theological category is a modern development, arising from the ever more impermeable partitions erected between philosophy and theology—or between "natural" and "supernatural" knowledge—at the end of the Middle Ages; and he is right that revelation consequently suffered a kind of "epistemological" reduction, as though revealed truth were merely another body of facts that, precisely because it is revealed rather than deduced, "irrationally" supplements the knowledge discovered by natural reason. Thus, too, faith came to be seen as an entirely supernatural capacity graciously bestowed, but not as the fullest expression of the intellect's natural intentionality toward Truth; thus, it too became essentially irrational. This followed the pattern of the debased, "two-tier" theology of Baroque Thomism, in which grace is by definition an extrinsic superimposition upon nature.

This is surely not what Paul meant by the *gnōsis* of God revealed in Christ by the Spirit who "knows the depths of God," nor an understanding of revelation that ever took root in Orthodox tradition. Where it did flourish, however, this simultaneous continuity of kind and discontinuity in content between natural and supernatural knowledge ultimately led to the estrangement of philosophy (including natural philosophy) from theology, as though they constituted two distinct or even competing systems of "information" (univocally understood). But surely it only exacerbates the problem if, having seen this, we widen the chasm by proposing an ultimate heterogeneity between natural forms of thought and supernatural *apokalypsis*, or between "metaphysical" and "phenomenological" approaches to revelation. This is the folly of so much popular Barthian theology: In rejecting every analogical metaphysics of being, supposedly to safeguard the transcendence of God against the presumptuous claims of creatures, it accomplishes the opposite, reducing God to just another *thing*, a "Wholly Other" who can actually be posed "over against" creation, and who must therefore logically be contained within some neutral medium of relation and alienation that encompasses both him and creation severally, as discrete "entities."

The tendency of the greatest Christian thinkers of the last century—Blondel, de Lubac, Przywara, Bulgakov—was to reject the dialectical in favor of a genuine metaphysics of participation, which allows us to recognize nature as more originally creation, human nature as more originally God's image, and divine revelation as a consummation of natural vision and intentionality. Created spirit is constitutively open to transcendence—is indeed, as de Lubac said, *nothing but* the insatiable desire for God. Hence, our rational and conceptual intentions do in some sense "constitute" the phenomena of revelation. They must, as we can know nothing—experience nothing—as purely patient, purely recipient beings. Spiritual natures can provide this intentional hospitality to revelation, in their limited and corrigible way, because all movements of natural intellect and will toward finite ends are sustained within a prior inexorable orientation of the mind toward the infinite horizon of Being's fullness in God.

In Maximus the Confessor's terms, the gnomic will's wanderings are animated by and embraced within the natural will's inalienable longing for God. Revelation quickens this primitive movement of love; but, apart from this natural agent capacity—including intentions, concepts, anticipations, and even some indispensable metaphysical predispositions—there could be no revelation at all. Except for this primordial relation of the natural will to the whole of Being—which, far from frustrating the apocalyptic freedom of revelation, is its womb within nature, the *fiat mihi* where the Logos condescends to be made manifest—the appearance of the divine within creation would be neither enlightenment nor redemption, but merely a magical transition or monstrous amalgamation: either nature's destruction and replacement by something alien, or an extrinsic and hence chimerical alliance of nature and supernature.

Commendably, Marion wants to open a path to a renewed receptivity to revelation that never risks petrifying into the sort of monstrous metaphysical systems that characterized early modern thought; and, if the only alternative were something like manualist Thomism or the Leibnizian-Wolffian system of predicates and principles, this rapt, dilatory, perpetually astounded phenomenological encounter with the sheer, unanticipated event of revelation would be the only civilized option. Happily, there are far better alternatives. In one of his readings of Paul, Marion speaks engagingly of "God's right to overstep the distinction between being and non-being," which presumably no one doubts, but then adds: "The difference between being and non-being is cancelled out because God excludes himself from Being, and thus from the very difference between Being and beings."[27] Now,

---

27. Marion, *Givenness and Revelation*, 68.

on a first reading I take this not so much false as meaningless: Who is this fabulous gentleman who "excludes himself from Being," and where does he come from? At second glance, however, I find it perverse. Surely the more theologically coherent claim is that God *transcends* the difference between beings and non-being—between existence and nonexistence—*precisely because of* the difference between Being and beings. Precisely because God is not an entity among other entities, comprised within finite existence, but is instead absolute Being—the infinite and supereminent wellspring of all reality, the unconditioned "to-be" upon which all beings depend—he is *absolved* of all ontic distinctions, as well as of the ontological contingency manifested in the difference between finite existence and nonexistence, and so is never absent from beings.

Again, as Maximus says, infinite Being cannot be negated or have nonexistence as its contrary. God is not modally qualified by any relation to nonbeing, as he is himself the "is" both of "it is" and of "it is not." He is the creator *ex nihilo*, because for him the difference between beings and nonbeing is literally nothing at all. But it requires a rigorous metaphysical language to affirm this truth properly. And such a language is unavailable to the theologian who confines all talk of "Being" within the narrow ambit that this style of phenomenological reasoning permits. It is not surprising that Marion also speaks of "the essentially *finite* horizon of Being and beings."[28] But this is completely backwards. Here the classical Christian metaphysical tradition more correctly asserts that every created essence is by nature finite, and that for this reason the distance between its existence and nonbeing is qualitatively infinite. In itself, any finite thing is impossible; insofar as it exists, it has arrived (so to speak) from across an infinite distance that it never had the power to traverse on its own.

Marion's language, by contrast, clearly invokes Heidegger's insistence on "the finitude of Being" and the economy of the "*Ereignis*," in which possibility presides over actuality. But was this not just a symptom of Heidegger's ontological purblindness? For, in the end, both the *Sein* and the *Seiendes* of Heidegger's thought turn out to be only distinct aspects of a wholly ontic process of arising, "whiling," and passing away, which differ from one another only as finite possibility and finite actuality. Both are situated on *this* side of the "difference." The truly "ontological" dimension of reality is never addressed by Heidegger. The true difference between Being and beings, which alone makes any finite economy of existence possible—the difference

28. Marion, *Givenness and Revelation*, 70.

between transcendent actuality and the contingency of finite becoming—is something he singularly failed to grasp (principally by blunderingly confusing it with the "onto-theology" of early modernity). Hence the ever more nebulous inconclusiveness of his attempts to articulate an ontology without metaphysical premise. Heidegger's true distinction as a philosopher was not to have recalled the ontological difference, but to have forgotten it more completely than any other. It seems a pity, then, cavalierly to dispense with the language of Being, which Christian tradition addressed with such exquisite subtlety, out of deference to a philosopher who addressed it with such unprecedented incompetence.

Perhaps, though, I assume too much. Perhaps the post-metaphysical theologian's eye is turned only to the Aristotelian definition of metaphysics as the science of *on hē on, ens in quantum ens.* But, if so, this too raises questions. Certainly metaphysics in this sense is a science not yet properly aware of what later Christian thought understands by such terms as *to ontōs on,* or *to einai,* or *esse ipsum,* or *actus essendi subsistens.* The best way of rendering the Aristotelian formula would not be "being qua being," but rather something like "entity qua (the condition of) entity": that is, the science of entities not as specific kinds of things, but solely in the abstract, as individuated substantial forms in act. Here, philosophy is preoccupied solely with the realm of beings, in relation to which the divine is always simply *epeikeina tēs ousias, super substantiam,* or *super essentiam.* A distinct concept of "Being itself" has not yet emerged; it has merely been adumbrated, as the answer to a question that metaphysics must ask, but has not yet properly posed. And it was, arguably, the special achievement of Christian thought both to discover the correct question and to supply its answer, specifically in light of revelation. In part, this was because the notion of *creatio ex nihilo* obliged it to think through the absolute difference between Being and nothingness, and so more properly to conceive of God's transcendence of contingent existence and nonexistence. But it was also the result of that most mysterious aspect of Christian thought, Trinitarian doctrine.

III

In the three centuries before Nicaea, in the eastern empire especially, the philosophical grammars of most religious schools—Pagan, Jewish, Christian—encompassed what we might call a "Logos metaphysics," since nearly all concurred that the divine was connected to this world by some kind of "subordinationist" hierarchy of beings. In Alexandria, most Christian factions conceived of the Trinity in terms of one God Most High, the Father, who in his inaccessible transcendence could express himself *ad extra* only in a derivative, secondary divine principle; they accepted the common premise that, to overcome the measureless disproportion between the immanent and the transcendent, there must be some intermediary reality or realities inhabiting the interval, constituting both a hypostatic continuum and a qualitative disjunction between the One or Father above and the realm of unlikeness below.

The second "moment" of the real—*Logos, Nous,* or whatever—was understood as an economical embassy, sufficiently reduced in nature to enter into contact with the realm of discrete beings, yet capable of communicating some of the supreme principle's power to creation. For everyone in this tradition, of any adherence, the disproportion between the supreme principle and the secondary principle of manifestation was absolute. Thus, no revelation of the divine could be complete or transparent; it could be only the paradoxical manifestation of a transcendence never *truly* manifest—perhaps even to itself, as it possessed no Logos immanent to itself. We see this in Plotinus, for instance, for whom the first metaphysical moment of intellectual reflection "there above" is already a departure from unity. Nous contemplates the One, but only under the form of a duality that already belies the One's simplicity, then acts as an ontological prism, refracting the One's light into multiplicity. The One itself "knows" itself not as an object, but only "beyond intellection"; in itself, it has no "specular" other, it infinitely exceeds reflection or self-contemplation.[29] Here, the difference between Being and beings, as conceived in later Western thought, remains unaddressed. After all, how could that which absolutely transcends intuition, conceptualization, and knowledge, even within itself, be said to exist at all? Being *is* manifestation, and insofar as anything is wholly beyond thought, and hence not "rational," it does not "exist" in the normal sense.

Thus later Platonist tradition placed "being" second in the scale of emanation: as the purely unmanifest, unthinkable, transfinite unity that grants all things their identities, the One admits of no inner distinctions, no manifestation *to* itself, and so in some sense *is* not (though neither is it *not*). None of these systems, then, was so much ontological as "henological" in logic. None had any real concept of "Being" as wholly distinct from beings; each had some notion of a "being principle," but only as a "hypostasis"

29. See Plotinus, *Enneads,* 6:7.37.15–7.38.26; 9.6.50–55.

within the hierarchy of emanations, occupying a particular station within the structure of reality. And that structure can be correctly characterized as a "hierarchy within totality," secured at its apex by a principle so exalted as to be both the negation of all finite reality and also only the highest occupant of that continuum. Even then, none of these systems can be called a form of "onto-theology"; while each of them "grounded" being in its highest principle, none reciprocally "grounded" that principle in "Being"; they always preserved a sense that the Most High is beyond all "ground." Still, nowhere did this tradition descry any real "ontological difference" or "analogy of being," because it lacked a coherent ontology of divine transcendence. Hence, when "Being" did eventually become conceivable as infinite source, rather than as a discrete principle among others, far from being mistaken for the "ground" of a God who was just a supreme being among lesser beings, it was recognized as one of the proper names of God in his transcendence.

This, though, became possible only after the advent of Nicene theology had altered the late antique conceptual world and slowly forced Christian thinkers to conceive God's relation to the world in a properly "ontological" fashion. With the gradual defeat of subordinationist trinitarian theologies, and the definition of the divine Persons as coequal, the old metaphysics had implicitly been abandoned. The Logos of Nicaea was not a lesser manifestation of a God beyond all manifestation, but rather the eternal actuality of God's essence. The perfectly proportionate convertibility of God with his own manifestation of himself to himself is God's own act of self-knowledge and self-love in the mystery of his transcendent life. Thus his being is an infinite intelligibility; even his hiddenness—his transcendence—is always already a movement of infinite disclosure. And, if "being" is somehow convertible with manifestation or intelligibility, then the God who is always Logos is also eternal Being in its fullness. Once the notion of a graduated hierarchy of hypostases mediating between the world and its absolute principle had been abandoned, it became possible to understand true transcendence not merely as dialectical supremacy, and so to affirm that the transcendent God gives creation existence not through an economic reduction of his power in lesser principles, but by his immediate presence. He is at once *superior summo meo* and *interior intimo meo*. Rather than the supreme being at the summit of the hierarchy of beings, he is the infinite act within and beyond every finite act, the immediate source of the being of the whole who is also infinitely beyond the reach of the whole, even in its highest principles.

In discovering that God is not situated within the ontic continuum of creation, as some other "thing" mediated to creatures by his simultaneous absolute absence *from* and dialectical involvement *in* the totality of beings, Christian thought discovered him to be the truly *ontological* cause of creation. The true difference of Being from beings becomes visible for the first time in God's simultaneous transcendence of and intimacy to creation. But this *metaphysics* of *Being* did not enter thought merely as a paradox overturning all prior concepts; rather, it detached the thought of Being from the mythology of a hierarchy of essences, and so helped to complete God's revelation in Christ *as revelation*. Here the metaphysical and the apocalyptic prove inseparable. This metaphysics prepares us to receive and respond to what God reveals precisely by forbidding us to imagine that anything can limit or condition what appears within Being's horizon: *to ontōs on, esse ipsum*—what is this but the aptitude for everything?

And, because Being's infinite actuality, purged of all ontic determinations, constitutes the proper horizon of rational spirit's natural intentionality—such that the givenness of Being and the natural orientation of mind are teleologically the same event—it is possible for the mind to experience a surfeit of meaning in any finite phenomenon, an excess of intuition over concept, that does not dissolve into mere unintelligibility, but that instead summons the soul to an ever higher and deeper knowing (even if that terminates in the "super-conceptual intimacy" of divinization).

IV

If God's revelation to his creatures is a gift, then the labor of metaphysics is thanksgiving, a pious act of intellectual acceptance, a kind of prayer. But it is also a necessary modality of spiritual openness, which makes it possible to receive revelation at an otherwise unreachable depth. Any phenomenological reduction of revelation that comes at the cost of a hyperbolic, hyper-Kantian abstention from ontology is just another expression of a particularly pernicious modern pathology: the priority of the subjective vantage, the unwillingness to defer to the "objectivity" of metaphysical deduction. It was this that prompted Descartes to collapse the authority of the phenomenal into the intentionality of the reasoning self in reconstructing reality from the subjective position, and then to invoke the "god" of the *causa sui* as an adventitious source of epistemological certainty. It was this also that prompted Kant to erect the Great Wall of his antinomies and to reduce God to a postulate of practical reason, or that prompted Heidegger to contract ontology to the insipid immanence of "Being's finitude," and so on. Admittedly, a rigorously phenomenological approach to revelation might discourage us from allowing any metaphysical prejudice to foreclose the possibility of God's self-manifestation violating those boundaries. But, at the same time, it invites us to accept modern philosophy's equally metaphysical denial of reason's power to receive transcendent truths within the embrace of its *natural* intentionality toward the divine, and so to exceed the limits of the phenomenal. The result, predictably, is a mysticism of the incoherent.

This, at least, is my reaction to the enthusiasm of some theologians for Marion's accounts of the "saturated phenomenon."[30] Where they see a way of return to the apocalyptic novelty of revelation, and a theological diction evacuated of the philosopher's will to power, I see a reduction of revelation to a non-event. When described in qualitative and quantitative terms, this phenomenal saturation seems indistinguishable from mere cognitive dissonance, which is only (at least, potentially) a corrigible failure of intentionality. When described as an excess of meaning over intuition in certain experiences, however, it seems not only to assume an unwarrantably dialectical and static form, but also to generate formulae more rhetorically stirring than conceptually solvent. Granted, as regards revelation, I can agree with Marion that the phenomenon of *apokalypsis* ought not *simply* to be reduced to an object predetermined by prior concepts, "based on the gaze," but should *also* be allowed to "appear based on itself"[31]—though I find the danger vanishingly tiny—but I cannot agree that this constitutes an either-or.

I certainly cannot conceive of a "*paradox* that brings about counter-experience" or that "defines [those phenomena] that do happen (like events) only by *contra*-dicting the conditions of my experience," or that "extends experience . . . by allowing us to describe an experience that is non-objectifiable and thus all the *more* manifest in that it comes from phenomena that manifest themselves in themselves, because they give themselves from themselves."[32] Yes, revelation surprises us, overturns our expectations, ex-

---

30. This is, of course, one of the richest and most fascinating themes in Marion's work of the last two decades, and one that he expounds and develops in a variety of texts. Perhaps the best text to consult for some sense of the full range of meanings he gives the idea, and its relations to theological language, is Jean-Luc Marion, *In Excess.*

31. Marion, *Givenness and Revelation*, 47.

32. Marion, *Givenness and Revelation*, 55, 57.

ceeds our normal ability to articulate what we have seen and felt, offers us ever more than we can comprehend, and so on. But this is very different from saying that it simply contradicts the conditions of experience—which would mean that it is not an experience of anything at all. There is a difference between the apophatic and the meaningless, and the word "paradox" is worthless if not confined to its proper reference: a *seeming* contradiction that is really no rational contradiction at all.

Much of the language of phenomenal saturation comes perilously close to treating paradox as a thing in itself, an ultimate contrariety never dissoluble into a higher order of rational vision. Is revelation really revelation at all if our experience of it remains frozen in that initial moment of pure phenomenality, pure surprise? And how can any phenomenon give itself without a prior rational intentionality within which it can show itself? No phenomenon proceeds from itself alone. True, finite intention can be thwarted or overwhelmed at the level of the empirical self. But it would be a crude psychologism to imagine that this exhausts experience's intentional conditions, or that experience cannot be legitimately extended beyond its initial phenomenal moment by a further logical deduction. And it would be an even cruder obscurantism to think one can experience anything without *any* natural intentional capacity for it. At that empirical level, perhaps, given the psychological self's "gnomic" wanderings of attention, the limits of intentionality can be reached well before experience has been exhausted.

At the level of the *natural* will, however, in its pure and transcendental ecstasy, there is only a primordial orientation toward—and openness to— the infinite, not constituted by, but instead constituting, the psychological self as a phenomenon; and within the full scope of this orientation any phenomenon can appear, and any seeming contradiction be resolved. True, that highest intelligibility cannot be reduced to calculative or quantitative cognition; final knowledge is unitive, not merely cognitive, and must ultimately transcend concepts. Still, even that first moment of surprise is experienced as a vocation of the mind, in its inextinguishable love for Truth, to follow the phenomenon back to its original principles, and perhaps even to that original act of Being from which all things flow. And this corresponds to that one undoubted "saturation" that we can experience in any phenomenon, in those rare moments when we become all at once aware of the uncanny inexplicability of things—when we experience, in addition to even the commonest object of attention, the mysterious fortuity of existence, the infinite interval of Being's surfeit over beings.

In those moments, we discover an intentional range within ourselves capable of that interval, and of going beyond the finite occasion of experience toward the inexhaustible source of its event. We awaken, however briefly, to a deeper natural intentionality within us, whose end is convertible with the whole of Being, one that allows us to discern the invisible difference of Being from beings, and to respond to it by, in part, our metaphysical conjectures. Every phenomenon appears within the infinite horizon of Being's gratuity, and within the interval of analogical thought's movement from the conditions of beings to the unconditionality of Being, which is a natural capacity within us always open to God. Supernatural faith is only another name, granted from an inverse perspective, for the natural intentionality of the rational intellect toward Truth.

Some of Marion's most brilliant reflections on the "saturated phenomenon," I should note, concern events that seem somehow to precede or exceed their causes. But I do have to ask whether even this precedence and excess are not conditions of *every* phenomenon, *every* experience, in the moment of its event. I say this partly because I believe in final causality, and so in real causes that would be invisible to any inventory of a phenomenon's antecedent causes. But I also believe that the priority of *every* event over its causes is intrinsic to any experience that is truly *phenomenal*. Temporally speaking, causes and their effects are simultaneous, as classical and mediaeval philosophical tradition asserts, even in the case of causes that "arrive" from past or future. In the order of being, however, all causes are logically prior to their effects. But in the order of knowing just the reverse is true: all causes are posterior discoveries, preceded by a sheer event that is a phenomenal experience *before* it is an intelligible truth; the event comes first for us, while its causes lie only at the end of the wakened intellect's journey toward a reality that the event has made manifest, but not yet rendered wholly intelligible.

Every metaphysical truth *sub specie aeternitatis* is firstly, for the time-bound soul, sheer apocalypse, utter novelty breaking in upon the rational will's patient capacity. This is simply the noetic expression of the structure of participated being: For us, whose existence is a gift ceaselessly imparted by a source beyond us, every moment of being's advent is a pure *novum*, calling us out of ourselves toward the *novissima* of the divine nature, and out of nothingness toward our last end. In even the most ordinary experience, the fortuity of the phenomenon precedes its meaning; and in certain extraordinary experiences the normally entirely tacit surprise of the phenomenal is amplified into shock, alarm, delight, confusion. In either case, nothing is known or even truly experienced so long as the mind remains fixed in that initial moment of the unexpected. Here the desire to go "beyond" metaphysics amounts only to a desire to be fixed forever in thought's most infantile state, that delightful or terrific state of guileless wonder before the wholly unexpected. But when childish innocence is artificially prolonged it becomes mere perversion. Thought *must* take that surprise as a vocation to understand, because the natural will irrepressibly desires to ascend to the source of every phenomenon—to what in the *ordo cognoscendi* is most ultimate precisely because in the *ordo essendi* it is what is most original.

In that most extraordinary event of all, the disclosure of the divine within creation, this means an ascent of the mind to God, the infinite source of all; and this must involve every capacity of the rational spirit, including the speculative. It is this second movement—this response to the provocation of the unanticipated event of God's revelation and its power to surpass our existing concepts—that translates revelation's phenomena into gnosis. Thus, phenomenology is rescued from banality by metaphysics: by its ceaseless labor to find the true inverse proportion between the orders of knowledge and of being, thereby demonstrating that, in the end, they are one and the same.

V

Where do these reflections lead? Or, rather, where might an Orthodox thinker then look for a proper model of, at once, acceptance of theology's necessary metaphysical dimension and openness to the apocalyptic novelty of God's self-disclosure? Surely to someone who presumes, but also creatively interprets, the whole grammar of classical Christian metaphysics: someone, too, who recognizes that metaphysics, being first regulative rather than fully prescriptive, is not merely a grammar of assent, but also a provocation to think beyond conventional boundaries, to reconsider and reinterpret the tradition ever anew, to engage fully with every movement in the greater philosophical and theological world rather than retreating into the safe redoubt of purely catechetical dogmatics; someone able to conceive coherently of God's act in creation without mistaking it *either* for an arbitrary determination of the divine will (thus reducing God to a finite deliberative agent whose own actuality is surpassed by a larger realm of extrinsic possibility) *or* for a dialectical process whereby God achieves his essence (thus compromising his transcendence and making his goodness contingent upon the violence of nature and history); someone able to see that the participatory structure of Being forbids any form of extrinsicism in the relation of grace or supernature to creation, or in that of creation to God, and requires instead a proper sense of the analogical distinction between the divine and the creaturely; someone who sees (for the same reason) that there can be nothing accidental or "additional" to the divine nature in the relation between the Son's incarnation and the creature's divinization, or between divine humanity and human divinity, or between the Son's *kenosis* in time and his eternal procession from the Father; someone with the philosophical sophistication properly to grasp the modal difference of transcendent Being from created existence, and so the folly of attempting to understand the former in terms of freedom and necessity logically apposite only to the latter; above all, someone who, as a specifically Orthodox thinker, is able—with scrupulous attention to scripture, tradition, and logic—to overcome the most pernicious sickness of so much Western theology, the recurrent formal or even material distinction (to the point of opposition) between grace and nature, which in its most decadent form allows for any number of conceptual monstrosities: the possibility of *natura pura* and of a rational nature capable of resting sufficed in a wholly natural end, an entirely infralapsarian understanding of the Incarnation, an understanding of the supernatural as a true superaddition to the natural that activates (at most) a teleologically neutral *potentia oboedientialis*, and so on.

A truly accomplished Orthodox metaphysician, that is, must be one who takes *theosis* to be the theological master-key—especially to traditional Christology—that allows us to think of the incarnate Logos not as a mythic demigod or divine-human chimaera composed of disparate natures, but instead as truly wholly human and wholly divine, without conflict, separation, or diminishment. Such a thinker would start always from the necessary conviction that deification is the *natural* end of all we are, and so the eternal foundation of our nature. Such a metaphysician would see creation and salvation as a single divine act: the way whereby the eternal divine Wisdom, "repeated" in creation, brings all things into being by drawing them to their divine source and end—which for us here, at the furthest extreme of the *ordo essendi*, is the greatest of surprises, the awakening of everything out of pure nothingness into the divine glory, but which for God is merely the perfect expression of his absolute freedom, his infinite love. In modern

Orthodox thought, of course, only one thinker provides such a model in its entirety: Sergei Bulgakov. But that is an essay for another time.

Bibliography

Augustine. *Contra Maximinum Arianorum Episcopum.* In vol. 42 of *Patrologia Latina,* edited by J.-P. Migne, 743–814. Paris, 1841.

———. *De Trinitate.* Edited by W. J. Mountain and F. Glorie. Vols. 50–50A of *Corpus Christianorum Series Latina.* Turnhout: Brepols, 1968.

———. *Enarrationes in Psalmos.* Edited by E. Dekkers and J. Fraipoint. Vols. 38–40 of *Corpus Christianorum Series Latina.* Turnhout: Brepols, 1956.

———. *In Iohannis evanglium tractatus CXXIV.* Edited by R. Willems. Vol. 36 of *Corpus Christianorum Series Latina.* Turnhout: Brepols, 1954.

———. *Sermons (51–94): On the New Testament.* Translated by Edmund Hill. Vol. 3.3 of *The Works of Saint Augustine: A Translation for the Twenty-First Century.* Brooklyn: New City, 1991.

———. *Sermons (94A–147A): On the New Testament.* Translated by Edmund Hill. Vol. 3.4 of *The Works of Saint Augustine: A Translation for the Twenty-First Century.* Hyde Park, NY: New City, 1992.

———. *Soliloquies.* Translated by Kim Paffenroth. Hyde Park, NY: New City, 2000.

Gregory Nazianzen. *Faith Gives Fullness to Reasoning: The Five Theological Orations of Gregory Nazianzen.* Introduction and Commentary by Frederick W. Norris. Translation by Lionel Wickham and Frederick Williams. Leiden: Brill 1991.

Gregory of Nyssa. *De Vita Moysis.* Edited by Herbertus Musurillo. Vol. 7 of *Gregori Nyseeni Opera.* Leiden: Brill, 1964.

———. *In Canticum Canticorum.* Edited by Hermannus Langerbeck. Vol. 6 of *Gregori Nyseeni Opera.* Leiden: Brill, 1960.

Heidegger, Martin. "Die onto-theo-logische Verfassung der Metaphysik." In *Identität und Differenz,* edited by F.-W. von Herrmann, 51–79. Frankfurt am Main: Vittorio Klostermann, 2006.

Johannes Damascenus. "Expositio fidei [De fidei orthodoxa]." In *Die Schriften des Johannes von Damaskos,* edited by Bonifatius Kotter. Vol 2. Berlin: De Gruyter, 1973.

Marion, Jean-Luc. *Givenness and Revelation.* Translated by Stephen E. Lewis. Oxford: Oxford University Press, 2016.

———. *In Excess: Studies of Saturated Phenomena.* Translated by Robyn Horner. New York: Fordham University Press, 2004.

Maximus the Confessor. "Ambigua." In *Patrologiae Cursus Completus,* edited by Jacques Paul Migne, 1031–1418. Vol. 91 of *Series Graeca.* Paris: Migne 1863.

———. "Mystagogia." In *Patrologiae Cursus Completus,* edited by Jacques Paul Migne, 657–718. Vol. 91 of *Series Graeca.* Paris: Migne 1863.

Plotinus. *Enneads.* Translated by A. H. Armstrong. Vols 1–7. London: Heinemann; Cambridge, Massachusetts: Harvard University Press, 1966–1988.

Pseudo-Dionysius. *The Divine Names and Mystical Theology.* Translated and with an introduction by John D. Jones. Milwaukee: Marquette University Press, 1980.

5

Orthodox Theology and Philosophy of Self

Sergey S. Horujy

The subject of this chapter includes two different problem fields. First, Orthodox theology had always its own view of self, personhood, identity, and all related principles and notions. There is a rich Orthodox personalism,[1] the core of which is the conception of personhood as identified with divine hypostasis. Today this patristic conception, which can be called the theocentric personalistic paradigm (TPP), continues to be studied and developed further. Second, there is a rich secular personalism based on the identification of the notion of personhood with that of the individual human being. This conception of personhood can be called the anthropological personalistic paradigm (APP). After the "death of the subject," it went through radical changes, and is now in the intense search for new modes of human subjectivity. In this search, it analyzes closely the present-day anthropological reality, and Orthodoxy must take this analysis into account.

Thus, after describing the TPP in its modern state, presented in the recent personalistic synthesis by Metropolitan John Zizioulas, we briefly discuss the APP. But there is also the problem of the relationship between the two paradigms. After a long period of mutual misunderstanding and confrontation, the modern crisis of secularism stimulated the emergence of new dialogical models of the relationship between religious and secular thought. In the area of anthropology and personalism, the dialogue can

1. Let me note that the term "personalism" in this text means the theory of personhood in general, which should not be confused with the well-known schools in modern philosophy, like the French or the Russian personalism.

97

develop on the phenomenological ground, in the study of anthropological experience. In the concluding part of the chapter, I will describe personalist conceptions of synergic anthropology, a theory in which religious and secular discourse are in conjunction in a new way.

Principle of Personality in Orthodoxy: The Theocentric Personalistic Paradigm

Here we discuss the conception of personhood created in Orthodox theology. Development of Orthodox thought is often seen as a chain of reproducing syntheses. The teaching of Orthodoxy never took the form of a rigid, compulsory doctrine. Based on the quintessential Christian experience, Orthodox thought produces a wide spectrum of conceptions, studies, opinions, and from time to time, this rich intellectual landscape needs to be summarized or synthesized into a coherent conceptual unity. The earliest example of the Orthodox synthesis is the Niceno-Constantinopolitan Creed (381). Then followed the "Greek patristic synthesis," embracing the work of Greek Fathers from the Cappadocians to Maximus the Confessor; the Palamite synthesis of the fourteenth century, which revealed the theological meaning of ascetical (hesychast) practice and created a theology of the divine energies; the neo-patristic and neo-Palamite synthesis of the twentieth century; and finally the personalist synthesis of John Zizioulas, which is still in its formative stage. Regarding its key ideas, the synthesis of Zizioulas develops the approach of modern Orthodox theology of personhood, which originated almost a century ago in the works of several Russian thinkers, the most important of whom were Lev Karsavin, Vladimir Lossky and George Florovsky. After these first authors, many others took part in the creation of this theology—Fr. Dumitru Staniloae, Archimandrite Sophrony (Sakharov), Metropolitan Kallistos Ware, Jean-Claude Larchet, and some Greek and Serbian theologians. The work of Zizioulas provided a profound and systematic synthesis of this area of research.

Zizioulas begins with an exposition of the general principles of the TPP, describing in detail their patristic (predominantly Cappadocian) origins. He chooses person as the basic term, considering the term personality as close to individuality, and so to the APP rather than the TPP. Right from the outset, he shapes patristic personalism in a new way, putting to the forefront its ontological aspects and demonstrating that it implies a special "ontology of personhood," distinct from the Greek "ontology of substance/essence." It must be noticed, however, that his version of ontology is distinct not only from "ontology of essence," but from philosophical ontology as such. It is a specific "theological ontology" (a term sometimes used by Zizioulas) based on Christian presuppositions. He writes, e.g., that "the Holy Trinity is a primordial ontological concept."[2] Evidently, in usual philosophical discourse, the Holy Trinity as well as the divine hypostases, Father, Son and Holy Spirit, are neither ontological nor philosophical concepts. These terms signify some realities, which members of a particular religious community, namely the Christian Church, believe in. The meanings of these terms were defined by dogmatic formulas of this community, which are by no means philosophical definitions. In addition, the terms Father and Son stem from biology, keeping some of the properties of their biological prototypes while ignoring others. It is possible to integrate this set of terms with their intricate relations into philosophical discourse by means of hermeneutical and conceptual analysis. This is the strategy represented by some types of theology, which are called "religious philosophy," and some mystical theories. But Zizioulas rejects this approach. Instead of trying to define or explain these fundamental Christian realities, he regards them as the *explanans* and not the *explanandum*, considering them as the cornerstones of a new discourse. This new discourse adopts the main bulk of ontological categories, but its structure and basic laws are nevertheless determined by specifically theological principles. Hence this discourse is essentially incommensurable with philosophical discourse. For instance, the term "being" in the two discourses represents a homonym rather than an identical concept.

In Zizioulas's theological ontology, person, or more precisely, the Father, emerges as the basic ontological principle, which implies a new "personalist" conception of being. Now "Being is not an absolute category in itself. . . . The person becomes the being itself"[3] and "the ultimate ontological category which makes something really *be*, is . . . the person."[4] The ontological primacy of personhood is underlined in all aspects. "The person *constitutes* being, that is, enables entities to be entities."[5] Due to "the identification of hypostasis with person . . . the being of God Himself was

2. Zizioulas, *Being as Communion*, 17.

3. Zizioulas, *Being as Communion*, 39.

4. Zizioulas, *Being as Communion*, 17–18 (italics added).

5. Zizioulas, *Being as Communion*, 39 (italics added).

identified with the person."[6] The person has also priority over substance, *ousia*: "Being is traced back not to substance but to person.[7] . . . God 'exists' on account of a person, the Father, and not on account of a substance."[8] This priority is rooted in the Orthodox principle of the "monarchy of the Father," which is one of the divergences between the Christian East and West. This principle is of fundamental ontological significance. It is not the person as such, but the Father that is the ultimate ontological principle: "the Father . . . [is] that person which 'hypostasizes' God, which makes God to be three persons."[9] Due to the postulate of the creation *ex nihilo*, the Father is the cause of being, and Zizioulas stresses that "the Cappadocians introduced the concept of 'cause' into the being of God."[10] Contrary to an ontology of essence, an ontology of personhood does not define its notions. Rather, they are introduced *in medias res*, being characterized by their relations and functions in the discourse. It means that these notions are of relational nature.

In Zizioulas, communion is another primary ontological principle, in addition to person and before being. "It is communion that makes beings 'be': nothing exists without it, even God. . . . God exists thanks to an event of communion."[11] He stresses that communion is not one of the properties or functions of person, or God, since person as well as God *are* communion and love. Contrary to this, the notion of the individual does not include the necessity of communion. The closest principle to communion is love. It also possesses ontological primacy: "We must speak of an ontology of love as replacing the ontology of *ousia*, that is, we must attribute to love the role attributed to substance in classical ontology."[12] Like communion, "Love is not an emanation or 'property' of the substance of God. . . . Love as God's mode of existence 'hypostasizes' God, *constitutes* His being." Moreover, love always comes from one concrete person, in God's case from the Father: "[Love] is not something 'common' to the three persons . . . like the

---

6. Zizioulas, *Being as Communion*, 40.

7. Zizioulas, *Being as Communion*, 42.

8. Zizioulas, *Being as Communion*, 42.

9. Zizioulas, *Being as Communion*, 46.

10. Zizioulas, *Being as Communion*, 18.

11. Zizioulas, *Being as Communion*, 17.

12. Zizioulas, *Communion and Otherness*, 108.

common nature of God, but is identified with the Father. When we say that 'God is love,' we refer to the Father."[13]

Identity and uniqueness are predicates of personhood, which manifest that "the person . . . wants to exist as a *concrete, unique and unrepeatable* entity . . . as a *hypostasis* of the substance, as a concrete and unique identity."[14] According to Zizioulas, identity is created in the relationship of love, but more concretely, "man acquires personal identity and ontological particularity only by basing his being on the Father-Son relationship,"[15] which demands a "'new birth,' which is the essence of Baptism."[16] Thus his concept of identity is basically theological, though structurally it is close to the usual philosophical model of identity acquired in the relationship with the Other. As for uniqueness, it implies that the person cannot be identified by means of any set of properties, since any property singles out not a unique being, but some class of them. Rather, uniqueness is acquired in communion: "In a reality of communion . . . each particular is affirmed as *unique* and irreplaceable by the others—a uniqueness which is ontological."[17] Communion is not only the sufficient, but also the necessary condition of uniqueness: "Outside the communion of love the person loses its uniqueness and becomes a being like other beings, a 'thing.'"[18]

Reflecting on the notion of personhood, Zizioulas considers it necessary to focus on the principle of otherness. This decision is in accordance with trends in modern thought: In the last decades, a profound, tectonic shift occurred, from the long-standing primacy of the self (subject, individual, ego, etc.) to the primacy of the Other. As Zizioulas himself points out: "The problem of the Other has been central to philosophy in our time . . . philosophers such as M. Buber and E. Levinas . . . made the idea of the Other a key subject of philosophical discourse."[19] On the ontological level, the most radical example of otherness is the gulf, *chasma*, between God and the world as uncreated and created being. This is the difference of natures, or *natural otherness*. Furthermore, there is the difference of persons, since persons are all unique: this is *personal otherness*. The idea of *creatio*

13. Zizioulas, *Being as Communion*, 46 (italics added).

14. Zizioulas, *Being as Communion*, 46–47.

15. Zizioulas, *Communion and Otherness*, 109.

16. Zizioulas, *Communion and Otherness*, 109.

17. Zizioulas, *Communion and Otherness*, 107.

18. Zizioulas, *Being as Communion*, 49.

19. Zizioulas, *Communion and Otherness*, 13.

ex nihilo implies the connection between otherness and personal freedom, and so the discourse of otherness as an ontological principle is integrated into ontology of personhood.

The central problem in this discourse is the relationship between otherness and communion. This relationship is very different in the Holy Trinity and among human beings. According to Zizioulas, Western culture tends to consider communion and otherness as mutually incompatible, since it cultivates the "protection from the other." In contrast to such a practice of individuals, communion of persons, that is hypostases, manifests an opposite relation to otherness. Two corresponding types of the relation are described by means of Maximus's pair of categories, difference (*diaphora*) and division (*diairesis*). Otherness always means difference, but difference may involve or not involve division. Division implies separation and is considered as a negative predicate; otherness, which includes division, characterizes a disunited and discordant order of things. "Diaphora (difference) must be maintained, for it is good. Diairesis (division) is a perversion of diaphora, and is bad."[20] If otherness represents difference without division, then communion and otherness form a harmonious relationship, in which otherness and difference do not exclude unity, and communion does not exclude otherness. One can even say that "otherness and communion coincide."[21] According to Zizioulas, this harmonious relationship is the basic structure of person/hypostasis as such: "The Person is otherness in communion and communion in otherness,"[22] and the necessary condition of this relationship is that otherness does not include division.

This is the relationship between communion and otherness in the Holy Trinity. In human existence, this relationship is distorted in many ways. As a result, the empirical human being is not a person, in full accordance with the TPP. The distortion begins with Adam's Fall, which "meant that otherness and communion could not ultimately coincide." One of the principal distortions is the emergence of the self. On Zizioulas's view, "in personhood there is no 'self,'" and the self is treated as a disruptive factor: "Once the affirmation of the 'self' is realized through the rejection and not acceptance of the other—this is what Adam chose in his freedom to do—it is only natural and inevitable for the other to become enemy and

20. Zizioulas, *Communion and Otherness*, 3.
21. Zizioulas, *Communion and Otherness*, 42.
22. Zizioulas, *Communion and Otherness*, 9.

a threat."[23] Criticism of the notion of the self is one of the main themes in Zizioulas's discussion of Western philosophy. Above all, he objects to the primacy and dominance of the self over the other, which took place in Western philosophy "almost from its beginnings," being firmly established by Augustine and Descartes. He describes the forms of this dominance in Husserl, psychoanalysis, Heidegger, and singles out two thinkers, M. Buber and E. Levinas, who chose the opposite position by taking the Other as the primary principle. Levinas is "closer to the patristic understanding of otherness" and Zizioulas approves many of his ideas, although he "rejects the idea of communion."[24] He also approves the postmodern position regarding the problem of self and writes that "One must acknowledge with appreciation . . . the proclamation of the death of the Self by leading thinkers of postmodernism. . . . Any attempt to question the idea of Self at a philosophical level should be applauded."[25] However, postmodernists proclaim the "death of the subject," but not "the death of the self." In the next section, we will show that at least in some postmodern conceptions, the self is present and conceived of as not self-affirming, and as not rejecting the other. Thus, Zizioulas's argument that "in human existence there is a fundamental conflict between the self and the other,"[26] is too sweeping.

There are many more factors in fallen existence that destroy the trinitarian coincidence of otherness and communion, that is, the personal structure of the human being. An important role belongs to consciousness and the body, but the most decisive factor is death, which destroys both communion and otherness. Looking for ways of overcoming these factors, man discovers that he and his mode of being are separated from God by a gulf, but this gulf is bridged by Christ and in Christ. "It is Christ who links God and the world ontologically."[27] Thus, the strategy leading man to the overcoming of the ontological damage of the human mode of being must be Christocentric.

The christocentric strategy of human existence unfolds in Christianity into an integral way of life. It begins with the new birth, baptism, which establishes a new *ecclesial* dimension of man's existence. In this dimension, man is capable of overcoming the bounds of his empiric nature, both

23. Zizioulas, *Communion and Otherness*, 2.

24. Zizioulas, *Communion and Otherness*, 2.

25. Zizioulas, *Communion and Otherness*, 51–52.

26. Zizioulas, *Communion and Otherness*, 68.

27. Zizioulas, *Communion and Otherness*, 203.

biological and social, and of becoming a person. "In the Church . . . man is born as 'hypostasis,' as person. This new hypostasis of man has all the characteristics of . . . authentic personhood."[28] This means, in particular, that in the Church the coincidence of communion and otherness is restored: "In the Church . . . communion with the other fully reflects the relation between communion and otherness in the holy Trinity."[29] Such a supernatural character of the church is ensured by its key element, the Eucharist. It is in the Eucharist that God communicates himself to us, so that we enter into communion with him. Consequently, "difference ceases to be divisive and becomes good. *Diaphora* does not lead to *diairesis*, and unity or communion does not destroy but rather affirms diversity and otherness."[30] In personalist terms, "the Eucharist . . . has as its object man's transcendence of his biological hypostasis and his becoming an authentic person."[31] This "becoming a person" in the Eucharist is the realization of the union of God and man, and this union is nothing but deification (*theosis*): "Union between God and the human being . . . is called *theosis* in the Orthodox tradition."[32] The Eucharist and *theosis* are key concepts in Zizioulas's personalism. *Theosis* means union in the hypostasis of the Son: "*Theosis* is realized through our adoption by grace (= in the Spirit) as sons in the Son. . . . The human being can reach deification in and through the *hypostatic* union of God and man in Christ."[33] Zizioulas's exposition of *theosis* retrieves principal components of the patristic doctrine, and presents the structure of this sacred event in logical order: The preconditions of deification—Incarnation and Baptism; the process of deification in this world; and finally the eschatological consummation of deification.

Zizioulas's thought is usually considered as belonging to Eucharistic ecclesiology, since it is centered firmly on the church and the Eucharist. Following Maximus, he states repeatedly that it is in the Eucharist, above all, that the union of God and man is realized. He states also that *theosis* has an ecclesial nature, which is ensured by baptism. He stresses the personalist nature of *theosis*, describing it as the event of the transcendence of the human being which preserves, however, its otherness and particularity, its

28. Zizioulas, *Being as Communion*, 56.

29. Zizioulas, *Communion and Otherness*, 6.

30. Zizioulas, *Communion and Otherness*, 7.

31. Zizioulas, *Being as Communion*, 61.

32. Zizioulas, *Communion and Otherness*, 32.

33. Zizioulas, *Communion and Otherness*, 31, 42 (italics added).

identity and uniqueness. As for the eschatological dimension of *theosis*, it means, according to him, the "constitutive role of the future" in all economy of the ecclesiastic and sacramental life.

Questions that are more complicated arise when we penetrate deeper into the theological structures of *theosis*. It is here that we encounter the majority of disputable and controversial points in Zizioulas's synthesis. Developing his own approach, he criticizes the preceding formation of Orthodox theology usually called "Neo-Palamism." His disagreements with this theological movement are concentrated mainly in the interpretation of *theosis*. The Palamite theology of divine energies, which is the foundation of the Neo-Palamism, describes the union between God and man as the union of divine and human energies. Palamas reiterates this position many times (e.g., "the union between God and those who are worthy of Him . . . is realized in the divine and supernatural energy. . . . Saints like angels . . . partake in divine energies"[34]), and this character of the union is articulated in the "Palamite dogma" adopted by the Council of Constantiople of 1351 (items 6, 13 in the *Tomos* of the Council). Zizioulas never objects to Palamas, but states that modern proponents of Neo-Palamism exaggerate the role of energy at the expense of other theological principles, the *hypostasis*, above all. As he points out, "the employment of the energy language should not obscure the importance of personal communion in God's relationship with us in the Economy. . . . 'Maximizing' the role of divine energies may obscure the decisive significance of personhood for the God-world relationship."[35] He finds such maximization especially in the interpretation of *theosis*.

> The view that union between God and the human being . . . is not realized at the level of *hypostasis*, but only at that of *energeia*, appears to be questionable. Such view . . . would make it difficult to identify *theosis* with *hyiothesia* (filial adoption), an identification with deep roots in the Bible and in the Fathers. . . . Theosis is not simply a matter of participating in God's glory and other *natural* qualities, common to all three persons of the Trinity; it is also or rather above all, our recognition and acceptance by the Father as his sons by grace, in and through our incorporation into his only-begotten Son by nature. . . . It is at the hypostatic level—the hypostasis of the Son—that theosis is realized.[36]

34. Palamas, "On Divine and Deifying Communion," 109–110.

35. Zizioulas, *Communion and Otherness*, 139, 30.

36. Zizioulas, *Communion and Otherness*, 31 (italics added).

However, in his criticism Zizioulas goes to the opposite extreme, almost completely excluding the discourse of divine energies from his personalist synthesis. For this synthesis excludes all subjects, which cannot be dealt with without the discourse about the divine energies. It is the subjects, which play an important role in the hesychast practice, and which were put to the forefront in both Palamism and Neo-Palamism. The Palamite position in Orthodox theology is that hesychast ascesis is the source and the school of quintessential Christian experience of the union with Christ, and this position gives birth to a series of new theological problems: The theology of hesychast prayer; the theology of the transfiguration and the contemplation of the light of Tabor; the connection of *theosis* with the hesychast practice; conceptions of divine energy and the essence-energy distinction. The elaboration on these topics resulted in a considerable re-configuration of Orthodox theology. It overcame definitively the age-old dependence on Western stereotypes and (re)gained its experiential nature. Independently, due to the philokalic renaissance, a similar reconfiguration centered on hesychasm took place in the religious consciousness of large parts of the pan-Orthodox community. Hesychasm was recognized as the core of the Orthodox mentality and way of life, and as an important theo-logical *topos*.

According to Zizioulas, the hesychast understanding of *theosis* as the energetic union of God and man is unsatisfactory, because energies convey only impersonal, unhypostasized properties and contents. However, this argument is disputable. First, hesychast experience is thoroughly christo-centric in all its principal aspects, as it is based on hesychast prayer, which is the *Jesus* prayer. Dumitru Staniloae writes: "We make the ascent by ascet-ic efforts to the mystical contemplation of Christ, through Christ, toward Christ."[37] In contrast to non-Christian ascetic practices, hesychast practice includes Baptism and the Eucharist—and hence the hypostatic union be-tween God and man—as its necessary precondition. Staniloae shows the necessary connection of the two kinds of the union: "What is the Eucha-rist? . . . Not the change, but the deification of the creature . . . the union between God and man. . . . With this our deification starts."[38] These words clearly distinguish between two horizons of deification: The Eucharist *is* the deification, however, "our deification," i.e., our union with divine energies is not achieved but only starts with it. Thus, the energetic union represents

37. Staniloae, *Orthodox Spirituality*, 60.
38. Staniloae, *Orthodox Spirituality*, 55.

the continuation and completion of the hypostatic union, while the latter is the ontological precondition of the former, ensuring its christocentric character. We also see that the hesychast experience and the experience of the Eucharist are two aspects of the constitutive Christian experience connected by an ontological succession. Moreover, at least some conceptions of the divine energy imply that this energy can carry not only impersonal characteristics. For instance, John Meyendorff writes that "divine 'energy' is not only unique but tri-hypostatic, since the 'energy' reflects the common life of the three Persons. The personal aspects of the divine subsistence do not disappear in the one 'energy.'"[39] In the last section, we will show that in the hesychast ascent, the constitution of the human person according to the TPP is achieved.

Modern Philosophy of Self: The Anthropological Personalistic Paradigm

Philosophies of self, which adopt the APP are far from Orthodoxy, and I will only briefly summarize them here. The "death of the subject" led to the emergence of many new nonclassical conceptions of personality, which evolved from conceptions close to the old classical model to more and more radical new theories. Less radical conceptions are somewhat in between the APP and the TPP: here the human person is usually constituted by actualizing its relation to the ontological Other, though the Other is not conceived as the Holy Trinity. The central place in this class of theories belongs to Heidegger's fundamental ontology, which transformed philosophical discourse, opening wide horizons for nonclassical anthropology and personalism.

The conception of man as *Dasein*, "being-there," or "presence," is not theocentric, but has a structural resemblance to the TPP. The main common element is the relational constitution, shaped in the relation to the ontological Other. In its relation to being, *Dasein* forms the fold, *die Zwiefalt*, between being and the existent, *das Seiende*. The fold is the ontological difference, and *Dasein* is a special kind of the existent, which actualizes and overcomes the ontological difference. But the radical difference to the TPP is no less important. Heidegger's conception of being does not include any basic notions of the TPP such as person, hypostasis, Trinity, and being is not conceived as communion and otherness. However, these principles

39. Meyendorff, *Byzantine Theology*, 186.

take part in the economy (the analytic) of *Dasein* developed in the book *Being and Time* (1927), which presents a rich personalism based on a system of special predicates, *existentialia*, embracing all aspects of man's existence. The main organizing principle of this system is being-toward-death, a mode of being constituted by the fundamental predicate of the finitude/mortality of *Dasein*. In later texts, shifting the accents of existential analytic and reinterpreting principal *existentialia*, Heidegger describes the destination of *Dasein* as the ecstatic stepping-out into the clearing (*die Lichtung*) of being.

Both the earlier and the later forms of Heidegger's philosophy had and continue to have a strong influence on philosophical development, since they provided a full-fledged alternative discourse to classical metaphysics. The later form, which entails elements that are close to the TPP, attracted considerable attention from Christian thinkers, and in all Christian confessions there emerged theological conceptions that in some way or other adopted Heidegger's ideas. The most notable receptions of Heidegger are those of Christos Yannaras in Orthodoxy, Jean-Luc Marion in Roman Catholicism, and Rudolf Bultmann in Protestantism.

Both Zizioulas and Yannaras represent the modern reception of the Greek Fathers, which puts at the center the concept of the person that is identified with that of divine hypostasis. Their versions of this "neopatristic" reception both entail a mixed discourse, combining theology and philosophy—although these two disciplines are given a different weight. In contrast to Zizioulas, in Yannaras's discourse philosophy always prevails: His discussion of specific problems often follows closely that of some philosopher, Heidegger in most cases, so that the thought of the Greek Fathers constantly alternates with modern philosophical discourse. But these two kinds of discourse are of different nature and obey different rules, and their careless merging results in a discourse with an indeterminate and diminished epistemology. For these reasons, I regard his personalism not as belonging to the TPP as such, but rather to the intermediate zone between the TPP and APP. Yannaras's ontology is basically the same patristic onto-theology as that of Zizioulas. Communion and otherness are among its key principles, and the mode of personal being is defined as ecstatic self-transcending, realized as the "event of relation and communion." In other words, his personalism is essentially in accordance with both the TPP and Heidegger's conception of the constitution of man as *Dasein*. However, the economy of personal being is envisaged in a different way compared to Zizioulas, with a considerable change of priorities and accents. Due to the priority of philosophy over theology and Heidegger's influence, Zizioulas's emphasis on hypostasis and hypostatic union gives way to the primacy of the discourse of energies. Ecstasy and *eros*/love become the key principles of personal being, while the constitutive principle of the hypostatic union is absent. Accordingly, the hypostatic, eucharistic, and ecclesial dimensions of this mode of being remain underdeveloped in comparison with Zizioulas.

Further away from the TPP, but still preserving some of its basic features, is the personalism of Levinas. According to Levinas, the human constitution is formed in relation to the other, but his rejection of ontology gives to this constitutive relation very specific features. The main feature is his famous *principle of responsibility for the Other*. Responsibility is the highest form of the relation to the other. Here the "to-the-other" is converted into the "for-the-other," which is not an ontological, but an ethical relation. It includes kindness, charity, commitment, compassion, and "compassionate suffering." At the same time, the responsibility for the other is the source and the constitutive principle of human subjectivity as such: "Responsibility for the other is the place where the non-place of subjectivity is located.[40] . . . To be the I means impossibility to avoid responsibility. . . . But the responsibility does not turn I into an element of the universal order, it confirms its uniqueness. The uniqueness of I means that nobody can answer instead of me.[41] . . . Responsibility is an individuation, a principle of individuation."[42] Thus the personalism of Levinas is essentially identical to his ethics, they both are based on his fundamental principle. Levinas's other is not the Ontological Other, and not God, although the relation to God is not denied: "In the other, there is a real presence of God."[43] There is some resemblance here with God's role in the philosophy of Descartes and Kant: Man's constitutive relation is not the relation to God, but God is the precondition making it possible for this relation to be constitutive. "[God] helps you to be responsible. . . . The relation to God is . . . a relation to another person."[44]

In more radical personalist conceptions, the figure of the constitutive other disappears and the human being is represented in more and more depersonalized and fragmented way. Foucault's personalism is at the border

40. Lévinas, *Autrement*, 12.

41. Lévinas, "Humanism of the Other Human," 171.

42. Lévinas, "Philosophy, Justice, and Love," 108.

43. Lévinas, "Philosophy, Justice, and Love," 110.

44. Lévinas, "Philosophy, Justice, and Love," 109–110.

between moderate integral and radical fragmented models. In the main work of his early period, "Les mots et les choses" (1966), he propounds the idea of the "death of man," predicting the disappearance of the episteme based on some "image of man." In this period, he considers the human being as a fully reducible and decomposable entity, "a certain secondary derivative of systems of knowledge and power," as his commentator F. Gros says. It means that he certainly tends towards a fragmented anthropology. But then an unexpected turn takes place.

About 1980, Foucault launches a large program of the study of "practices of the self." These anthropological practices are defined as "certain procedures which indisputably exist in every civilization and which are proposed or prescribed to individuals for establishing their identity and for maintaining or transforming it.[45] . . . They can be practices of purification, ascesis, renunciation, conversion, or change of one's mode of life."[46] They are constitutive: they shape the human constitution in relation to a certain "true self," who is the goal of the practice. When they have a popular character, they create a rich culture of the self, based on such principles as "conversion to the self," "care of the self," etc. They can be religious practices, but Foucault interprets them in a positivist way as practices actualizing man's relation not to God, but exclusively to himself. Thus, his personalism is strictly secular and excluding the TPP.

Like in all his theories, Foucault develops his personalism within the framework of historical studies. He reconstructs the history of practices of the self in Western culture from the fourth century BCE to the fourth and fifth century CE. He summarizes this reconstruction as follows: "There are three great models, which followed one another in historical succession. The model which I call the "Platonic" model, and which gravitates around recollection. The "Hellenistic" model, which is centered on the relation to the self as the final end. And the Christian model, which is centered on self-exegesis and self-renunciation."[47] He presents a thorough analysis of these models, but the Christian model is described less systematically. Its basis is early Christian asceticism (although the only author studied in detail is John Cassian), but according to Foucault, it is sufficiently representative of the entire Christian tradition. It has one central idea (rooted in Nietzsche): the goal of Christian ascesis as well as all Christian culture of

45. Foucault, "Subjectivité et vérité," 1032.

46. Foucault, L'herméneutique du sujet, 17.

47. Foucault, L'herméneutique du sujet, 247.

the self is "self-renunciation." As Foucault tries to prove, all basic elements of Christian practices of the self were borrowed from the practices of antiquity, and all changes that Christianity made regarding these practices were aimed at the destruction of the subject, and hence played a negative role anthropologically. However, his model and its conclusions are extremely disputable. They do not consider the most important aspects of hesychast practice, and the detailed critical analysis[48] shows that Foucault's model presents an incomplete and distorted picture of Christian personalism.

Besides the historical models, Foucault outlined also a personalist model for modern and future society called "esthetics of existence." Here the human constitution is supposed to be shaped by all thinkable practices through which man seeks to obtain physical pleasure. Such a project discards basic features of man and society and gets close to the most radical postmodernist conceptions, which represent the human being as "singularity" and correspond to the destruction of the self and depersonalization.

Thus, with Foucault we reach the limits of the territory of the APP. Theories based on singularity cannot contain fully-fledged conceptions of self or personality, and thus they do not belong to the philosophy of self. It is the next stage of depersonalization after the "death of the subject" that demonstrates "what comes after the self." The best examples in this respect are provided by Gilles Deleuze and Jean-Luc Nancy. Nancy's postpersonalism is less radical. In his conception of "being singular plural" the human being is singularity, but singularity is conceived as compatible with communion and unity, and some concept of the self is still used. Deleuze, by contrast, interprets singularity as "total plurality, which excludes any unity," and goes to the extreme of representing reality as "purely scattered and anarchic plurality." Here the human being does not have predicates of integrity and wholeness, but is a topological phenomenon represented by configurations of dynamic elements, which permanently emerge and disappear. Such being can correspond to the virtual human or post-human. Here the depersonalization is complete.

Synergic Anthropology and Concluding Remarks

I will now briefly present my own approach of *synergic anthropology*, which aims to embrace the full diversity of anthropological experience and personalist structures. Like structuralist anthropology, it starts with the

48. Horujy, *Practices of the Self* 2.1.

analysis of a particular domain of anthropological experience, and gains in this analysis the source of notions and principles, which constitute the basis of a general anthropological theory. However, in my case the starting point is the experience of hesychast practice. This practice is a process of man's self-transformation, having the structure of a ladder with steps ascending from the *metanoia* to the meta-anthropological *telos* of the *theosis*. In the ascension on the hesychast ladder, the constitution of the human being is formed, and abundant descriptions of the practice in hesychast literature make it possible to reconstruct this constitution in great detail. It is a relational constitution, shaped by the actualization of man's relation to God. This step-by-step transformation of the totality of all energies of the human being advances first to the encounter and collaboration with the divine energies (*synergia*), and then to the union with divine energies, that is the deification (that includes also the hypostatic union, due to the ecclesial and Eucharistic dimensions of the practice). Evidently, this constitution corresponds to the TPP. We notice that from the anthropological point of view, it is based on a mechanism, which we call the *anthropological unlocking*. It is the act in which man becomes open or unlocked towards the contact with the Other. If the Other is beyond the horizon of man's experience and existence, in the unlocking, man reaches the boundaries of this horizon, i.e., he realizes the "unlocking in extreme experience."[49] Such unlocking has a special characteristic: man's constitution is shaped by it. The unlocking in hesychast practice has also another characteristic: It is the unlocking towards God as personal being-communion, which is separated by the ontological difference from man's mode of being. It is thus called the *ontological unlocking*. More precisely, the unlocking in hesychast practice can be identified with synergy understood in the anthropological sense, and therefore anthropology based on the principle of unlocking is called synergic anthropology.

Thus, the reconstruction of hesychast anthropology shows that hesychast practice realizes the paradigm of the human constitution in the ontological unlocking. Considering other areas of anthropological experience, synergic anthropology discovers that spiritual practices of other world religions such as Sufism, yoga, Zen, Taoism, are also constitutive practices realizing different representations of the same paradigm. Furthermore, it notices that the ontological unlocking is not the only kind of unlocking in extreme experience. By definition, in such unlocking we reach

49. Horujy, "Man's Three Far-Away Kingdoms."

contact with the Other that is beyond the horizon of our consciousness and existence. But such an Other is not necessarily the ontological Other belonging to another mode of being. The horizon of human existence is a heterogeneous reality, and consequently, the Other experienced by the human being as such is diversified. Besides the ontological Other, another kind of Other is provided by the unconscious. Indeed, the unconscious is *ex definitione* beyond the horizon of consciousness, but there is a certain class of anthropological manifestations in which we are open to its influence, i.e., in our terms, the unlocking towards the unconscious is accomplished. Corresponding manifestations express extreme experience, and so this unlocking is a constitutive practice actualizing a certain paradigm of the human constitution. The unconscious is ontologically not different from empirical being whence it follows that this paradigm is not the same as the constitution in the ontological unlocking. Adopting Heidegger's terminology, we call this new kind of the unlocking in extreme experience the *ontic unlocking*.

The last conclusion is of prime importance: it means that the anthropology of unlocking is pluralistic. We discovered that there are at least two different paradigms of the constitution of the human being as such, or, in other words, two different anthropological formations. These formations, called the *Ontological Human* and the *Ontic Human*, are two autonomous representations, or variants, of the human being. But the description of anthropological reality in the prism of unlocking is not finished yet. The ontic unlocking is the unlocking towards the other, not different ontologically from present (empirical) being. The unlocking towards the unconscious is one example of such unlocking, and it is possible a priori that there are other examples (a posteriori we discover that such examples do exist). Moreover, today's anthropological experience provides an example of such constitutive unlocking, which is neither ontological nor ontic. Man makes himself unlocked also in his virtual practices, in the going-out into anthropological virtual reality. Since virtual reality is different from actual one, such going-out is extreme experience, and so the *virtual unlocking* is a constitutive practice. In this unlocking a certain anthropological formation is constituted, which is called the *Virtual Human*.

All possible kinds of the unlocking in extreme experience are exhausted by these three formations, because in our framework there are three and only three ontologically different kinds of reality: being as such or Divine being, present (empirical) being, and virtual, or under-actualized being.

Thus, the human being is presented in synergic anthropology as an existent, which is constituted in unlocking itself in three different ways, and thus is represented in three independent anthropological formations respectively: the Ontological, the Ontic and the Virtual Human. In addition, analysis of anthropological practices shows that these three basic formations can combine with each other, constituting so called "hybrid formations" (e.g., popular practices of the New Age subculture such as "trips," imitating mystical experience, correspond to the combination of the ontological and virtual unlocking).

The outlined framework represents the basis of a project with far-reaching aims, directed at the creation of a new kind of anthropology: the "science of human sciences," or the episteme for humanistic knowledge. In this essay, however, I will only discuss the personalist aspects. Synergic anthropology makes it possible to reconstruct the full ensemble of personalist structures. Arguing that the universal paradigm of the human constitution is the unlocking in extreme experience, it discovers that this paradigm has three (and only three) independent representations: the ontological, ontic and virtual unlocking, each of which generates a certain anthropological formation. The problem of personalism is to reconstruct the set of personalist structures corresponding to each of these formations: i.e., the personalist structures of the Ontological, Ontic and Virtual Human. They are radically different, and this fact confirms that our formations represent three different independent varieties of the human being. It is thus confirmed that the anthropological reality demands a pluralistic anthropology.

The constitution of the Ontological Human has two different variants corresponding to two representations of the Ontological Other: In the Abrahamic traditions (Judaism, Christianity, Islam) it is conceived according to the personalist paradigm, while in all religions and spiritual traditions of the East, the Ontological Other is an impersonal principle. The first variant, the constitution formed in the ontological unlocking towards personal being, is exactly the TPP. Synergic anthropology describes the ontological dynamics of the ascension to deification based on the discourse of communion. It reconstructs the hierarchy of modes of communion, which ascends from the trivial everyday communication, the exchange of information, to the *perichōrēsis*, the exchange on the level of being, the perfect and absolute mode of communion. It is the being of love, in which man's consciousness and identity are not lost, but converted into the higher form of hypostasis. The second variant, the constitution shaped in the unlocking towards some impersonal *telos* like Nirvana, Heaven, or the Great Void, is in a sense the opposite of the first variant. Here the constitution is also shaped in a certain practice of the self, representing the step-by-step self-transformation of the human being. However, in the former case the transformation is directed at the creation of structures of personality, while in latter case its steps lead to the dismantling and dissolving of such structures; it is the process of the type known as *haplosis*, the simplification, in Neoplatonic mysticism.

The constitution of the Ontic Human is formed in the unlocking to the Ontic Other, which is within the existent. Such a nature of the constitutive Other implies a very specific character of the corresponding constitution.[50] The Ontic Other is nothing but a certain domain in the existent, inaccessible for man's experience. It is a certain lacuna, shortage, deficiency, which is caused by man's particular circumstances, and becomes the paradigm of his constitution. It is completely individual and accidental and hence it does not coincide with the Ontic Other of any other ontic individual. Thus, any two ontic individuals implement different paradigms of the constitution. Realizing his/her own constitutional paradigm different from all others, each ontic individual is a singled-out human being, a *singularity*. It is the central concept of a poststructuralist radical anthropology; and we see that the human being, which eliminates its relation to being or God, is really a singularity. Singularity is a topological concept, and our description of the Ontic Human, like the anthropology of Deleuze, is a kind of topological anthropology. Although the mode of existence of the Ontic Human is characterized by total disjointedness, ontic constitutions can have common elements, and hence can form groups or classes. Synergic anthropology identifies two big groups or sub-formations of the Ontic Human: *Freud's Human* is the set of all constitutions, shaped in the unlocking towards the unconscious; *Nietzsche's Human* is the set of all constitutions shaped in the actualization of Nietzsche's principles of the Superman and will to power. The Ontic Human is a vast formation, which may also include other sub-formations. Under various names it is now the focus of attention of anthropological thought.

The Virtual Human is a new formation, which emerged in the last decades, and its constitution has been very little studied so far. Nevertheless, it is easy to understand the general character of this constitution proceeding from the interpretation of virtuality in synergic anthropology. Generalizing

50. For the detailed discussion of the Ontic Human see Horujy, "Zametki ob onticheskich konstitutsiyakh."

the conception of virtuality in natural science, we characterize virtual phenomena by the property of the unfinished or incomplete actualization. Such interpretation leads to what we call the paradox of virtuality. Although phenomena of the virtual world seem to be most unusual and unlike phenomena of actual reality, in fact they are nothing but "virtual doubles" of these actual phenomena, their various under-actualizations. Turning to personalism, we conclude that practices of the virtual unlocking, even those that do not have any evident actual prototypes, do not create really new personalist structures. Thus, virtual constitutions must be considered as combinations of disjoint parts of every possible actual constitutions, belonging to the Ontological and Ontic Human. Examples of such constitutions corresponding to some popular virtual and digital practices (above all, those of virtual communion) are described in my book "*Socium and Synergy: Colonization of the Interface*" (2016). Due to its piecewise nature, any virtual constitution excludes the wholeness and integrity of the human being, the key predicates of personality in both the TPP and APP, which means that the current virtualization of reality implies the depersonalization. Increasing virtualization leads to the emergence of transitory forms approaching the Post-Human. Here the depersonalization develops into the deanthropologization, and we come to the end of man's path.

We can see that synergic anthropology reconstructs the full set of personalist structures corresponding to the anthropological reality in all its present diversity. Thus, it represents an anthropological synthesis based on the paradigm of the unlocking as universal principle of the human constitution. Being pluralistic, it combines the TPP and the APP: the Ontological Human implements the TPP, while the Ontic and Virtual Human can be considered as variations of the APP. Finally, this anthropological synthesis must be compared to Zizioulas's theological synthesis. *Grosso modo*, they complement each other. They conform to each other on the common ground of Christian experience described on the basis of the TPP, and then they advance from this ground in different directions. Zizioulas deepens the analysis of ecclesiastical, liturgical and sacramental dimensions, while synergic anthropology studies other domains of anthropological experience aiming to achieve an integral vision.

But there are also significant divergences between the two anthropologies. Zizioulas's theological anthropology is strictly monistic. It allows only one anthropological formation, the Ontological Human, in terms of synergic anthropology, and completely excludes the idea of the human devoid of the relation to God. Here is his argument in favor of this uncompromising position (resembling the equally unbending ontologism of Heidegger): "The act of creation *ex nihilo* involves the emergence of so absolute and radical otherness between God and the world that unless otherness is bridged by communion the world would ontologically collapse."[51] Indeed, this argument looks very shaky today! Who is afraid of the ontological collapse? Maybe, we are already living in it, or, maybe, it is prevented by prayers of the righteous. . . . Here we are entering the realm of eschatology, where there are no incontrovertible proofs. On the other hand, there are obviously large groups of humans, who never actualize their relation to God, or being, but still have the extreme experience in which the full-dimensional human constitution is formed up. Synergic anthropology articulates and solves the problem of the reconstruction of these non-ontological constitutions.

The next difference concerns the concept of self. As mentioned above, Zizioulas treats the self exclusively as the principle of self-affirmation and self-isolation, which suppresses otherness and is not relational. However, modern studies of the self—in particular, in synergic anthropology—contradict such an interpretation. The self is actively involved in the modern search for new subjectivities, and there appeared several profound studies of this concept by Michel Foucault, Paul Ricoeur and Vladimir Bibikhin. They are very different, but they all agree about some basic properties of the self. Above all, the self is of relational nature. This is not obvious, because the self is the deepest core of the human being, in which its uniqueness is concentrated and preserved. Its contents are intimately its own, they represent what Plato calls *auto-to-auto*, the "self itself." Nevertheless, these contents *can* be acquired in the relation to the Other! The actualization of this relation includes the appropriation and assimilation of elements of the Other, and assimilated elements can be integrated into my core and thus become maximally mine, *auto-to-auto*. It is the subtle dialectics of one's own property and that of another, subtly analyzed by Bibikhin: I seize some *property* and then it gets converted into my *properties*, it becomes myself, my self. And he argues that such seizure is the principal paradigm of being and reason reflected in European cultures already on the level of language (e.g., *Begriff*, the notion, means ethymologically "what is seized," from *greifen*, to seize). Thus, all mentioned theories including synergic anthropology state that the constitution of self is relational. Consequently, the relation of the self to the personhood is also different from Zizioulas's approach.

51. Zizioulas, *Communion and Otherness*, 12.

According to Zizioulas, the self is the obstacle in the way to the person-hood, but in synergic anthropology it is exactly the self that realizes the ascension to personhood.

Summing up, I agree that personalist positions of Orthodoxy find the most capital presentation in Zizioulas's theological synthesis. Synergic anthropology complements it with the anthropological synthesis embracing all the diversity of modern anthropological experience. In fact, Zizioulas's conception bears the strong imprint of age-old Byzantine mentality, which had always the tendency to be closed in the ecclesiastic world. Thus, his personalism refers predominantly not to the human being as such but rather to *Homo Ecclesiasticus* and, above all, *Homo Eucharisticus*. Such a personalism was not quite sufficient in Byzantium, and is much less sufficient in our time. Regarding some questions, Zizioulas holds extreme and unjustified views: The most significant examples are his banishment of the self and the almost total rejection of the discourse of divine energies. In these respects, synergic anthropology disagrees with Zizioulas's position. And last but not least, none of the two theories can present the comprehensive solution to the problem of the relationship between the economies of personality/hypostasis and energy. This problem came to the forefront of Orthodox theology as a result of Vladimir Lossky's work, and now, several decades later, it continues to be one of its principal unsolved problems. The subtle balance between hypostatic and energetic elements in the economy of man's ascension to God still awaits resolution.

Bibliography

Foucault, Michel. *L'herméneutique du sujet: cours au Collège de France (1981–1982)*. Edited by François Ewald. Paris: Gallimard, 2001.

———. "Subjectivité et vérité." In *Dits et écrits II, 1976–1988*, edited by Daniel Defert and François Ewald, 1032–37. Paris: Gallimard, 2001.

Heidegger, Martin. "Die onto-theo-logische Verfassung der Metaphysik." In *Identität und Differenz*, edited by F.-W. von Herrmann, 51–79. Frankfurt am Main: Vittorio Klostermann, 2006.

Horujy, Sergey S. "Man's Three Far-Away Kingdoms: Ascetic Experience as a Ground for a New Anthropology." *Philotheos: International Journal for Philosophy and Theology* 3 (2003) 53–77.

————. *Practices of the Self and Spiritual Practices: Michel Foucault and the Eastern Christian Discourse*. Translated by Boris Jakim. Edited by Kristina Stoeckl. Grand Rapids: Eerdmanns, 2015.

————. "Zametki ob onticheskich konstitutsiyakh." *Fonar' Diogena* 1 (2015) 17–42.

Lévinas, Emmanuel. *Autrement qu'être ou au-delà de l'essence. Phaenomenologica*. La Haye: Martinus Nijhoff, 1974.

————. "Humanism of the Other Human." In *Vremya i Drugoy*, 123–258. Russian. St. Petersburg: Vysshaya Religiozno-Filosofskaya Shkola, 1998.

————. "Philosophy, Justice, and Love." In *Entre Nous: On Thinking-of-the-Other*, by Emmanuel Lévinas, 103–121. New York: Columbia University Press, 1998.

Meyendorff, John. *Byzantine Theology: Historical Trends and Doctrinal Themes*. London: Mowbrays, 1975.

Palamas, Gregory. "On Divine and Deifying Communion." In *Traktaty*, 90–120. Russian. Krasnodar: Tekst, 2007.

Staniloae, Dumitru. *Orthodox Spirituality: A Practical Guide for the Faithful and a Definitive Manual for the Scholar*. Translated by Archimandrite Jerome (Newville), et al. South Canaan: St. Tikhon's Seminary Press, 2003.

Zizioulas, John. *Being as Communion: Studies in Personhood and the Church*. London: Darton, Longman, and Todd, 1985.

————. *Communion and Otherness: Further Studies in Personhood and the Church*. Edited by Paul McPartland. London: T & T Clark, 2006.

6

Orthodoxy and Logic

The Case of Pavel Florensky's Theory of Antinomy[1]

Paweł Rojek

O rthodox theology is often thought to be essentially antinomic. The fundamental principles of Christian faith, such as the dogmas of the Holy Trinity or the two natures of Christ, are supposed to be true, yet self-contradictory statements. Recently this idea has spread among Orthodox theologian most of all thanks to Vladimir Lossky, who in his influential *Mystical Theology of the Eastern Church* claimed that "the dogmas of the Church often present themselves to the human reason as antinomies; the more difficult to resolve, the more sublime the mystery which they express."[2] Exactly this "spirit of antinomy," for Lossky, was supposed to be a characteristic feature of Eastern theology, in contrast to more rational character of Western thinking.[3] This account of the nature of Orthodox theology became very influential, and can also be found in works of Sergei Bulgakov, Paul Evdokimov, John Meyendorff, and many others.[4]

1. This publication has been generously supported by a grant from the National Science Center, Poland (2014/15/B/HS1/01620). I am grateful to Ewelina Jaskiewicz, Viacheslav Moiseev, Teresa Obolevitch, Katarzyna Popowicz, Igor' Priadko, Tat'iana Rezvykh, and Christoph Schneider for their comments and help.

2. Lossky, *Mystical Theology*, 43.

3. Lossky, *Mystical Theology*, 68, 215. For the idea of antinomy in Russian philosophy and literature in general see Rezvykh, "Florenskii—Rozanov—Frank—Trubetskoi," and Blank, "Rabbit and The Duck."

4. See Bulgakov, *Unfading Light*; Evdokimov, *Orthodoxy*; Meyendorff, *Byzantine Theology*.

However, this widespread idea of the antinomic character of Christian doctrine raises serious problems. Classical logic, which is supposed to express the rules of rational thinking, is based on the principle of noncontradiction. Therefore, the claim that Christian truth is essentially antinomic either leads to radical irrationalism, or implies a kind of non-classical logic. The former case seems to undermine the very nature of theology, which is thought as a rational enquiry into divinity. The latter case, however, entails a rather arduous task of formulating higher, non-classical logic, which would tackle divine contradictions. No one, including theologians, can claim the antinomic nature of truth without facing consequences.

The contemporary idea of the antinomic nature of Orthodox theology, popularized by Lossky and others, was originally formulated by Pavel Florensky, an Orthodox priest, theologian, philosopher and mathematician, in his famous book *The Pillar and the Ground of Truth*, published in 1914. Florensky aimed to express the truth of Orthodoxy by various means of his contemporary culture, including art, literature, philosophy, science, and, notably, mathematical logic. Regarding logic, Florensky argued that the ultimate truth goes beyond the available formal categories, and that Christianity is essentially antinomical. There is no question that, as regards the teaching on antinomy, Lossky gravely relied on Florensky. He even directly referred to his book in *Mystical Theology*:

> According to a modern Russian theologian, Father Florensky, there is no other way in which human thought may find perfect stability save that of accepting the trinitarian antinomy. . . . This question is, indeed, crucial—in the literal sense of that word. The dogma of the Trinity is a cross for human ways of thought. The apophatic ascent is a mounting of calvary.[5]

The religious antinomy, therefore, for both Lossky and Florensky, was seen as a kind of intellectual torture. To continue this analogy, one might ask whether these Orthodox authors also anticipated the resurrection and final salvation of human reason. I believe that Florensky not only pointed out the antinomies of the reason, but also sketched the idea of a new logic of antinomy, which could deal with religious contradictions.

In this essay, I am going to present, discuss, and systematize Florensky's idea of antinomy of religion. I hope that it will also make a contribution to the more general issue of the relationship between logic and Orthodoxy. In the first part of the paper, I will sketch Florensky's views on antinomies

5. Lossky, *Mystical Theology*, 65–66.

as they stand in *The Pillar and the Ground of Truth*, in the second one I shall take a look at four types of its interpretations, proposed by various contemporary commentators. Only recently, at the beginning of the new century, mostly among Russian logicians, the logical ideas of Florensky finally raised serious discussions. In conclusion, I am going to offer a unified interpretation, which combines some elements from the previous ones. In sum, I believe that Florensky's views might be interpreted and developed into a consistent and insightful theory of religious discourse, finding indeed, as Christoph Schneider suggested, a third way between the rational ontotheology on the one hand, and irrational fideism on the other.[6] Thus, Florensky's theory is a valuable contribution to the logical structure of the theological philosophy.

Florensky's Theory of Religious Antinomy

Pavel Florensky's expressed his view on antinomies most of all in the two passages in *The Pillar and the Ground of Truth*: in Letter Six, directly devoted to the problem of contradiction, and in one of the additional chapters, in which he analyzed a logical paradox posed by Lewis Carroll.[7] Letter Six is more general and philosophical, whereas the appendix on Carroll's problem is more specific and logical.

The General Idea of Antinomy

Florensky believed that the ultimate truth is essentially antinomic. This is definitely the most striking and—for many—the most inspiring logical idea of his *Pillar and Ground of Truth*. In Letter Six he states clearly:

> For rationality [*rassudok*], *truth is contradiction*, and this contradiction becomes explicit as soon as truth acquires a verbal formulation. . . . The thesis and the antithesis together form the expression of truth. In other words, truth is an antinomy, and it cannot fail to be such.[8]

---

6. Schneider, "Will the Truth," 37.
7. Florensky, *Pillar*, 106–123, 355–58.
8. Florensky, *Pillar*, 109.

This is a perfectly clear expression of radical dialetheism.[9] Florensky openly allowed for some contradictory sentences to be both true. He was fully aware that by doing this, he undermined the foundation of rational thinking, namely the principle of noncontradiction. His personal attack on this principle was as passionate as its famous defense by Aristotle in *Metaphysics* IV. He urged: "We must not, we dare not, cover contradiction over with the paste of our philosophemes! Let contradiction remain as profound as it is."[10] It seems therefore, that Florensky might be seen as an early proponent of the non-classical logic, based on the rejection of the principle of noncontradiction.

Florensky not only put forward the idea of dialetheism, but also attempted to sketch a kind of formal theory of antinomy. First of all, he proposed the following "symbolic definition of the antinomy":

(1) $P = (p \land \neg p) \land V$.[11]

An antinomy P is a conjunction of thesis and antithesis accompanied by a sign "V" meaning "truth" (*veritas*). The addition of that symbol was intended to distinguish the necessary philosophical antinomies, rooted in the nature of things, and mere contingent formal contradictions, resulting from simple mistakes. In a deeper sense, this symbol "raises the antinomy above the plane of rationality,"[12] and represents "the spiritual unity, the supersensuous reality of antinomy," which is "experienced and perceived directly" in "the Holy Spirit."[13]

It is unclear what the intended scope of Florensky's claim was. In some places he suggested that every truth is in fact antinomic. "Here, on earth—he wrote—there are contradictions in everything."[14] Florensky even attempted to formulate a general, purely logical "proof of antinomy." He recalled two versions of the valid *reductio ad absurdum* principle:

(2) $(\neg p \to p) \to p$,
(3) $(p \to \neg p) \to \neg p$.

---

9. Priest, "Paraconsistency and Dialetheism."

10. Florensky, *Pillar*, 116.

11. Florensky adopted the old-fashioned symbolism of Peano and Russell; here and henceforth, I will translate it into a more accessible notation.

12. Florensky, *Pillar*, 113.

13. Florensky, *Pillar*, 113–14.

14. Florensky, *Pillar*, 117.

Florensky easily proved (2) by the definition of implication and the law of double negation, and then obtained (3) by the substitution of p in (2) by ¬p.[15] Both formulas (2) and (3) are plain tautologies of classical logic. Surprisingly enough, Florovsky claimed that the deduction of (2) and (3) somehow forms a logical proof of antinomy. He concluded: "Using the methods of pure logic we have shown the possibility of antinomy in the strictest sense of the word."[16] Strictly speaking, this proof, if it was sound, would prove not merely the possibility, but rather the necessity of antinomy.

Florensky nevertheless focused mainly on religious contradictions. "Antinomies—he wrote—are the constituent elements of religion, if we conceive it rationally."[17] Florensky pointed to three main sources of antinomies in religious discourse. The first one is the religious experience. As he claimed, "an object of religion, in falling from the heaven of spiritual experience into the fleshiness of rationality inevitably splits apart into aspects that exclude one another."[18] The nature of religious experience is expressed by the theological formulas, dogmatics therefore is also supposed to be essentially antinomic. This is true, for Florensky, first of all about the dogma of the Holy Trinity, which accepts one substance and three hypostases at the same time,[19] and about the dogma of two natures of Christ, which are thought to be both "unmerged and unchanging" and "indivisible and inseparable."[20] Finally, according to Florensky, "the Holy Scripture is full of antinomies."[21] Florensky closed the Sixth Letter by a huge table displaying most striking Christian contradictions, for instance the nature of grace (Rom 5:20 vs. Rom 6:1–2) and faith (John 3:16–28 vs. John 6:44) or the character of the coming of the Christ (John 9:39 vs. John 12:47).

The Analysis of Lewis Carroll's Puzzle

Lewis Carroll, an English mathematician and logician, famous as the author of *Alice in Wonderland*, published in 1894 a logical puzzle known as the Barbershop Paradox. He introduced it as a story about two uncles

15. Florensky, *Pillar*, 112.
16. Florensky, *Pillar*, 112–13.
17. Florensky, *Pillar*, 120.
18. Florensky, *Pillar*, 119.
19. Florensky, *Pillar*, 121.
20. Florensky, *Pillar*, 121.
21. Florensky, *Pillar*, 120.

discussing the customs of three local barbers: Allen, Brown, and Carr. One of them is always in the shop, and Brown appears there only with Allen. The discussion results in the following two statements:

(4) If Allen is out, then Brown is out,

(5) If Carr is out, then, if Allen is out, then Brown is in.

Uncle Joe argues that from these premises follows that Carr is in, since the case "Allen is out" would lead to contradiction. Carroll himself believed that this conclusion was a kind of paradox and saw this as "a very real difficulty in the Theory of Hypotheticals."[22] His paradox raised a considerable debate, which engaged such authors as Alfred Sidgwick, W. E. Johnson, and Irving M. Copi.

Quite surprisingly, Florensky saw in this logical puzzle a profound expression of a crucial problem of the logic of religion, namely the relationship between rationality and faith. That is why he believed that "for a greater understanding of the step we take when we believe in the Truth" it is useful to "solve the aforementioned logical problem."[23] First, he reconstructed the paradox in a standard propositional calculus:

(6) $q \rightarrow r$,

(7) $p \rightarrow (q \rightarrow \neg r)$.

The question is what follows from these two premises. Florensky briefly reviewed two competing solutions. The first one, proposed by Carroll himself, states that if $q \rightarrow r$ then it is impossible that $q \rightarrow \neg r$, therefore p entails a contradiction and thus should be rejected. The second one, which he (rather mistakenly) attributed to the French logician Louis Couturat, states the opposite, namely that $\neg q$. Florensky himself claimed that the proper solution is neither $\neg p$, nor $\neg q$ but $p \rightarrow \neg q$. He proved it in the following way:

(8) $\neg r \rightarrow \neg q$	contraposition of (6),
(9) $p \rightarrow (\neg q \lor \neg r)$	from (7) and the definition of implication,
(10) $p \rightarrow (\neg q \lor \neg q)$	substitution in (9) by (8),
(11) $p \rightarrow \neg q$	conclusion.[24]

22. Carroll, "Logical Paradox."

23. Carroll, "Logical Paradox," 438.

24. Florensky, *Pillar*, 356. See also Sidorenko, "Logistika i teoditseia," 173–75; Biriukov, "Iz istorii," 164–65; Biriukov and Priadko, "Florenskii," 30.

Ironically, in the Russian original text there is a typo in the conclusion, which has not been noticed yet by all the editors and translators.[25] Florensky noticed that his conclusion somehow unites the two above mentioned competing solutions. Neither p, nor q are *prima facie* absurd, but they might not be true at the same time. His proof is obviously correct. The same solution of the Barbershop Paradox was given, for instance, by Bertrand Russell in his *Principles of Mathematics*.[26] That is why nowadays Carroll's puzzle is not considered as a deep logical paradox, but rather as a mere logical mistake resulting from the early unclear understanding of the peculiarities of the logical connectives.

Florensky believed that his solution of Carroll's problem may help us understand the relation between faith and reason. The suggestion was that the premise p somehow changes the logical status of the other propositions. As he clarified, "in the presence of p, q is revoked; but in all other cases, it is in force," that is in some special conditions p "the usual, everyday, ubiquitous q stops being such."[27] The condition p, therefore, might be compared with faith, whereas the other propositions correspond with the rational thought. The leap of faith consists in the acceptance of p, which modifies the entire worldview. Logics, Florensky suggested, leaves room for such change.

This interesting general suggestion was developed in one of Florensky's examples of the application of the Carroll's scheme. Florensky proposed the following puzzle:

> A rationalist says that contradiction of the Holy Scripture and of dogmas prove their non-divine origin, whereas a mystic affirms that in a state of spiritual illumination these contradictions precisely prove the divinity of the Holy Scripture and the dogmas. The question is, what conclusion should be drawn from these declarations?[28]

This is clearly a particular case of the general scheme discussed above. Here q is "The Scripture is contradictory," r is "The Scripture is not-divine," and p is "There is spiritual illumination." The problem might be therefore formulated as follows: (1) If the Scripture is contradictory, then the Scripture

25. Florensky, *Pillar*, 356.

26. Russell, *Principles of Mathematics*, 16–18. Russell influenced Couturat, so he had also indirect effect on Florensky. See Rhodes, "Note on Florensky's Solution," 611.

27. Florensky, *Pillar*, 357.

28. Florensky, *Pillar*, 357–58.

is not-divine, and (2) If there is spiritual illumination then (if the Scripture is contradictory then the Scripture is divine). Florensky rejected two one-sided answers, namely, that there is no spiritual illumination ($\neg$p) on one hand, and that there is no contradictions in the Scripture ($\neg$q), on the other. The logic, he remained, suggests merely that p $\rightarrow$ $\neg$q, that is, in a state of spiritual illumination, there is no scriptural contradictions. Again, it leaves open the question whether such mystical states take place or not.

This particular example of illumination and contradictions links the consideration about Carroll's puzzle with the general problem of antinomy discussed above. The suggestion is that there are real contradictions in religion, but they might be somehow removed or accepted in a special state of mind. As Florensky put it:

> That which is a contradiction, and an unquestionable contradiction, for the *ratio*, stops being a contradiction at the highest level, is not perceived as a contradiction, is synthesized. And, then, in a state of spiritual illumination, there are no contradictions.[29]

This is, as Florensky points out, "the same conclusion at which we have arrived in the present text," that is in the body of the book.

Logical Interpretations

What is the worth of Florensky's logical ideas? Most commentators believe that Florensky received an "excellent mathematical education,"[30] was "quite familiar with his contemporary symbolic logic,"[31] and his *Pillar and the Ground of Truth* was "a work of great logical, mathematical, and philosophical rigor."[32] It is often suggested that he anticipated many logical ideas developed only long after his death. In short, Florensky is considered a genius and "the adequate and deeper understanding of the greatness of that personage is a matter of future."[33]

There is, however, also the other side of Florensky's logic. First of all, suspiciously many of his logical formulas *prima facie* make no sense. Perhaps some of them are simple misprints; others might be the result

---

29. Florensky, *Pillar*, 358.
30. Biriukov and Priadko, "Problema," 38.
31. Sidorenko, "Logistika i teoditseia," 172.
32. Foltz, "Fluttering of Autumn Leaves," 175.
33. Biriukow and Priadko, "Florenskii," 21.

of the ambiguity of logical connectives. Nevertheless, too many formulas seems to be plainly wrong. What is worse, his own clarifications are often not helpful at all, and in some cases even directly contradict the symbolic formulas.[34] Not surprisingly, some commentators simply reject Florensky's logical views as meaningless. For instance, Viacheslav Bocharov, a famous Soviet logician, took his ideas as plain "abracadabra in Hegel's spirit."[35] He was also disgusted by his colleagues, Biriukov and Priadko, who believed that they may contain profound truths.[36] Andrei Bronnikov even opposes calling Florensky a scientist; for him, he was rather "a poet of the language of science."[37]

I adopt here a moderate view. I believe that Florensky aimed to provide a real logical analysis, even though in many cases he simply failed to do it. Logical mistakes and oddities should not however veil his deep insights and intuitions. What we need now, is a careful and sympathetic interpretation and development of his ideas.

Florensky held that religion is essentially antinomic. This claim seems to be ambiguous in two ways. The first question is, whether he understood logical contradiction in the literal sense. Perhaps, as some authors suggested, he was talking about some oppositions, contrasts, or dialectical tensions, which in fact are not necessarily formally inconsistent. This question is legitimate, since most of Florensky's examples, such as Christian dogmas or Holy Scripture, are *prima facie* not logical antinomies, but at most merely epistemological paradoxes. The second question concerns the level of thinking where the alleged contradictions were supposed to occur. Florensky himself distinguished two kinds of thought—the lower "rationality" (*rassudok*) and the higher "reason" (*razum*).[38] Roughly, the rationality is supposed to be discursive and conceptual, whereas reason is thought rather as an intellectual intuition immediately grasping the truth.

Now, combining the possible answers for these two questions, we arrive at four possible interpretations of Florensky's view (see Fig. 1).

34. Gerasimova, "Florenskii o protivorechii," 79. See Rojek, "Sens idealizmu," 138.
35. Bocharov, "Florenskii i logika," 122–23.
36. Bocharov, "Florenskii i logika," 124.
37. Bronnikov, "Florensky and Science," 113.
38. Florensky, *Pillar*, 7 [translator's note].

Type of Interpretation	Rationality	Reason
paraconsistent	inconsistent	inconsistent
L-inconsistent	consistent	inconsistent
non-monotonic	inconsistent	consistent
rhetorical	consistent	consistent

Fig. 1. The Classification of Florensky's Interpretations

The first one holds that there are true logical antinomies, and that they are everywhere, both on the level of rationality and the reason; the second holds that there are true contradictions but only on the level of reason, not rationality; opposed to this is the third interpretation, in which contradictions appear on the level of rationality, but not on the level of reason; finally, there is an option according to which there are no true contradictions in Florensky at all, neither on the level of rational, nor reasonable thought. Now I am going to elaborate on these four interpretations.

Paraconsistent Logics

Florensky held that the truth is contradictory and therefore rejected the logical law of noncontradiction. As I indicated, that was not a unique idea among logicians of his time. Florensky shared some intuitions with Łukasiewicz or Vasiliev, which are now recognized as forerunners of the idea of paraconsistency.[39] Paraconsistent logic seems therefore to be the most natural context for the interpretation of Florensky's views.

Florensky claimed that religious truth is contradictory, but at the same time he was not willing to accept any sentences as true. This strongly suggests that he implicitly rejected the notorious principle of classical logic called the law of Duns Scotus:

(12) $(p \wedge \neg p) \rightarrow q$.

39. Arruda, "Development of Paraconsistent Logic"; Bazhanov, "Dawn of Paraconsistency."

According to (12), a contradiction entails any propositions. As a result, any formal theory which happened to contain a contradiction, turns out to be trivial since every possible formula of its language become its thesis. The embarrassing principle (12) is, however, well founded in classical logic, and thus not so easy to remove. It follows from the disjunctive introduction and disjunctive syllogism: if p, then for every q, p∨q, and thus if also ¬p, then q. The alternative logics, which do not allow such deductions, are called paraconsistent. Such formal systems were first outlined by a Łukasiewicz's student Stanisław Jaśkowski, then flourished among Latin American logicians, such as Florencio Asenjo or Newton da Costa, and finally were widely popularized by Graham Priest.[40] Nowadays it is perhaps the most established and the most developed branch of non-classical logic.

Florensky wanted to accept antinomy without accepting its classical consequences, and therefore might be seen as a forerunner of paraconsistent logic. Such suggestion has been made independently by Russian logicians, such as Boris Biriukov, Igor' Priadko, Evgenii Sidorenko, and American philosopher Michael Rhodes.[41] According to the latter, Florensky was "the first Orthodox philosopher to understand both the form of logical reasoning endemic to Orthodox thought as well as its paraconsistent implications."[42] According to this interpretation, the contradictions in Florensky are literal, not rhetorical. This was clearly expressed by Rhodes: the dogmas of Orthodox thought "are reckoned to be true, in spite of the obvious inconsistencies," and for Florensky "the antinomy . . . is robust. It is a contradiction. . . . This is not hyperbole; it is clarity."[43] The acceptance of the contradictions, however, did not lead to trivialization of his theory. Again, as Rhodes notices, "Florensky's paraconsistent logic being grounded in the Holy Trinity does not allow that 'anything follows,' rather . . . that orthodoxy follows."[44]

What is important here is that contradictions are thought to be present not only on the level of rationality, but remain also on the level of reason. For Rhodes, Florensky's solution of Carroll's problem was not supposed

40. See Perzanowski "Fifty Years of Parainconsistent logics."

41. Biriukov and Priadko "Problema," 31, 62; "Florenskii," 20; Sidorenko, "Logistika i teoditseia," 167, 176; Rhodes, "On Contradiction," 98; "Logical Proof of Antinomy."

42. Rhodes, "On Contradiction," 83.

43. Rhodes, "On Contradiction," 95.

44. Rhodes, "Logical Proof of Antinomy."

to remove, but rather to emphasize the contradiction.[45] Similarly, Biriukov and Priadko suggest that the difference between the rationality and the reason lies simply in that the former does not allow contradictions, whereas the latter accepts it. "The contradiction of reason—they write—is seen only by person in the state of spiritual enlightenment."[46] Supposedly, without spiritual enlightenment, antinomies would be seen as mere mistakes. It is clear, therefore, at least, that even in the state of enlightenment, the truths of religion remain inconsistent, only the attitude to them is changed. That which was unacceptable for rationality becomes welcome for the reason.

Commentators disagree as to the value of Florensky's efforts to develop a formal theory of antinomies. Biriukov and Priadko appreciate his intuition but criticize its formal expression. "Here it turns out," they wrote, "that though he mastered logical technique, he did not really think through the problem of how to combine the logical calculus with his own theological position."[47] This results, for instance, in the futile definition of antinomy (1). As they indicate, the sign "V" fails to change the contradiction into truth, since the whole formula remains false, as previously.[48] Alas, Florensky's bald proof of antinomy is also a simple "logical mistake." There is nothing antinomic in tautologies (2) and (3).[49] Nevertheless, Biriukov and Priadko are not confused by all these results. They believed that they could merely show that "most of the ideas of Father Paul, concerning the formal aspects of thinking, go beyond the limits of [classical] logics."[50]

Michael Rhodes is even less critical than Biriukov and Priadko. For instance, he takes Florensky's formal proof of antinomy seriously. Though Rhodes sees some "logical peccadilloes" in Florensky's writings, he nevertheless believes that Florensky really proved that "both p and ¬p are derived from their opposites, making together the antinomy."[51] Unfortunately, instead of analyzing Florensky's proof, which is plainly wrong, Rhodes merely reproduces his formulas. Even if we agree that Florensky had some deep

45. Rhodes, "Note on Florensky's Solution," 613.

46. Biriukov and Priadko, "Problema," 59.

47. Biriukov and Priadko, "Problema," 55.

48. Biriukov and Priadko, "Problema," 56.

49. Biriukov and Priadko, "Florenskii," 27–29. See also Biriukov, "Iz istorii," 168; Bocharov, "Florenskii i logika," 123.

50. Biriukov and Priadko, "Florenskii," 28.

51. Rhodes, "Logical Proof of Antinomy."

insights into logic, we should not lock our eyes on the grave nonsenses in his logical writings.

The Theory of L-contradiction

Now I will turn to the second type of interpretation, which holds that the religious truths are essentially antinomic, but that contradictions do not in fact appear on the level of rational thinking, but only on the level of reason. Ordinary thinking cannot deal with contradictions and therefore always finds a way to avoid them. That is why rational thought reaches only the surface of reality. Its ultimate nature is revealed only in the suprarational illumination. The task of religious philosophy is to show the limitations of rationality, and to prepare for the encounter with the ultimate reality.

A logical theory roughly corresponding to this type of interpretation was formulated by Viacheslav Moiseev.[52] The fundamental idea of this theory was directly inspired by Florensky's remarks in the Sixth Letter of the *Pillar and Ground of Truth*. Moiseev's aim, however, is not to give an interpretation of Florensky's views. He pursues only his general idea of the "formal logical theory of antinomy," which should provide a "symbolic-logic algorithm"[53] for the analysis of antinomies. Moiseev criticizes Florensky's own attempts to realize that program, in particular his formula (1). The problem is that in fact every formula can be completed by the sign "V." Florensky therefore failed to express his own insights. "It is clear," Moiseev concludes, "that the use of sign V by Florensky has a metaphorical meaning, which goes beyond the means of logistics."[54] Moiseev's own theory of antinomies was supposed to capture that missing meaning of the symbol "V" and thus became a "more adequate" realization of Florensky's project.[55]

Moiseev suggests that the rational mind can always find some logical tricks to avoid contradictions. In the face of contradictory statements, we usually differentiate their subjects or predicates obtaining more specific and thus consistent propositions. In some cases, however, these solutions themselves pose a similar problem, which requires corresponding logical treatments. The true philosophical antinomies, for Moiseev, can be merely

---

52. Moiseev, *Logika vseedinstva*, 329–39; "Properties of L-Inconsistent Theories"; *Chelovek i obshchestvo*, 97–121. See also Rojek, "Antynomia Russella."

53. Florensky, *Pillar*, 110.

54. Moiseev, *Logika vseedinstva*, 176.

55. Moiseev, *Logika vseedinstva*, 176.

shifted, but never finally solved. Rational thought arrives as a result to an infinite series of successive solutions. According to Moiseev, in the case of true philosophical antinomies, that infinite series of solutions reaches at its limit the robust contradiction. Such formulas he calls L-contradictions ("L" for "limit").

The formal theory of L-contradictions is based on the concept of a sequence of formulas, inspired by the analogy between logic and topology. Such sequences might be finite or infinite and, just like in mathematics, might have their limits. L-contradiction is defined as infinite sequence of formulas with a contradiction in its limit. Such a sequence corresponds to the idea of logical antinomy. Nevertheless, the formal theory of L-contradiction is consistent.[56] Therefore, it is not a kind of paraconsistent logic, but an alternative way of dealing with contradictions.

Moiseev does not intend to give an interpretation of Florensky's view, but he nevertheless notices that his own theory may help explain the crucial distinction between the rational and reasonable thought. "The rational thought (*rassudok*) works through devices of formal logic," whereas "the reason (*razum*) adds to the structures of rationality devices of logic of antinomy."[57] It is clear, therefore, that the rational thinking for Moiseev is free from contradictions, whereas the reason ultimately admits them. The antinomies, however, are accepted only as the limits of the infinite sequences of consistent rational formulas.

Now I would like to illustrate Moiseev's approach by an analysis of a simple version of his antinomy of the Absolute, claiming that the Absolute is everything, and at the same time that the Absolute is nothing.[58]

The absolute being is usually said to be both immanent and transcendent. God might be thought as being a part of the world and at the same time as transcending the whole reality. It seems to be a contradiction. If P means "is a part of the universe," and ¬P means "is not a part of the universe," then the antinomy of immanence and transcendence might be formulated as follows:

(13) $P(a) \land \neg P(a)$.

Now, the rational thinking might easily resolve that contradiction. It might, for instance, differentiate the subject of the contradictory statement. We can

56. Moiseev, "Properties of L-Inconsistent Theories," 10.

57. Moiseev, *Chelovek i obshchestvo*, 121.

58. Moiseev, *Chelovek i obshchestvo*, 105.

split the subject a into two distinct subjects a_1 and a_2, say, the "immanent absolute" and the "transcendent absolute," to obtain a consistent formula:

(14) $P(a_1) \land \neg P(a_2)$.

The immanent absolute a_1 is a part of the universe, whereas the transcendent absolute a_2 is not. Unfortunately, the price for this move is the relativization of the concept of the Absolute. The general concept of the Absolute forces us the go beyond all the limits. The transcendent absolute a_2, on its way, still seems to be a part of a world, though it is not our initial world, but a wider one. That world also should be exceeded. This suggests that we should split not only the concept of the Absolute, but also the concepts of the world W and the property of being in the world P. Therefore, there is a sequence of sets $W_1, W_2, W_3, \ldots$, such that $W_n \subseteq W_{n+1}$ and $W_n \neq W_{n+1}$, $n = 1, 2, 3 \ldots$ and the corresponding sequence of properties $P_1, P_2, P_3, \ldots$, such that P_1 means "being in W_1," P_2 means "being in W_2" and so on. The absolute a_1 is a part of W_1 and hence has P_1, and the absolute a_2 is not a part of W_1 and thus has $\neg P_1$. Next, the absolute a_2 is a part of W_2, that is has P_2, though the following absolute a_3 is not a part of W_2 and hence has $\neg P_2$. In general, the relative immanent absolute a_n is a part of W_n, that is has P_n, whereas the relative transcendent absolute a_{n+1} is not a part of W_n and has $\neg P_n$:

(15) $P_1(a_1) \land \neg P_1(a_2)$,
(16) $P_2(a_2) \land \neg P_2(a_3)$,

$\ldots$

(17) $P_n(a_n) \land \neg P_n(a_{n+1})$.

Now, Moiseev introduces here a concept of infinite sequences of formulas. In this case we obtain the following:

(18) $\{P_n(a_n) \land \neg P_n(a_{n+1})\}_{n=1}^{\infty}$

Once we have accepted these sequences of formulas, we can speak about their limits. It seems plausible that the infinite sequence of relative absolutes $a_1, a_2, a_3, \ldots$ approaches the absolute Absolute a: $\lim_{n \to \infty}\{a_n\} = a$. Similarly, the infinite sequence of restricted $P_1, P_2, P_3, \ldots$ tends to the unrestricted P: $\lim_{n \to \infty}\{P_n\} = P$. So we can analyze the formula (18) as follows:

(19) $\lim_{n \to \infty}\{P_n(a_n) \land \neg P_n(a_{n+1})\}_{n=1}^{\infty} = P(a) \land \neg P(a)$.

The limit of the infinite sequence of consistent formulas turns out to be the initial contradiction (13). In other words, we can solve each case of contradictions, but nevertheless the infinite sequence of such solutions tend to the robust contradiction in its limit case. It is, therefore, an example of "L-contradiction." This particular form, according to Moiseev, is characteristic for the true philosophical antinomies.

Non-Monotonic Logics

Now I will turn to the third type of interpretation of Florensky's view. It holds that there are true contradictions in religious discourse, but that they occur only for lower rationality, not for the higher, transformed reason. It is, therefore, a direct opposition of the previous reading. The general idea behind it is that rational thought cannot grasp religious truth without contradiction, whereas the higher reason is able to see a higher unity of supposedly contradictory statements. The antinomies of rational thought may thus somehow be solved by divine illumination. I will try to show that the difference between the rationality and the reason might be explained in the terms of additional premises implicitly denied by the rationality and explicitly accepted by the reason.

This kind of interpretation was first proposed by a Russian logician Evgenii Sidorenko.[59] He believes that "Florensky put forward a number of ideas, which were made explicit in our times in the systems of non-monotonic . . . logics."[60] To reveal this, Sidorenko provides a careful analysis of Florensky's discussion on Carroll's problem.

Sidorenko suggests that Florensky's main concern in his discussion of the Barbershop Paradox was the idea that some of our conclusions might be withdrawn in the face of certain supernatural circumstances. This might be thought, as Sidorenko argues, as an expression of the fundamental intuition of non-monotonic logics. Classical logic is based on the relation of logical consequence Cn which satisfies condition of monotonicity:

$$(20)\ X \subseteq Y \to Cn(X) \subseteq Cn(Y).$$

It states that any extension of a set of premises preserves the possibility of inferring the same conclusions as from the previous set. Non-monotonic logics rejects that condition and accept the weakened relation of logical consequence C. On the ground of non-monotonic logics the extension of the set of premises may lead to rejection of the previous conclusions, or

59. Sidorenko, "Logistika i teoditseia."
60. Sidorenko, "Logistika i teoditseia," 167.

even to acceptance of their negations. That is, when $a \in C(X)$ then it is possible that for some set of additional premises Y holds that $a \notin C(X \cup Y)$, or even $\neg a \in C(X \cup Y)$. The operator of consequence C might be also relativized to some set of implicitly or explicitly accepted premises K: $C_K(X)$. That set K might also contains the principles and rules of interpretation of X, which is very important in the analysis of religious discourse.[61] It is believed that non-monotonic logics are more adequate to the real human reasoning in the conditions of restricted time, or limited access to information.

The point of Florensky's interpretation of Carroll's problem is that in the normal situation $q \to r$ holds, but under some special condition p, which is supposed to be illumination of faith, it is not the case that $q \to r$ but rather that $q \to \neg r$. Note, the fact that in Florensky's reading the proposition q concerns the contradictory character of Holy Scripture, is irrelevant here. The most insightful is the role of the additional premise p, which changes the final conclusion. This is clearly non-monotonic reasoning, which might be further analyzed with the help of the concept of default assumptions. As Sidorenko says, "the implication $q \to \neg r$ is taken as true because it is actually true that $\neg p \to (q \to \neg r)$, and $\neg p$ is accepted by default."[62] The hidden premise of the natural reason is therefore the lack of spiritual illumination $\neg p$. This mysterious illumination might be understood not in psychological or spiritual terms, but simply as the addition of some extra premises replacing the implicitly assumed default conditions. The religious illumination is thus an extension of the set of the explicit premises.

Now, the problem was that Florensky tried to express that non-monotonic intuitions with the help of classical logic, whereas "classical logic of propositions . . . is simply not able to adequately take into account the reasons underlying Florensky's reasoning."[63] Sidorenko points out a number of grave inadequacies between Florensky's informal intentions and their logical expression. First, the characteristic of material implication undermines his efforts to present p as an additional premise, which transforms the conclusion. The problem is that in classical logic, an implication stays true even when false implies truth, therefore every true proposition might be preceded by any p. Florensky's additional premise p becomes thus in fact superfluous, since it could be inferred from any true proposition. Next, the conclusion of his whole reasoning is somewhat ambiguous. Florensky

---

61. Trepczyński, "Logika teologii"; "Non-monotonic logic"

62. Sidorenko, "Logistika i teoditseia," 176.

63. Sidorenko, "Logistika i teoditseia," 177.

welcomed the formula p→ ¬q, which he read as "If there is a spiritual illumination, then there are no contradiction in Holy Scripture," but this
conclusion is—by contraposition—equivalent to q→ ¬p, that is, "if there
are contradictions in Holy Scripture, there is no spiritual illumination." The
problem here is that Florensky openly admitted the presence of contradictions. Unfortunately, if there are contradictions, then there is no illumination, and, what is worse, from the implication q → r it follows also that the
Scripture is not-divine. Finally, Florensky's conclusion fails to express his
belief that in the state of illumination the contradictions in Holy Scripture
prove its divine origin. If there is the state of illumination, then there are
simply no contradictions in Scripture. If p, then both q → r and q → ¬r, and
therefore ¬q. The problem is that this conclusion obviously cannot support
the divine character of Scripture. If ¬q then there is no way to get ¬r. Florensky simply did not notice that problem. As a result, it seems that Florensky's formal reasoning is dramatically inadequate to his initial intuitions.
That is why we should reject the formalization of Florensky's reasoning in
classical logic and seek a way to more adequate expressions.

Sidorenko outlines an alternative non-monotonic interpretation of
Florensky's analysis of Carroll's problem. Florensky's suggestion was that
it usually holds that q → r, but not in the face of the premise p. It means
therefore that it is as a rule implicitly assumed that ¬p, and that assumption
is explicitly rejected in the case p. The premises of the Barbershop Paradox
should be therefore reformulated as:

(6') ¬p → (q → r),
(7) p → (q →¬r).

Proposition p simply blocks the inference to q → r and implies that q → ¬r.
In this formalization there is no way to make a use of the removed antecedent q → r. So, the inference to the misleading conclusion that p → ¬q
is finally blocked. It turns out, as Florensky initially suggested, that in the
state of spiritual illumination there are true contradictions, but now they
are seen as evidences of the divine character of Holy Scripture. As a result,
the logic shows that though there is no way to prove the divine character of
the Scripture, there is also no way to obtain its non-divine character. The
additional premises may always change the supposed charges into benefits.

In this interpretation, Florensky implicitly suggested a new solution
to the Barbershop Paradox. He did neither, as Carroll himself, reject p, nor,
as Couturat, reject q. Though he explicitly accepted p→ ¬q, that is ¬ (p∧q),

he really wanted to say something completely opposite, namely that both p and q might be true. As Sidorenko clarifies, "the point of this is that p undermines the claim q→ r. . . . And this is, as it seems, exactly the result, which Florensky wanted to reach."[64] Going back to the Carroll's story, it might be said that only if Carr is in then, if Allen is out, then Brown is out, while if Carr is out, then, if Allen is out, then Brown is in. One cannot prove therefore that Carr is in. That is how Florensky should solve the Carroll's problem. Unfortunately, the monotonic logic, which he adapted for his purposes, made impossible the adequate expression of his own insights.

Rhetorical Turn

Finally, I would like to look at the last possible kind of interpretation of Florensky's views, which fundamentally opposes the previous ones. According to it, there are in fact no real logical contradictions, neither on the level of rationality, nor on the level of reason. Florensky's so called antinomies are merely hyperboles aimed at shocking the reader and making him think in a new way. This interpretation obviously undermines all attempts to construct formal theories of antinomies.

Many readers of Florensky's work are confused by his reckless use of the concept of antinomy. Are the Holy Scripture or Christian dogmatics truly antinomic? The Church Fathers, who put so much effort into consistent exegesis of the Bible and coherent clarification of the Christian teaching, would probably be deeply disappointed by such a view. The thesis that God is one in nature and three in hypostasis is *prima facie* not a case of contradiction, since it obviously concerns two different aspects of the divine reality. The same is true about Christ, who is one person with two natures. Perhaps dogmatic definitions indeed involve implicit contradiction, but this should be argued, not simply assumed.

This consideration leads to the hypothesis that Florensky used the term "antinomy" in a loose and wide sense, not adequately captured by the concept of contradiction in formal logic. Recently, Irina Gerasimova proposed a kind of rhetorical interpretation of Florensky's theory of antinomies.[65] She reminds us that Florensky was more poet, writer, and preacher than mathematician or logician. His concept of antinomy derived therefore not from logic, but rather from rhetoric, where the contrast of

64. Sidorenko, "Logistika i teoditseia," 182–83.

65. Gerasimova, "Florenskii o protivorechii."

the thesis and the antithesis is a well known classical device. Making striking comparisons, using abundant hyperbolas, highlighting contrasts, and
introducing thought-provoking oppositions, Florensky was simply a faithful student of the ancient art of speaking. The point is, however, that in
fact none of these rhetorical devices are adequately analyzable as formal
contradiction.

More specifically, Gerasimova distinguishes three aspects of so called
antinomies in Florensky's writings. Firstly, the logical (or rather epistemological) one helps to see complements and alternatives for the accepted
thesis. Secondly, the communicative aspect concerns the use of antinomy
in rhetoric. Thirdly, the psychological aspects reveals the role of such
formulations in stimulating emotions and creative thinking. In all these
cases antinomies are not thought literally as logical contradictions. As she
concludes,

> In most cases the logical connective "and" uniting the thesis and
> the antithesis represents the level of the metalanguage. . . . The
> proposition p combined with negation ¬p changes its meaning in
> virtue of the change of its context. It would be more appropriate to
> write, for example, "p" for thesis and "q" for antithesis.[66]

In other words, Florensky's basic formula for antinomy (1), which involves
a true logical contradiction, turns out to be fundamentally misleading.

Gerasimova carefully analyzes Florensky's list of the alleged contradictions in the Holy Scripture form Letter Six of *The Pillar and Ground of
Truth*.[67] The antinomy of grace, for instance, is only an apparent contradiction since Rome 5:20 describes the actual state of being, whereas Rome 6:10
and 6:15 concern the desired state. Similarly the antinomy of faith between
John 3:16–18 and John 6:44 consist in fact of two complementary, not contradictory statements. Finally, the antinomy of Jesus's judgement simply describes the different moments in history: his first coming in John 12:47 and
the second coming in John 9:39. In all these cases we have merely rhetorical figures, not logical contradictions. They are rather cases of complement
statements concerning the different aspects of reality, describing the different stages of the one process, or addressed to different audiences. As she
concludes, "the opposition between the thesis and antithesis is not a formal
or logical contradiction," and the figure of antinomy, was merely supposed

66. Gerasimova, "Florenskii o protivorechii," 86–87.
67. Gerasimova, "Florenskii o protivorechii," 89–95.

to "produce an intense rhetorical effect."[68] If this is true, the whole project of the logical theory of antinomy seems to be a result of a misunderstanding of a rhetorical device. What we really need here is not a new logic but rather proper hermeneutics.

Towards the Integral Theory of Antinomy

As I have pointed out, it is not easy to determine what exactly Florensky's logical view on religious antinomies was. His original statements are so unclear, vague, and in many cases incoherent that they allow for many different interpretations. I briefly reviewed here four different types of analysis of Florensky. None of them were supposed to be comprehensive studies of his views. Most commentators take into account only selected passages from Florensky's writings; others are just inspired by his general ideas. While the paraconsistent, L-contradictory, and rhetorical interpretations focus on Florensky's idea of the theory of antinomies from Letter Six, the non-monotonic interpretation departs mainly from the discussion of Carroll's Paradox. Nevertheless, I believe that all of them, to some extent, express Florensky's views. Now I would like to sketch an integral interpretation which unites the results of all discussed approaches.

First of all, it seems clear that many, perhaps most, of Florensky's antinomies are in fact merely rhetorical devices, not true logical contradictions. Accordingly, in many cases, the rhetorical interpretation is the best reading of Florensky's reflections on antinomy. This insight particularly applies to the alleged antinomies of Holy Scripture, which usually can be resolved in many ways, without violating the laws of classical logic. The same is true about many supposed contradictions in dogmatics.

However, in some limited cases, the issue is more complicated. It seems plausible that some religious statements might indeed be truly contradictory. Notwithstanding, the admission of contradictions is definitely not supposed to make it logically trivial. Contradictions are allowed only in isolated spheres and should not affect the rest of the system of beliefs. Paraconsistent logic is then very useful here.

Nevertheless, even such tamed antinomies in religious thinking are not the desired and the ultimate state. The contradictions appear only within natural thinking, which is not able to express the religious experience. The development of the religious system consists of making it consistent

68. Gerasimova, "Florenskii o protivorechii," 94.

through the formulation of dogmas. The process starts with contradictions appearing in an initial conceptual scheme, and then transforms that scheme to resolve the contradictions. The dogmas might be seen as concepts and principles which make possible the adequate and consistent description of the reality of religion. Dogmas therefore are not to reproduce, but rather to reduce antinomies.

This whole development might be described in the general frame of non-monotonic logic. Let R be a set of religious statements, such as the data of the revelation and/or the reports of the religious experience. At the first level, R contains some real contradictions. That is, for some p,

(21) $p \wedge \neg p \in C(R)$.

It is crucial here to avoid the triviality of $C(R)$. That is why we really need to adopt a paraconsistent approach on this level. This is not the end, however. The contradictions in the religious discourse are only the beginning of the process of enhancement of natural rationality. This process might be thought simply as an enrichment of operation C by a set of additional premises and heuristics. Such a set, say D, is supposed to correspond to the dogmatics of religious discourse. This suggests a clear interpretation of the distinction between rational and reasonable thought. The concept of rationality might be identified with the natural consequence C, whereas the concept of reason with the consequences C enabled with the premises D, that is C_D. Hence, we obtain two supersets of the religious statements R, closed under the operations C or C_D, that is containing solely formulas produced by the operations of natural or dogmatic consequences. The enlightenment by faith is seen here not as a spiritual change of the person, but rather as an enrichment of the operation of logical consequence. Now, the point is that the contradictions which appear for C might not appear for C_D:

(22) $p \wedge \neg p \notin C_D(R)$.

In other words, contradictions are really a matter of lower rationality, not of the higher reason. What is important, we need not deny here the presence of true contradictions in religious discourse. The formula (21) is still valid, though not ultimate. The religious experience is not consistently expressible in natural language, but might transform the language to a non-contradictory description of the divine reality.

Finally, it seems that also L-contradictory interpretation might help to clarify the development of dogmas. We start with an inconsistent set of R, which might be made consistent by the addition of premises D. There might be, however, a new revelation which could add some statements making R inconsistent again and therefore inducing the need of a new dogmatic modifications. It seems that this might be the historical case of, for instance, the development of judaic monotheistic theology into Christian trinitarian dogmatics. Now, this situation might suggest that in fact there is a sequence of sets $R_1, R_2, \ldots, R_n$, such that $R_n \subseteq R_{n+1}$ and $R_n \neq R_{n+1}$, n= 1, 2, 3 $\ldots$, and the corresponding sequence $D_1, D_2, \ldots, D_n$, such that D_1 makes R_1 consistent, D_2 makes R_2 consistent and so on. The sequence of statements

$$(23)\ \{C_{Dn}(R_n) \text{ is consistent} \wedge C_{Dn}(R_{n+1}) \text{ is not consistent}\}_{n=1}^{\infty}$$

would be of course L-contradictory. But this is not a necessary move. Recall that in the case of the true L-contradiction the solution of the problem at level n produces the same problem at the level n+1. For instance, as we have seen, the concept of the Absolute goes beyond all possible limitations. It is not clear, however, whether it is the case with the revelation and its dogmatic expression. It might be that dogmatics on a particular level simply succeed in making the available religious discourse consistent. If that would be the case, the sequence of the statements would be consistent and finite, and thus there would be no L-contradiction in its infinite limit.

I believe that such a complex, non-monotonic model is the best interpretation of Florensky's views. Though he boldly emphasized the antinomic character of religious discourse for rationality, he also clearly allowed for the possibility of a consistent expression of the faith for illuminated reason. Natural philosophy might therefore transform into supranatural thought. This takes places, as Florensky once suggested, in the minds of the saints, purified by ascesis and filled by divine grace.

> In this mind, the healing of the fissures and cracks has begun; the sickness of being is being cured; the wounds of the world are being healed. For this mind itself is the healing organ of the world.[69]

As I propose, such a mind might be identified with the non-monotonic operation of the logical consequence, and the illumination by grace might be interpreted as the addition of a set of dogmatic premises. Suprarational

---

69. Florensky, *Pillar*, 118.

thought is therefore a new consistent superset of the religious discourse closed under the operation of dogmatic consequence.

Bibliography

Arruda, Ayda I. "Aspects of the Historical Development of Paraconsistent Logic." In *Paraconsistent Logic: Essays on the Inconsistent*, edited by Graham Priest, et al., 99–130. München: Philosophia Verlag, 1989.

Bazhanov, Valentin A. "The Dawn of Paraconsistency: Russia's Logical Thought in the Turn of XX Century." *Manuscrito* 34.1 (2011) 89–98.

Biriukov, Boris V. "Iz istorii matematicheskoi logiki v Rossii: Zadacha Kerolla v traktovke o. Pavla Florenskogo." *Logicheskie issledovaniia* 6 (1999) 163–69.

Biriukov Boris V., and Igor' P. Priadko. "P. A. Florenskii: Filosofsko-logicheskie idei kak sredstvo eksplikatsii filosofsko-teologicheskikh vozzrenii." *Vestnik Moskovskogo Universiteta. Seriia 7: Filosofiia* 1 (2011) 20–35.

——. "Problema logicheskogo protivorechiia i russkaia religioznaia filosofiia." *Logicheskie issledovaniia* 16 (2010) 23–84.

Blank, Ksana. "The Rabbit and The Duck: Antinomic Unity in Dostoevskij, the Russian Religious Tradition, and Mikhail Bakhtin." *Studies in East European Thought* 59 (2007) 21–37.

Bocharov, Viacheslav A. "Pavel Florenskii i logika." In *Sed'mye Smirnovskie chteniia*, 121–124. Moscow: Sovremennye tetradi, 2011.

Bronnikov, Andrei. "Florensky and Science." In *Faith and Reason in Russian Thought*, edited by Teresa Obolevitch and Paweł Rojek, 91–116. Krakow: Copernicus Center, 2015.

Bulgakov, Sergius. *Unfading Light.* Translated by Thomas Allan Smith. Grand Rapids: Eerdmans, 2012.

Carroll, Lewis. "A Logical Paradox." *Mind* 11.3 (1894) 436–38.

Evdokimov, Paul. *Orthodoxy.* Translated by Jeremy Hummerstone. Hyde Park, NY: New City, 2011.

Florensky, Pavel. *The Pillar and Ground of the Truth.* Translated by Boris Jakim. Princeton: Princeton University Press, 2004.

Foltz, Bruce. "The Fluttering of Autumn Leaves: Logic, Mathematics, and Metaphysics in Florensky's *The Pillar and Ground of Truth*." In *Logic in Orthodox Christian Thinking*, edited by Andrew Schumann, 174–203. Hausenstamm: Ontos Verlag, 2013.

Gerasimova, Irina A. "P. A. Florenskii o protivorechii." *Logicheskie issledovaniia* 18 (2012) 77–96.

Lossky, Vladimir. *The Mystical Theology of the Eastern Church.* Cambridge: James Clarke, 1973.

Meyendorff, John. *Byzantine Theology: Historical Trends and Doctrinal Themes.* New York: Fordham University Press, 1983.

Moiseev, Viacheslav I. "About Properties of L-Inconsistent Theories." *Sorites* 17 (2006) 7–16.

——. *Chelovek i obshchestvo: obrazy sinteza.* Vol. 1. Moscow: Navigator, 2012.

——. *Logika vseedinstva.* Moscow: Per Se, 2002.

Perzanowski, Jerzy. "Fifty years of Parainconsistent Logics." *Logic and Logical Philosophy* 7 (1999) 21–24.

Priest, Graham. "Paraconsistency and Dialetheism." In *The Many Valued and Nonmonotonic Turn in Logic*, edited by Dov M. Gabbay and John Woods, 129–204. Vol. 8 of *Handbook of the History of Logic*. Amsterdam: North Holland, 2007.

Rezvykh Tat'iana N. "Florenskii—Rozanov—Frank—Trubetskoi: ideia antinomii." In *Pavel Aleksandrovich Florenskii*, edited by Aleksei N. Parshin and Oksana M. Sedykh, 82–96. Moscow: Rossiiskaia politicheskaia entsiklopediia, 2013.

Rhodes, Michael Craig. "Logical Proof of Antinomy." *Theandros* 3.2 (2005). Online. http://www.theandros.com/lawofident.html.

———. "Note on Florensky's Solution to Carroll's Barbershop Paradox." *Philosophia* 40.3 (2012) 607–616.

———. "On Contradiction in Orthodox Philosophy." In *Logic in Orthodox Christian Thinking*, edited by Andrew Schumann, 82–103. Hausenstamm: Ontos Verlag, 2013.

Rojek, Paweł. "Antynomia Russella, twierdzenie Gödla i logika absolutnego." *Semina Scientiarum* 3 (2004) 101–110.

———. "Sens idealizmu według Pawła Florenskiego." *Logos i Ethos* 27 (2008) 131–39.

Russell, Bertrand. *Principles of Mathematics*. London: Allen & Unwin, 1903.

Schneider, Christoph. "Will the Truth not Demand a Sacrifice from Us? Reflections on Pavel A. Florensky's Idea of Truth as Antinomy in the *Pillar and Ground of the Truth* (1914)." *Sobornost* 34.2 (2013) 34–51.

Sidorenko, Evgenii A. "Logistika i teoditseia." In *Logika. Paradoksy. Vozmozhnye miry*, by Evgenii A. Sidorenko, 167–83. Moscow: Editorial URSS, 2002.

Trepczyński, Marcin. "Logika teologii objawionej w pismach Alberta Wielkiego i Tomasza z Akwinu." *Roczniki Filozoficzne* 61.3 (2013) 61–76

———. "Non-Monotonic Logic in Favor of Science and Religion Compatibility." In *The Second World Congress on Logic and Religion: The Book of Abstracts*, 96. Warsaw: IF UW, 2017.

7

Orthodoxy, Philosophy, and Ethics

Rico Vitz

B eing members of a family can lead to awkward conversations—well intended perhaps but awkward nonetheless. This is true not only of one's natural family, but of one's spiritual family as well. For instance, since becoming an Orthodox Christian a little over a decade ago, I have had a number of awkward conversations with Orthodox brothers and sisters along the following lines. Upon learning that I am both an Orthodox Christian and a philosopher who does research in ethics, some have apparently felt compelled to inform me that "Orthodox Christianity is not a philosophical system," or that "Orthodox Christianity is completely opposed to Western philosophy," or that "Orthodox Christianity does not have an ethical theory." These conversations became more awkward when they found out that I am one of a number of contemporary philosophers who came to Orthodoxy not *in spite of* but *because of* my studies in Western philosophy.[1] As members of loving families should, we then sorted through what initially seemed like starkly opposing views to discover that we were largely in agreement about both the value of and the problems with academic philosophy.

I have had similar conversations with philosophers when they found out that I am religious, not as a matter of pragmatic cultural affiliation, but as a matter of sincere faith and practice. In each case, the conversations

---

1. For similar stories, see Vitz, *Turning East*, and St. Gregory Palamas's observation regarding the role of secular learning in acquiring wisdom (Palamas, *Homilies*, 260). I will discuss more noteworthy examples of Orthodox Christian philosopher saints below.

seem to have been motivated by an underlying suspicion that Orthodox Christianity and philosophy are deeply incompatible.

Now, I obviously do not share that view. Nevertheless, these experiences cause me to approach my work in this chapter with some trepidation, since I contend that Orthodox Christians can and ought to be engaged with philosophical conceptions of ethics. So, in the hope of avoiding a similarly awkward experience, let me begin by clarifying briefly what I take to be the relationship between Orthodox Christianity and philosophy.[2] I recognize that not every reader will share the view, but I hope, at the very least, to make it sufficiently understandable so that those who are willing to read this chapter charitably can find in it something of value.

There are, broadly construed, two erroneous ways for Orthodox Christians to approach philosophy. On the one hand is the temptation to err by adopting something like the view of Tertullian, who valued philosophy too lowly. Those who take this approach suggest that "Athens" (philosophy) should have little, if anything, to do with "Jerusalem" (Christianity). On the other hand is the temptation to err by adopting something like the view of Origen or of Barlaam, who seemed to value philosophy too highly. Those who take this approach try to get Christianity to conform to an antithetical system of philosophy.

Each of these approaches misapplies the wise counsel of St. Paul, not to be taken captive by vain and deceptive philosophy in accordance with the traditions of men, and not in accordance with Christ (Col 2:8). Notice two points about St. Paul's teaching. First, not every engagement with philosophy is an instance of being taken captive by philosophy. Second, not every form of philosophy is both in accordance with the principles of men and not in accordance with Christ. With these points in mind, we can rightly see that St. Paul's teaching is not a prohibition against philosophy *per se*, as those who adopt a view like that of Tertullain seem to think. Rather, it is a prohibition against *being taken captive* by *a certain kind* of philosophy: namely, by embracing too uncritically one or another "humanistic" school of philosophy that is essentially opposed to Christian tradition, as those who adopt a view like that of Origen or of Barlaam are seemingly inclined to do.

Between these two erroneous views, there are at least three ways that faithful and traditionally-minded Orthodox Christians both have been

---

2. The following is, essentially, the same view I expressed in Petcu, "Unicity of Orthodox Spirituality."

and can be engaged with philosophy. First, as St. Clement of Alexandria notes, philosophy can be a preparation for those who are being perfected in Christ.[3] Second, as both the theoretical work of the Cappadocian fathers and the practical work of the neptic tradition illustrate, philosophy can be a source of concepts and methods that can be appropriated in new ways to help explain the faith once delivered to the saints (Jude 1:3).[4] Third, as the lives of St. Paul,[5] St. Aristides, St. Justin Martyr, St. John Damascene, St. Catherine the Great, and others suggest, philosophy can be a source for evangelization and for apologetic debates.

My aim in this chapter is to help develop the groundwork for greater dialogue on ethical issues at the intersection of philosophy, psychology, and the neptic tradition of Orthodox Christianity. My efforts towards this end proceed in three steps. In the first section, I offer some preliminary conceptual clarifications concerning the field of ethics. In the second section, I explain the Orthodox tradition in light of these conceptual clarifications and show that the Orthodox Christian way of life embodies a type of virtue ethics. In the third section, I suggest the significance of Orthodox Christian virtue ethics for a contemporary debate concerning evidence from social psychology.

Philosophical Conceptions of Ethics

A key challenge in writing for an interdisciplinary audience like the one for which this chapter is intended, is to communicate effectively with people who have a diverse set of interests and may not be especially familiar with the subtleties of one's own area of expertise. So, for the sake of clarity, let me begin by providing an overview of contemporary philosophical approaches to ethics.[6]

---

3. Clement of Alexandria, *Stromata* 1.5.

4. Consider, for instance, St. John Damascene's *De Fide Orthodoxa*, or the way that the Church Fathers appropriate a philosophical concept like *energeiai* to explain God's relationship to the world, what can be known of God, or the concept of theosis. Regarding the latter, see, e.g., David Bradshaw's excellent work, especially Bradshaw, *Aristotle East and West*. Regarding the neptic tradition's appropriation of philosophical terms related to human nature and moral development, see below.

5. See, e.g., Acts 17:18.

6. What follows in this section is a general survey intended to give non-specialists a framework for understanding how philosophers who specialize in ethics tend to approach the subject.

Among contemporary philosophers, there are three general approaches to ethical reflection:[7] (1) *virtue ethics*, which focuses principally on character,[8] (2) *deontology*, which focuses principally on autonomy and related concepts concerning individual rights and duties,[9] and (3) *utilitarianism*, which focuses principally on collective welfare of all sentient creatures.[10] Although some might be tempted to view these as rigidly siloed approaches to ethics, this is not the case. Systems of virtue ethics regard virtuous people as rational agents, who exercise their autonomy wisely in such a way that they promote the common good. Thus, it is not as if the primary foci of deontology and of utilitarianism are antithetical to systems of virtue ethics. Likewise, systems of deontology regard autonomous rational agents as ones who cultivate good character and promote the common good. Hence, it is not as if the primary foci of virtue ethics and of utilitarianism are antithetical to deontology. Similarly, systems of utilitarianism regard character and autonomy as qualities that are important for promoting the common good. Therefore, it is not as if the primary foci of virtue ethics and deontology are antithetical to utilitarianism.

In short, reflective versions of each of these three approaches to ethics ought to be regarded as competing ways of trying to articulate *proper conceptions* of character, autonomy, rights, duties, and the common good, on the one hand, and the *right ordering and balance* of these concepts, on the other. The debate regarding the conception, order, and balance of these key concepts focuses, in large part, on how to answer four questions. First, is ethical reflection and discourse principally *character-centered*, as virtue ethics tends suggests, or *act-centered*, as deontology and utilitarianism tend to suggest? Second, is ethical learning primarily centered on recognizing and imitating *exemplars*, as virtue ethics tends to suggest,[11] or is it primarily

7. See Baron et al., *Three Methods of Ethics*.

8. One finds varying conceptions of virtue ethics not only in ancient Greece (e.g., Plato, Epictetus) and in ancient Rome (e.g., Seneca, Cicero), but also in ancient China (e.g., Confucius, Mencius, Xunzi), among medieval theistic philosopher theologians (e.g., Aquinas), among early modern philosophers (e.g., Descartes, Hume), and among contemporary figures (e.g., Foot, Hursthouse, Noddings). For ease of presentation, I have chosen to characterize natural law ethics (e.g., Aquinas) and the ethics of care (e.g., Noddings) as variations of virtue ethics, broadly construed. It should be noted, however, that some might prefer to consider these either as distinct types of character-centered approaches to ethics or as unique categories of ethics altogether.

9. See, e.g., the works of Kant, Ross, Rawls, Scanlon, and Korsgaard.

10. See, e.g., the works of Bentham, Mill, Sidgwick, Smart, Brandt, and Hare.

11. Especially, Confucian, Aristotelian, and Scholastic conceptions of virtue ethics.

centered on learning and applying *principles*, as deontology and utilitarianism suggest? Third, is *the good prior to the right*, as virtue ethics and utilitarianism suggest, or is *the right prior to the good*, as deontology suggests?[12] Fourth, must moral deliberations be *impartial* or may they be *partial*? In other words, are people naturally unencumbered moral agents, who have only natural duties (e.g., not to cause harm) and voluntary obligations (e.g., to keep one's promises), as deontology tends to suggest, or are they naturally encumbered moral agents with what Michael Sandel calls "obligations of solidarity"[13]—that is, special obligations, e.g., to one's family, religious community, or nation—as virtue ethics suggests?

These three approaches to ethical discourse are the essential touchstones for contemporary philosophers. With these points in mind, let me now use this three-part framework to elucidate the traditional Orthodox Christian conception of ethics.

Orthodox Christianity and Virtue Ethics

The traditional Orthodox Christian conception of ethics has strong affinities with the ancient virtue traditions of Greece and of Rome, as well as some distinctive affinities with classical Confucian virtue traditions. Nonetheless, even with respect to these affinities, it has a number of distinctive and key differences. For instance, like the Platonic and Aristotelian systems of ancient Greece, Orthodox Christianity conceives of human nature as teleologically-oriented and, thus, regards human life as objectively purposeful and inherently meaningful. Given its conceptions of God and of human nature, however, it retains a markedly different conception of the *telos* of human life. For instance, in place of a naturalistic conception of human flourishing that is contingent upon certain privileges of upbringing, as in Aristotle's conception of *eudaimonia*,[14] it posits a supernaturalistic concep-

12. To say that "the good is prior to the right" is to say, e.g., that (1) principles of right action are derived from a conception of the good life, and that (2) considerations concerning the common good may trump individual rights. To say that "the right is prior to the good" is to say, e.g., that (1) principles of right action are derived independently of a conception of the good life, and that (2) individual rights trump considerations concerning the common good. See Rawls, *Theory of Justice*, 30–33, 446–52; Sandel, "Political Liberalism."

13. See, e.g., Sandel, *Democracy's Discontent*, 11–17; "Political Liberalism"; Noddings, *Caring*, as well as the seminal works of Confucius, Mencius, and Xunzi.

14. See, e.g., Aristotle, *Nicomachean Ethics* 1.8.15 [1099a–b]; 7.13.3 [1153b].

tion of human flourishing that is available to everyone—namely, *theosis*, or *deification*, i.e., union with God.[15] To this extent, it is quite different from the philosophical systems of ancient Greece and of ancient Rome.

Systematically exploring these affinities and differences is interesting work.[16] For present purposes, however, I would simply like to highlight four key themes concerning (1) the soul, (2) the nature of virtue, (3) the significance of affective-motivational dispositions for a virtuous life, and (4) the significance of ritualistic practice for virtue acquisition and, consequently, human flourishing.

The Tripartite Soul

One key affinity between Orthodox Christian ethical discourse and ancient Greek virtue ethics is a common conceptual framework for discussing questions of philosophical anthropology. In Plato's system, this framework stems from a pair of distinctions. The first is a distinction between the body and the soul, or psychological aspect of human nature.[17] The second is a distinction among three parts of the soul: the intellective, the incensive, and the appetitive.[18]

Why would Plato bother making these distinctions, especially the distinctions among parts of the soul? The purpose is deeply practical: namely, to promote human flourishing. Ideally, such flourishing entails the well-being of the entire person, both body and soul. In ancient Greek philosophical discourse, medicine offers a method of caring for the body and ethics offers a method of caring for the soul.[19] To understand how to care

15. For philosophical descriptions of this doctrine with references to relevant patristic texts, see, e.g., Vitz and Espinoza, "Divine Energies"; Jacobs, "Eastern Orthodox Conception." For helpful theological descriptions, see, e.g., Mantzaridis, *Deification of Man*; Nellas, *Deification in Christ*.

16. For examples of some work done is this regard, see, e.g., Bradshaw, *Aristotle East and West*; Engelhardt, *Foundations of Christian Bioethics*; "Ritual, Virtue, and Human Flourishing"; *After God*; Vitz, *Turning East*; *Reforming the Art of Living*; "What is a Merciful Heart?"; Vitz and Goss, "Natural Law among Moral Strangers"; Vitz and Espinoza, "Divine Energies."

17. See, e.g., Plato, *Republic*, esp. book 4; *Phaedrus*; *Alcibiades I*.

18. See, e.g., Plato, *Republic*, esp. book 4; *Phaedrus*.

19. See, e.g., Plato, *Republic*, esp. book 4. For examples of traditional Christians expressing a similar view, see, e.g., Basil the Great, "Homily against Anger," esp. §1, 5; Isaac the Syrian, *Ascetical Homilies*, 128–33.

for the body, the physician distinguishes its various parts, identifies their proper functions, understands their diseased states, discovers methods of treatment, and learns when and how to apply these methods to promote the well-being of the body. Likewise, to understand how to care for the soul, the philosopher distinguishes its various parts, identifies their proper functions, understands their disordered states, discovers methods of treatment, and learns when and how to apply these methods to promote the well-being of the soul.

In short, according to ancient Greek philosophers like Plato, proper understandings of medicine and of ethics require a proper understanding of philosophical anthropology. Thus, Plato's account of the tripartite soul provides a conceptual framework of the human psyche with a very practical purpose.

With this practical aim in mind, the Church Fathers borrow and adapt this tripartite conception of the soul. For instance, in their discussions of virtues and vices, St. John Damascene, St. Philotheos of Sinai, Ilias the Presbyter, and St. Peter of Damaskos explicitly distinguish the three aspects of the soul: intellective, incensive, and appetitive, or "desiring."[20] St. Basil the Great employs the framework in his homily against anger, explaining how one can use the intellective part of the soul to regulate the incensive part. St. John Cassian does likewise in his discourse *On the Eight Vices*, distinguishing vices that afflict one part of the soul from vices that afflict "the whole soul." St. Maximos the Confessor uses the tripartite conceptual framework in similar ways in his *Four Hundred Texts on Love*, as do St. Isaac of Syria in his *Ascetical Homilies* and St. Gregory Palamas in his homilies.[21]

Since discussions of the relationship between Orthodox Christianity and philosophy are rife with misunderstandings, let me reiterate what I said above, for the sake of clarity. The Church Fathers *borrow and adapt* Plato's *conceptual framework* for discussing questions of philosophical anthropology. This phrasing is important because borrowing and adapting a philosopher's conceptual framework about a topic is not identical to endorsing the philosopher's views on the topic. I was careful to describe the Fathers' relationship to Plato's philosophical anthropology this way because they explicitly reject a number of Plato's views concerning the nature of

---

20. Palmer et al., *Philokalia*, 3:334–35 (cf. 20–21, 337, 340). See also Palmer et al., *Philokalia*, 3:63, 100, 253.

21. See, e.g., Basil, "Homily against Anger," §5; Palmer et al., *Philokalia*, 1:72–93; 2:48–113; Isaac the Syrian, *Ascetical Homilies*; Palamas, *Homilies*.

the human person. For the sake of brevity, let me simply highlight two. First, the Church Fathers adopt the conceptual distinction between body and soul, but reject the gnostic aspects of Plato's ontology, according to which the person is the soul and the body is its prison.[22] On the patristic account, a human being, properly constituted, is a *union* of body and soul, as evinced clearly in the doctrine of the resurrection. Second, the Fathers adopt the conceptual distinction between the intellective, incensive, and appetitive parts of the soul, but have notably different understandings both of the operations and of the aims of these parts of the soul. Consider, for instance, St. Maximos's claim that a "soul's motivation is rightly ordered when its desiring power is subordinated to self-control, when its incensive power rejects hatred and cleaves to love, and when its power of intelligence, through prayer and spiritual contemplation, advances toward God."[23] In this passage, St. Maximos offers a paradigmatic and distinctively Christian characterization of the operations and the aims of the incensive and intellective powers of the soul.[24]

In other words, the Church Fathers appropriate the *rhetoric* of Plato's philosophical anthropology insofar as it provides useful conceptual resources both for distinguishing different aspects of human nature, and for clarifying the proper means of caring for the soul. But they do so without endorsing the entirety of the *substance* of Plato's philosophical anthology, because they have fundamental disagreements with ancient Greek philosophers both about the nature of God and about human nature. Nonetheless, there remain key conceptual affinities between traditional Orthodox Christianity and ancient Greek philosophers about the nature of soul and related concepts like the virtues, as I will explain presently.

The Virtues

The English term "virtue" is a cognate of the Latin term *virtus*, which ancient and medieval philosophers used to translate the Greek term for excellence,

---

22. See Plato, *Pheado* 82e.

23. Palmer et al., *Philokalia*, 2:102.

24. To these two, we might also add a third key difference: namely, that although Plato's framework is a principal one used by the Church Fathers, it is not the only one. For instance, St. Theodoros characterizes the soul as having two aspects: the contemplative and the practical. See, e.g., Palmer et al., *Philokalia*, 1:47. See also Veniamin's comments on Palamas's homilies (e.g., Palamas, *Homilies*, 534n32). Regarding other differences, see, e.g., Palamas, *Homilies*, 546n117.

aretē. On the ancient Greek account, virtues are excellent dispositions[25] both of the different parts of the soul and of the soul itself. For instance, on Plato's account, the principal virtue of the intellective part is wisdom, the principal virtue of the incensive part is courage, the principal virtue of the appetitive part is temperance, and the principal virtue of the entire soul is justice, or righteousness (*dikaiosynē*), which is manifested when each of its parts is functioning excellently.

The Church Fathers characterize the virtues similarly, as dispositional states[26] of the soul and its various parts. For instance, St. Isaac of Syria describes virtue as "the natural health of the soul," St. Gregory Palamas suggests that each Christian is called to acquire "every virtue" in the image of Christ.[27] In a similar vein, St. Peter of Damaskos devotes a section of his "Treasury of Divine Knowledge" to the four cardinal virtues, which, he says, "constitute an image of the heavenly man." In fact, he not only identifies these virtues but also explains both their relationship to various parts of the soul and their nature as states between two unnatural passions.[28] St. John Damascene, St. Maximos the Confessor, and St. Philotheos of Sinai also explicitly discuss the nature and need for acquiring the cardinal virtues.[29] Evidently aware that their readers will be familiar with these virtues, other writers—e.g., Evagrius, St. Hesychios the Priest, St. Diodochos of Photiki—simply refer to "the four virtues," "the fourfold nature of the virtue," or the like.[30]

What's more, acquiring the virtues is emphasized not only in the Church's ascetic, but also in its sacramental way of life as evinced, for example, by St. Basil's emphasis on "the increase of virtue and perfection" as an aim of receiving the Eucharist.[31]

25. For a paradigmatic description of the nature of virtues as habitual dispositions of the soul, see Aristotle, *Nicomachean Ethics* esp. 2.1–5; 3.10–12.

26. For paradigmatic patristic descriptions of virtues—and more frequently of their correlative vices, or passions—as dispositions of the soul, see, e.g., Palmer et al., *Philokalia*, 2:261, 338; 3:160–61, 181–84, 227–28 (cf. 203–6, 251–53); Climacus, *Ladder* 15.74; 26.65. See also Isaac the Syrian, *Ascetical Homilies*, 295–98, 380–81; Palmer et al., *Philokalia*, 1:236–37, 248, 290–91; 2:39–40, 371–72.

27. Isaac the Syrian, *Ascetical Homilies*, 129–30; Palamas, *Homilies*, 213–14, 240, 376 (cf. 259–65).

28. Palmer et al., *Philokalia*, 3:100–101.

29. Palmer et al., *Philokalia*, 2:334 (cf. 341). See also 2:78; 3:23.

30. Palmer et al., *Philokalia*, 1:57, 162, 168, 272.

31. Isaac the Syrian, *Ascetical Homilies*, 129–30; Palamas, *Homilies*, 213–14, 240, 376

The relationship between the conception of virtue among ancient Greek philosophers, on the one hand, and the conception of virtue among the Church Fathers, on the other, is like that between the philosophical anthropology of Plato and the philosophical anthropology of the Church Fathers, as follows. The Fathers appropriate the *rhetoric* of the ancient Greek philosophers insofar as it provides useful conceptual resources for diagnosing the state of a people's souls and for prescribing therapeutic ascetic practices to heal them. But they do so without endorsing the entirety of the *substance* of their views because of their fundamental disagreements with ancient Greek philosophers concerning the nature of human excellence. In an effort both to be brief and yet to highlight the wide scope of the differences, let me simply identify five. First, as I mentioned above, Christians identify a different *telos* of human life: namely, *theosis*, or *deification*, i.e., union with God.[32] Second, they identify a distinct human exemplar, Jesus Christ.[33] Third, and consequently, they recognize fully virtuous people both as those who resemble God, as Plato emphasizes,[34] and as those who are excellent representatives of their class of beings, as Aristotle emphasizes.[35] Fourth, also stemming from the second difference, they recognize a different catalog of virtues—emphasizing, e.g., love as a principal virtue of the incensive power of the soul. Fourth, they recognize God as the ultimate source of human virtue, both potentially and actually.[36] Consequently, they emphasize the necessity of grace: what Christ is by nature, every person is called to be by grace.[37]

Explaining the nature of these differences would require a series of interesting and important projects. In this chapter, however, I would like to

(cf. 259–65).

32. For philosophical descriptions of this doctrine with references to relevant patristic texts, see, e.g., Vitz and Espinoza, "Divine Energies"; Jacobs, "Eastern Orthodox Conception"; Palmer et al., *Philokalia*, 2:40.

33. Regarding the significance of orthodox Christology for the traditional Christian conception of ethics, see, e.g., Vitz, *Reforming the Art of Living*; Vitz and Espinoza, "Divine Energies."

34. See, e.g., Russell, "Virtue as 'Likeness to God.'"

35. For a more detailed explanation of this point, see Vitz, "What is a Merciful Heart?"

36. See, e.g., Palamas, *Homilies*, 18; Climacus, *Ladder* 23.16; Palmer et al., *Philokalia*, 2:261.

37. See, e.g., Damascene, *De Fide Orthodoxa* 4.15; Palmer et al., *Philokalia*, 2:230. For similar patristic references, see Mantzaridis, *Deification of Man*; Panayiotis Nellas, *Deification in Christ*; Vitz and Espinoza, "Divine Energies," 487n45.

focus not on these more theoretical issues, but on one that is more practical. To attain the ultimate human *telos* requires the excellence of the intellective faculty—or, more specifically, of the *noetic* (as opposed to the *dianoetic*) aspect of the intellective faculty.[38] For that part to function excellently, however, one must first tame "the passions," a concept that I will turn to next.

The Passions[39]

One distinctive feature of ancient Greek virtue ethics is its emphasis on the need to cultivate not merely the rational, but also the irrational aspects of the soul: i.e., the incensive and appetitive faculties. This entails cultivating not only one's desires, but also one's affective-motivational dispositions. For instance, as Aristotle notes, having the right feelings "at the right times, about the right things, toward the right people, for the right end, and in the right way is the intermediate and best condition," that "is proper to virtue."[40]

One sees a similar, and even more noteworthy, emphasis on this theme in the Stoic concern with "the passions." The Stoics distinguished two types of human affections: namely, (1) *pathē*, like anger, delight at the misery of others, fear, and sorrow, and (2) *eupathē*, like wishing, joy, and watchfulness.[41] On their account, a key aspect of the good life is for a person to acquire the virtue of *apatheia*. To do so, one must eradicate the *pathē*, which are contrary to nature and bring disorder to the soul, and cultivate the *eupathē*, which are in accordance with nature and bring order to the soul.[42]

The Church Fathers express a similar concern. They recognize that the ability to cultivate the virtues is impeded by "the passions," which they characterize as (1) violent activities of the soul that are (2) not properly

38. The former is the principal faculty by which one "mystically" communes with God; the latter is the principal faculty by which one engages in discursive reasoning.

39. The following explanation of the passions is adapted from Vitz, "What is a Merciful Heart?"; "Situationism, Skepticism, and Asceticism." See Fagerberg, *On Liturgical Asceticism*, esp. 27–64.

40. Aristotle, *Nicomachean Ethics* 2.6.10–12 [1106b].

41. See, e.g., Annas, *Hellenistic Philosophy of Mind*, 114–15; Cottingham, *Philosophy and the Good Life*, 55–57; Pereboom, "Stoic Therapy," 594–98; Vitz, *Reforming the Art of Living*, 43.

42. See, e.g., Cicero, *De Officiis* 1.89; 2.2, 59; Seneca, "On Tranquillity of Mind" 2.4; 17.12.

directed primarily by the soul's intellective, or more specifically its noetic, power and, consequently, are both (3) contrary to nature, in the ancient teleological sense, as opposed to the contemporary biological sense, of the term, and (4) disobedient to the Word.[43] For instance, the author of *The Didache* exhorts Christians to eradicate anger, jealousy, lust, avarice, and arrogance.[44] St. Poemen echoes this concern, noting that the passions are disorders of the soul when he says, "God has given this way of life to Israel: to abstain from everything which is contrary to nature, that is to say, anger, fits of passion, jealousy, hatred and slandering the brethren."[45] One finds similar kinds of concerns with eradicating incensive passions in the writings of St. Basil the Great, St. Gregory Nazianzus, St. John the Dwarf, St. Isidore the Priest, St. Nilus, St. Isaac of Syria, and St. Peter of Damaskos.[46] In a similar vein, St. John Cassian and St. Gregory Palamas express a concern with eradicating not only irascible passions, like anger, dejection, and listlessness, but also concupiscible passions, like gluttony, lust, avarice, self-esteem, and pride.[47]

The Church Fathers are concerned not merely with eradicating the passions, but also—and more importantly—with cultivating penitential affective-motivational dispositions that purify the heart, like fear of God and compunction for sins, and, most importantly with cultivating Christlike affective-motivational dispositions aimed at perfecting the heart, like inner peace (*hesychia*) and dispassion (*apatheia*), as Abba Doulas, Abba Rufus, and St. Maximos suggest.[48] The proximate goal of this process is to

43. See, e.g., Clement of Alexandria, *Stromata* 2.12; John of Damascus, *De Fide Orthodoxa* 2.22; Fagerberg, *On Liturgical Asceticism*, 29. Examples of the "passions" include, e.g., anger (Matt 5:22–24; Jas 1:19), lust (Matt 5:27–30), vainglory (Matt 18:1–4; Mark 9:33–37; Luke 9:46–48), worry (Matt 6:25–34; 13:22; Luke 8:14; 12:22–32; Mark 4:19 [cf. Matt 11:28–30; 19:16–22; Mark 10:17–22; Luke 18:18–23]), profane fear (Matt 10:26, 28; Luke 12:4), unforgivingness (Matt 18:23–35), as well as bitterness, enviousness, ambition, and other self-indulgent desires (Jas 3:14–15; 4:1–3). For similar examples, see, e.g., Matt 6:19–21; 1 Cor 11:1; Gal 5:25.

44. Lightfoot and Harmer, *Apostolic Fathers*, 150–51.

45. Ward, *Sayings of the Desert Fathers*, 176 (cf. 179).

46. See, e.g., Basil the Great, "Homily against Anger"; Gregory of Nazianzus, *Poems on Scripture*, 81–121 (cf. 129); Ward, *Sayings of the Desert Fathers*, 86, 96, 153, 155 (cf. 156); Isaac the Syrian, *Ascetical Homilies*, 128–33, 276–80, 439–40 (cf. 468); Palmer et al., *Philokalia*, 3:205–6.

47. Palmer et al., *Philokalia*, 1:72–93; Palamas, *Homilies*, 260–65, 450–53.

48. See, e.g., Ward, *Sayings of the Desert Fathers*, 55, 210; Palmer et al., *Philokalia*, 2:53, 56.

reach the height of dispassion and to acquire what St. Isaac of Syria calls a "merciful heart," or what St. Maximos alludes to as a heart that is perfected and "completely transformed into divine love."[49] Without such love, St. Gregory Palamas says, echoing St. Paul (1 Cor 13), all the other virtues are useless and senseless.[50]

If the Church Fathers are concerned with the positive project of cultivating pro-social affective-motivational dispositions, then why do they spend as much time as they do on the negative project of eradicating "the passions"? The reason lies at the root of the passions and their relationship to the more Christ-like affective-motivational dispositions. The primary cause of the passions is what the ascetic fathers and mothers called "self-love," or "a senseless love of one's body and an impassioned attachment to it."[51] The most prominent secondary causes of the passions are pleasure, wealth, and praise.[52] In essence, these secondary causes are inordinate exercises of the appetitive power of the soul, directed at particular kinds of objects (e.g., food, drink, sex, money, honor, etc.), for the purpose of attempting to satiate "self-love," in their technical sense of the term. As a result, a person who is preoccupied with self-love will be preoccupied with trying to satisfy his or her desires for pleasure, for wealth, and for praise.

Consequently, such a person will fail to attend to, let alone to cultivate, the other-regarding affective-motivational dispositions and their corresponding virtues. Subsequently, such a person will tend to see others, for instance, either as rivals or as impediments to satisfying the desires of self-love. Thus, when confronted with others who make claims to those goods that such a person possesses or aims to possess, he or she will be disposed not to compassion but to some passion that inhibits love of neighbor. Thus, eradicating "the passions" is an ordinary pre-condition for cultivating a Christ-like heart—hence the Fathers' principal concern with the negative projects and secondary concern with the positive project. In other words, just as skillful physicians must stabilize their patients before they can begin to promote their health, let alone help them to maximize their well-being in the service of others, so too spiritual fathers and mothers must work to stabilize the souls of their children before they can begin to promote their

49. Isaac the Syrian, *Ascetical Homilies*, 491–98; Palmer et al., *Philokalia*, 2:70, 73, 82; Palamas, *Homilies*, 30–33, 346–52.

50. Palamas, *Homilies*, 29 (cf. 3, 33).

51. Palmer et al., *Philokalia*, 2:336.

52. Palmer et al., *Philokalia*, 2:339.

spiritual health, let alone lead them into the difficult work of Christ-like service to others.

To this point, I have highlighted three key conceptual similarities between traditional Orthodox Christianity and the virtue ethics of ancient Greece and ancient Rome. Before concluding this section, let me highlight one final conceptual similarity, this one from farther east, between Orthodox Christianity and classical Confucian virtue ethics, since this has important implications for a contemporary debate that I discuss briefly in the final section.

Ritual

One particularly distinctive element of classical Confucian virtue ethics[53] is the significance of ritual for the cultivation of character, in general, and the virtue of benevolence, or humaneness, in particular. To explain this distinctive element, let me say something briefly both about ritual (*li*) and about the virtue of benevolence (*ren*).[54]

In classical Confucianism, the term "ritual" (*li*) refers to a set of cultural prescriptions that govern a wide variety of human behavior "involving rite, ceremony, manners, or general deportment, that bind human beings and spirits together in networks of interacting roles within the family, within society, and with the numinous realm beyond."[55] These prescriptions include both (1) more formal and ornate *ceremonial rituals* governing family life and affairs of state, as well as (2) more mundane and informal *minute rituals* concerning manners, decorum, and etiquette.[56]

They are, however, more than mere customs or mores. They are careful aspects of human artifice designed to cultivate virtuous people, both individually and collectively.[57] On a classical Confucian view, as on an Aristotelian view, people are not born virtuous, but are born with the

53. I have in mind here the conceptions of character and of the virtues that are expressed in the seminal works of Confucius, Mencius, and Xunzi.

54. The following brief description of classical Confucian ethics is adapted from Vitz, "Character, Culture, and the Future."

55. Schwartz, *World of Thought*, 67. See Kim, "Early Confucianism"; Slingerland, "Situationist Critique."

56. See, Fan, "Confucian Ritualization"; Eno, *Confucian Creation of Heaven*; Hutton, "Character, Situationism," 56n34; Olberding, "Etiquette," 438; Slingerland, "Situationist Critique," 410; Li, "*Li* as Cultural Grammar."

57. See Slingerland, "Situationist Critique," 410.

potential to become virtuous. Their characters are shaped, for better or for worse, "from the steady accumulation of . . . seemingly minor events."[58] In other words, people become either virtuous or vicious depending both on whether and on how they participate in rituals that are designed to cultivate human excellence. Thus, on a Confucian account, it is necessary not merely to perform rituals, but to perform the *right kinds* of rituals, and to perform them well, such that in so doing one manifests both the proper external *form* and also the proper *inner disposition*.[59] Hence, one of the aims of Confucian ritual practice is to cultivate people's affective-motivational dispositions, in what Plato could call the irrational parts of the soul.[60] In particular, Confucian ritual practice aims to cultivate "virtuous emotions such as love, reverence, humility, gratitude, faith . . . loyalty,"[61] and, most importantly, the virtue of benevolence, or humaneness (*ren*), a principal affective-motivational disposition aimed at caring for others.[62] What's more, Confucian rituals aim not merely to cultivate the virtue of benevolence but to "extend" it such that it becomes more expansive in scope, thereby forming people who are motivated to care for a wider variety of people.[63]

In short, on classical Confucian accounts, the character both of people (i.e., of individuals) and, consequently, of a people (i.e., of society) will be determined, in large part, by the quality of the rituals in which they participate.[64] For this reason, classical Chinese philosophers like Confucius and Xunzi are deeply attuned to the need to develop a set of rituals that,

58. Kim, "Early Confucianism," 479 (cf. Olberding, "Etiquette," 443).

59. See, e.g., Confucius, "Analects," 8–9; Xunzi, "Xunzi," 280, 284 (cf. Kim, "Early Confucianism," 480). See also Mower, "Situationism and Confucian Virtue Ethics," 122.

60. Mower, "Situationism and Confucian Virtue Ethics," 118–19. See Xunzi, "Xunzi," 257, 274, 280; Slingerland, "Situationist Critique," 410–11; Sarkissian, "Confucius and the Effortless Life," 6.

61. Sarkissian, "Confucius and the Effortless Life," 3. Regarding aretaic obligations to cultivate affective-motivational dispositions, see Vitz, "What is a Merciful Heart?"; Vitz and Espinoza, "Divine Energies."

62. See Mower, "Situationism and Confucian Virtue Ethics," 126–27; Hutton, "Character, Situationism," 40. Thus, the concept of *ren* in Confucian virtue ethics is akin to the concept of *humanity* in Humean virtue ethics and to the concept of *care* in certain versions of feminist ethics. Regarding the latter, see, e.g., Pang-White, "Reconstructing Modern Ethics"; Li, "Confucian Concept of Jen."

63. See, e.g., Mencius, "Mengzi," 118–23; Slingerland, "Situationist Critique," 406–410.

64. See Sarkissian, "Confucius and the Effortless Life," 12.

cumulatively, help to constitute a distinctive "way of life,"[65] designed to help people develop hearts properly attuned to beauty and goodness.[66]

Orthodox Christianity also has a distinctively ritualistic orientation. Like classical Confucian philosophers, the Church Fathers prescribe specific rituals for cultivating virtues. That is, they prescribe (1) actions, (2) involving the mind and the body, (3) that people repeat regularly, (4) within specific contexts, (5) under specific conditions, (6) for the purpose not merely of cultivating character, in general, but of cultivating a Christ-like heart by which people are united in love both to God and to their neighbors. This comprehensive system of rituals, *embodying* authentic Christian doctrine, constitutes a distinctively Christian *way of life* that, according to the Church Fathers, distinguishes the "true philosophy" of Christianity from the philosophical systems of the Greeks and the Romans.[67]

Orthodox Christian Virtue Ethics and Contemporary Social Psychology

Let me conclude by describing briefly one way that this conception of Orthodox Christian ethics is significant for a contemporary debate at the intersection of philosophy and psychology. For the past two decades, philosophers have been developing a "situationist challenge" to virtue ethics.

65. Kim, "Early Confucianism," 48. See Slingerland, "Situationist Critique"; Olberding, "Etiquette."

66. See Mower, "Situationism and Confucian Virtue Ethics," 122.

67. In my experience, it is fairly common for Orthodox Christians to approach discussions of philosophy with a critical—sometimes all-too-critical—eye. So, let me note three things that I did *not* say above. First, I did not say that traditional Orthodox Christianity is attempting to offer a *philosophical theory* of ethics. I merely said that is has key affinities with virtue ethics, the significance of which will be made clear presently. Second, I did not say that traditional Orthodox Christianity is simply a derivative form of Greek or Roman virtue ethics dressed in Christian garb. I did not say that because, like the Fathers, I do not believe it. Third, I did not say that there is a *causal* relationship between Confucian conceptions of ritual and the Orthodox Christian uses of ritual. I merely noted an affinity between the conceptions of moral psychology and moral education between the Far East (i.e., classical Chinese philosophy) and the Near East (i.e., Orthodox Christianity), one which distinguishes each from "the West" (i.e., the philosophers of ancient Greece and Rome, as well as those of eighteenth-century Germany, like Kant, and nineteenth-century Britain, like Mill). In so doing, I have been careful to suggest that Orthodox Christianity conceives of ethics as a therapeutically-oriented discipline more akin to medicine than as a regulatively-oriented discipline like law—or, more importantly, as a punitively-oriented discipline like criminal law.

Proponents of the challenge highlight evidence from a series of studies in social psychology, which suggests that people's behavior is more probably predicted not in light of their character traits,[68] but in light of various features of their situations—e.g., whether they are in a hurry, are in a positive affective state, perceive a diffusion of responsibility, and so forth. This evidence, they argue, is sufficiently compelling to show that traditional virtue ethics is empirically inadequate.[69]

Why is the situationist challenge significant for Orthodox Christianity? The reason is pretty straightforward: if proponents of the challenge are right, there is compelling empirical evidence that Orthodox Christianity's emphasis on "the practice of the virtues" is rather deeply misguided. Thus, Orthodox Christians of today ought to respond to this challenge to their way of life as Orthodox Christians of prior times responded to similar challenges: namely, by developing a response that explains why the challenge is erroneous.

Why is Orthodox Christianity significant for philosophers interested in the situationist challenge? The essence of the answer to this question is pretty straightforward as well: Orthodox Christianity is remarkably well-suited to offer a compelling response to the situationist challenge in two ways. The first is Orthodoxy's conception of human nature, according to which (1) human beings in their fallen state are beleaguered by the passions, such that they are prone to the kinds of moral failings that are revealed in the studies on which the situationist challenge depends (e.g., Rom 7:14–24),[70] and (2) human beings are inherently social, such that their characters and behaviors rely on interdependent communal support. The second is that Orthodoxy Christianity's liturgical ascetic[71] way of life

---

68. Specifically, their "global" character traits—see Doris, *Lack of Character*; Harman, "Moral Philosophy Meets Social Psychology"; "Non-Existence of Character Traits"; Miller, *Character Gap*.

69. Given spacing limits for the purpose of this chapter, my description of the challenge here is exceedingly brief. For details concerning the details of the challenge, the empirical evidence, and the argument, see, e.g., Doris, *Lack of Character*; Harman, "Moral Philosophy Meets Social Psychology"; "Non-Existence of Character Traits." For a more popularly accessible presentation of the current state of the challenge, see Miller, *Character Gap*.

70. See Isaac the Syrian, *Ascetical Homilies*, 124–25, 127–33, 276–80, 283, 290–91; Palmer et al., *Philokalia*, 1:155; 2:167–68, 243–48; 3:75, 77, 236, 302; Palamas, *Homilies*, 101–2.

71. For an excellent and accessible description of this way of life, see Fagerberg, *On Liturgical Asceticism*.

is constituted by a socially rich set of rituals aimed at healing the soul by reforming its affective-motivational dispositions and, consequently, cultivating virtues. To illustrate these points in ways that might be clearer to readers less familiar with Orthodox faith and practice, let me restate them in light of other philosophical responses to the situationist challenge. Like Humean virtue ethics, Orthodox Christian virtue ethics is committed to a weaker conception of the motivational self-sufficiency of character and a stronger conception of the sustaining social contribution to character.[72] And like Confucian virtue ethics, Orthodox Christianity claims that human beings are born with the capacity to develop virtues[73] and that the development of this potential requires "long term-intensive training."[74] In essence, Orthodox Christian ethics is significant for philosophers interested in the situationist challenge in the same way that Humean and Confucian virtue ethics are. Thus, contemporary philosophers ought to respond to the Orthodox conception of virtue ethics as they have to other conceptions of virtue ethics: namely, by seeking to understand the view charitably so that they can evaluate it accurately.

There is obviously much more that can, and ought, to be said on this subject. For the purposes of the present volume, however, let me bring this chapter to a close. My aim has been to help develop the groundwork for greater dialogue on ethical issues at the intersection of philosophy, psychology, and the neptic tradition of Orthodox Christianity. I hope that in the space available, I have been able to make important progress toward accomplishing at least this modest task.

Bibliography

Annas, Julia. *Hellenistic Philosophy of Mind*. Berkeley, CA: University of California Press, 1992.
Aristotle. *Nicomachean Ethics*. In *The Basic Works of Aristotle*, edited by R. McKeon, 927–1112. Translated by W. D. Ross. New York: Random House, 1941.
Baron, Marcia W., et al. *Three Methods of Ethics: A Debate*. Malden, MA: Blackwell, 1997.

72. See Merritt, "Virtue Ethics."

73. See, e.g., Hutton, "Character, Situationism"; Mower, "Situationism and Confucian Virtue Ethics."

74. See, e.g., Slingerland, "Situationist Critique," 404–5; Sarkissian, "Confucius and the Effortless Life," 11; Hutton, "Character, Situationism," 53n15; Mencius, "Mengzi," 125–29, 149–51. Regarding similar claims about these first three points, see Aristotle, *Nicomachean Ethics* 2.1 [1103a–4a].

Basil the Great. "Homily against Anger." In *On the Human Condition*, by Basil the Great, 81–92. Translated by Nonna Verna Harrison. Crestwood, NY: St. Vladimir's Seminary Press, 2005.

Batson, C. Daniel. *Altruism in Humans*. Oxford: Oxford University Press, 2011.

Bradshaw, David. *Aristotle East and West: Metaphysics and the Division of Christendom*. Cambridge: Cambridge University Press, 2004.

Cicero, Marcus Tullius. *De Officiis*. Translated by Jeffery Henderson. Cambridge: Harvard University Press, 2005.

———. *Tusculan Disputations*. Translated by J. E. King. Cambridge: Harvard University Press, 2001.

Clement of Alexandria. "The Stromata." In Vol. 2 of *Anti-Nicene Fathers*, edited and translated by Philip Schaff, 638–1237. Grand Rapids: Eerdmans, 2001.

Confucius. "The Analects." In *Readings in Classical Chinese Philosophy*, edited by P. J. Ivanhoe and B. W. Van Norden, 1–57. Rev. ed. Indianapolis: Hackett, 2005.

Cottingham, John. *Philosophy and the Good Life: Reason and the Passions in Greek, Cartesian, and Psychoanalytic Ethics*. Cambridge: Cambridge University Press, 1998.

Doris, John. *Lack of Character*. Oxford: Oxford University Press, 2002.

Engelhardt, H. Tristram. *After God: Morality and Bioethics in a Secular Age*. Crestwood, NY: St. Vladimir's Seminary Press, 2014.

———. *The Foundations of Christian Bioethics*. Lisse: Swetz and Zeitlinger, 2000.

———. "Ritual, Virtue, and Human Flourishing: Rites as Bearers of Meaning." In *Ritual and the Moral Life: Reclaiming the Tradition*, edited by David Solomon, et al., 29–51. Dordrecht: Springer, 2012.

Eno, Robert. *The Confucian Creation of Heaven*. New York: State University of New York Press, 1990.

Fagerberg, David. *On Liturgical Asceticism*. Washington, DC: Catholic University of America Press, 2013.

Fan, Ruiping. "Confucian Ritualization: How and Why?" In *Ritual and the Moral Life: Reclaiming the Tradition*, edited by David Solomon, et al., 143–58. Dordrecht: Springer, 2012.

Gregory of Nazianzus. *Poems on Scripture*. Translated by Brian Dunkle. Crestwood, NY: St. Vladimir's Seminary Press, 2012.

Harman, Gilbert. "Moral Philosophy Meets Social Psychology: Virtue Ethics and the Fundamental Attribution Error." *Proceedings of the Aristotelian Society* 99 (1999) 315–31.

———. "The Non-Existence of Character Traits." *Proceedings of the Aristotelian Society* 100 (2000) 223–26.

Hutton, Eric. "Character, Situationism, and Early Confucian Thought." *Philosophical Studies* 127 (2006) 37–58.

Isaac the Syrian. *The Ascetical Homilies of Saint Isaac the Syrian*. Translated by Holy Transfiguration Monastery. Rev. 2nd ed. Boston, MA: Holy Transfiguration Monastery, 2011.

Jacobs, Jonathan D. "An Eastern Orthodox Conception of Theosis and Human Nature." *Faith and Philosophy* 26 (2009) 615–27.

John Climacus. *The Ladder of Divine Ascent*. Rev. ed. Brookline, MA: Holy Transfiguration Monastery, 2001.

John of Damascus. *De Fide Orthodoxa*. In Vol. 9 of *Nicene and Post-Nicene Fathers*, Series 2, edited by Philip Schaff, 546–781. London: T & T Clark, 1898.

Kim, Richard. "Early Confucianism and Contemporary Moral Psychology." *Philosophy Compass* 11 (2016) 473–85.

Li, Chenyang. "The Confucian Concept of Jen and the Feminist Ethics of Care: A Comparative Study." *Hypatia* 9 (1994) 70–89.

———. "*Li* as Cultural Grammar: The Relation between *Li* and *Ren* in the *Analects.*" *Philosophy East and West* 57 (2007) 311–29.

Lightfoot, J. B., and J. R. Harmer. *The Apostolic Fathers.* Edited by Michael W. Holmes. 2nd ed. Baker, 1989.

Mantzaridis, Georgios I. *The Deification of Man: St. Gregory Palamas and the Orthodox Tradition.* Crestwood, NY: St. Vladimir's Seminary Press, 1984.

Mencius. "Mengzi." In *Readings in Classical Chinese Philosophy,* edited by P. J. Ivanhoe and B. W. Van Norden, 115–59. Rev. ed. Indianapolis: Hackett, 2005.

Merritt, Maria. "Virtue Ethics and Situationist Social Psychology." *Ethical Theory and Moral Practice* 3 (2000) 365–83.

Miller, Christian. *The Character Gap.* Oxford: Oxford University Press, 2018.

Mower, Deborah. "Situationism and Confucian Virtue Ethics." *Ethical Theory and Moral Practice* 16 (2013) 113–37.

Nellas, Panayiotis. *Deification in Christ: The Nature of the Human Person.* Crestwood, NY: St. Vladimir's Seminary Press, 1987.

Noddings, Nel. *Caring: A Relational Approach to Ethics and Moral Education.* 2nd ed. Berkeley, CA: University of California Press, 2013.

Olberding, Amy. "Etiquette: A Confucian Contribution to Moral Philosophy." *Ethics* 126 (2016) 422–46.

Palamas, Gregory. *The Homilies.* Edited and translated by Christopher Veniamin. Dalton, PA: Mount Tabor, 2016.

Palmer, Gerald, et al., eds. *The Philokalia.* 4 vols. London: Faber and Faber, 1979–1995.

Pang-White, Ann A. "Reconstructing Modern Ethics: Confucian Care Ethics." *Journal of Chinese Philosophy* 35 (2009) 210–27.

Petcu, Tudor. "The Unicity of Orthodox Spirituality." *Studia Humana* 4.3 (2015) 51–55.

Plato. *Complete Works.* Edited by John M. Cooper. Indianapolis: Hackett, 1997.

Rawls, John. *A Theory of Justice.* Cambridge, MA: Harvard University Press, 1971.

Russell, Daniel C. 2004. "Virtue as 'Likeness to God' in Plato and Seneca." *Journal of the History of Philosophy* 42.3 (2004) 241–60.

Sarkissian, Hagop. "Confucius and the Effortless Life of Virtue." *History of Philosophy Quarterly* 27 (2010) 1–16.

Sandel, Michael. *Democracy's Discontent.* Cambridge, MA: Harvard University Press, 1996.

———. "Political Liberalism." *Harvard Law Review* 107 (1994) 1765–94.

Sarkissian, Hagop. "Confucius and the Effortless Life of Virtue." *History of Philosophy Quarterly* 27 (2010) 1–16.

Schwartz, Benjamin. *The World of Thought in Ancient China.* Cambridge, MA: Harvard University Press, 1985.

Seneca. "On Tranquility of Mind." In *Moral Essays,* edited by G. P. Goold, 202–285. Translated by John W. Basore. Vol. 2. Cambridge: Harvard University Press.

Slingerland, Edward. "The Situationist Critique and Early Confucian Virtue Ethics." *Ethics* 121 (2011) 390–419.

Vitz, Rico. "Character, Culture, and the Future of Humean Virtue Ethics: Insights from Situationism and Confucianism." In *Hume's Moral Philosophy and Contemporary Psychology*, edited by Philip Reed and Rico Vitz, 91–114. London: Routledge, 2018.

——. *Reforming the Art of Living: Nature, Virtue, and Religion in Descartes's Epistemology*. Dordrecht: Springer, 2015.

——. "Situationism, Skepticism, and Asceticism." Presentation at the Association for Moral Education, Pasadena, CA, November 8, 2014.

——. *Turning East: Contemporary Philosophers and the Ancient Christian Faith*. Crestwood, NY: St. Vladimir's Seminary Press, 2012.

——. "'What is a Merciful Heart?' Affective-Motivational Aspects of the Second Love Command." *Faith and Philosophy* 34 (2017) 298–320.

Vitz, Rico, and Boaz Goss. "Natural Law among Moral Strangers." *Christian Bioethics* 20 (2014) 283–300.

Vitz, Rico, and Marissa Espinoza. "The Divine Energies and the 'End of Human Life.'" *American Catholic Philosophical Quarterly* 91 (2017) 473–89.

Ward, Benedicta, trans. *The Sayings of the Desert Fathers*. Kalamzoo, MI: Cistercian, 1975.

Xunzi. "The Xunzi." In *Readings in Classical Chinese Philosophy*, edited by Philip J. Ivanhoe and Bryan W. Van Norder, 255–307. 2nd ed. Indianapolis: Hackett, 2005.

8

Orthodoxy and Philosophy of Language

CHRISTOPH SCHNEIDER

Introduction

A great deal of twentieth-century philosophy was characterized by what has become known as the "linguistic turn." Although language had been studied before, it now became for the first time the main object of investigation, both in the analytic and the Continental traditions. Yet, at least in the analytic tradition, this heightened interest in language was not concomitant with a positive attitude towards its epistemic and intellectual reliability. Rather, the discovery of the fundamental importance of language for philosophy went hand in hand with the conviction that language, or at least a certain usage of language, constitutes an obstacle to a truthful understanding of reality. In fact, the turn to language in the twentieth century was largely the culmination of a long history of *pessimism* about language.[1]

Elisabeth Leiss divides the history of philosophy of language into four eras.[2] First, it is believed that language, human reason and the structure of the world are closely interrelated, and that language enables us to know the world at it is in itself (e.g., Heraclitus, Aristotle).[3] Second, with the rise of

1. Leiss, *Sprachphilosophie*, 70.

2. Leiss, *Sprachphilosophie*, 1–15. This division only applies to the dominant and most influential approaches to language in the history of ideas. There are also significant thinkers who did not follow these general trends—such as Johann Gottfried Herder, Johann Georg Hamann, and Wilhelm von Humboldt. For a similar, but by no means identical periodization of history from a semiotic perspective, see Deely, *Four Ages of Understanding*.

3. Coseriu, *Geschichte der Sprachphilosophie*, 24; Graeser, "Aristoteles."

nominalism in the late Middle Ages, language is devalued in the sense that it can no longer represent the world, but only our thoughts (e.g., Ockham).[4] Third, the relationship between language and thought is also problematized. It is argued that natural language represents our thoughts unreliably and that it thwarts clear and precise cognition. Philosophy becomes *philosophy of language*, because its primary task is now to purge language of its distorting effects. As Gottlob Frege puts it, we need to "break the domination of the word over the human spirit."[5] Proponents of both "ideal language philosophy" and "ordinary language philosophy" agree that language is in need of a therapy, but they disagree about the sort of treatment that is appropriate to cure the patient.[6] For ideal language philosophy, natural language and the philosophical confusions that it causes, can be compared to cancerous tissue that metastasizes. The unhealthy tissue needs to be replaced by healthy tissue—that is, by an artificial, constructed language that eliminates these shortcomings. Ordinary language philosophy, by contrast, sees a philosophical problem more like a neurosis. While patients suffering from cancer can be cured without knowing how they have acquired this disease, the neurotic is more actively involved in his treatment, because s/he needs to understand why s/he became neurotic. Fourth, since the attempt at curing language does not succeed, the peak of pessimism about language is reached. Language is now viewed as separated from both world and reason. Sentences are merely "strings of marks and noises used by human beings in the development and pursuit of social practices—practices which enabled people to achieve their ends, ends which do not include 'representing reality as it is in in itself.'"[7]

Despite the above-outlined tendency towards a philosophical devaluation of language, only few attempts have been made to develop a consistently theological theory of language. This essay makes a contribution towards an Orthodox philosophy of language. Drawing on Pavel Florensky (1882–1937) and Sergii Bulgakov (1871–1944), two representatives of Russian religious thought, I will focus on three aspects of the "meaning of meaning": meaning as *reference*, meaning as *use*, and meaning as *sense*.[8]

4. Leffler, *Wilhelm von Ockham*.

5. Frege, "Begriffsschrift," 7.

6. Rorty, "Introduction," 16.

7. Rorty, "Twenty-Five Years After," 373.

8. I will use the term "meaning" in the broad sense, as including these three dimensions of meaning (reference, use and sense). A different use of terminology is possible

I will show that the neglection of, or one-sided emphasis on, one of these three aspects, prevents the formation of a theologically convincing theory of linguistic meaning and generates forms of reductionism.

Meaning as Reference: Ideal Language Philosophy

In the 1920s and 30s, the logical positivists (or logical empiricists) pursued the project of an "ideal language philosophy." They reduced the task of philosophy to correcting the problematic ambiguities of natural language that obscure rational thinking and reliable knowledge about the world. Before they adopted Alfred Tarski's theory of truth, they were suspicious about the notion of truth. The questions of what makes true sentences true and how we are to conceive of the connection between language and the world, were regarded to lie outside the scope of scientific philosophy.[9] Rather, the purpose of the so-called "principle of verification" was to distinguish between meaningful and meaningless statements. According to A. J. Ayer, who introduced logical positivism to the English-speaking world, "a sentence had literal meaning if and only if the proposition it expressed was either *analytic* or *empirically verifiable*."[10]

As far as analytic propositions are concerned, the logical positivists had learned from Russell and Whitehead that logical formulas can be regarded as tautologies. They are not about the world and thus cannot be empirically verified or refuted.[11] Frege's new concept-notation (*Begriffss-*

---

as well as common. See Nöth, *Handbook of Semiotics*, 92–94. Among the many different semantic theories, some advocate a monist approach to meaning, in the sense that only one of these three aspects (reference, use *or* sense) is taken into consideration to explain the meaning of meaning. Other theories have a dualist or pluralist character and combine two or three dimensions (Nöth, *Handbook of Semiotics*, 96).

9. McGee, "Truth," 405–6.

10. Ayer, *Language, Truth, and Logic*, 5 (italics added). A more elaborate version of the principle of verification reads as follows: "We say that a sentence is factually significant to any given person, if, and only if, he knows how to verify the proposition which it purports to express—that is, if he knows what observations would lead him, under certain conditions, to accept the proposition as being true, or reject it as being false. If, on the other hand, the putative proposition is of such a character that the assumption of its truth or falsehood, is consistent with any assumption whatsoever concerning the nature of his future experience, then, as far as he is concerned, it is, if not a tautology, a mere pseudo-proposition. The sentence expressing it may be emotionally significant to him; but it is not literally significant" (Ayer, *Language, Truth, and Logic*, 35).

11. Chapman, *Language and Empiricism*, 13.

chrift) for first-order predicate logic served as a tool for philosophy "to break the domination of the word over the human spirit."[12] The symbolic notation used in formal logic was supposed to eradicate the ambiguities of natural language such as the polysemy of word meaning, and the frequent discrepancy between grammatical and logical structure. Thought, the positivists believed, had to be freed from the imprecision of ordinary language. What was required was an analytically reconstructed language, an "ideal language" that could render the underlying logical relationships transparent and thus liberate pure thought from misconceptions.

Regarding the empirical verifiability of a sentence, the logical positivists were influenced by Locke and Hume, and to some extent by Wittgenstein's *Tractatus*. However, the concept of verifiability proved rather complex and they introduced some subtle qualifications to render it philosophically more plausible. They drew a distinction between *practical verifiability* and *verifiability in principle*, and argued that only the latter was required to make a sentence meaningful.[13] Furthermore, they realized that verifiability could be understood in the *strong* or in the *weak* sense: if a proposition is verifiable in the strong sense, "its truth could be conclusively established in experience"; and it is verifiable in the weak sense, "if it is possible for experience to render it probable."[14] According to Ayer, the weak version of the principle was sufficient to establish the meaningfulness of a sentence.[15] Thus, propositions are either analytic (tautologies), or probable hypotheses. Metaphysical and theological sentences, they argued, fall into neither of these two categories and are therefore literally nonsensical. At best, they express the attitude a person has adopted towards life and can only be of emotive, ethical, or aesthetic significance.[16]

For Pavel Florensky, the aim to construct an ideal language philosophy results from a one-sided emphasis on the "thingness" of language: language is viewed exclusively as *ergon*, as something objective, immovable, and universal. Thus, he criticized the Estonian linguist Iakov Lintsbakh (1874–1953), who—like the logical positivists—endeavoured to develop a philosophically precise language that overcomes the ambiguities of natural

12. Frege, "Begriffsschrift," 7.

13. Ayer, *Language, Truth, and Logic*, 36.

14. Ayer, *Language, Truth, and Logic*, 37.

15. The problems of the verification principal were discussed in detail by Hempel, "Empiricist Criteria of Cognitive Significance."

16. Carnap, "Elimination of Metaphysics," 78–79.

language.[17] Lintsbakh sought to eliminate the imprecision of vocabulary and syntax by means of mathematical and geometrical rules, and even considered the lack of symmetry in the classification of sounds in natural language a deficiency. Florensky rejects this project as a merciless, inhuman and perverse attempt to attack the central gift of humankind, our holiest good. Without a linguistically mediated self-manifestation, the self would no longer be an object even to itself, and thus be without reality.[18] Lintsbakh, Florensky argues, misses the organic, historically grown character of language, and takes a reductive and merely functional approach to language.

Florensky is equally critical of the attempt to define linguistic meaning in terms of the empirical verifiability of a sentence. At the beginning of the movement, the logical positivists believed in the possibility of drawing an unambiguous distinction between neutral, observational sets of facts that could not be questioned by any rational observer, and explanatory, scientific theories that need to be verified on the basis of these facts. Florensky questions any simplistic opposition between *describing* (*opisyvat'*) and *explaining* (*ob"iasniat'*) reality.[19] He argues that if by "explaining something" we mean that something can be explained exhaustively, then this kind of explanation can be found neither in the ordinary language of everyday life, nor in the sciences. Rather, an explanation is a *specific mode of description*, a description that is particularly compact, and the result of a particularly penetrating concentration.[20] Every explanation is conditional, i.e., diachronically and synchronically contingent, including scientific theories. Explanations are perspectival, they constitute models, symbols and fictive images that shape our perception of the world. The explanation is believed to be apodictic, but in fact only has a hypothetical character.[21]

Accordingly, Florensky understands the history of science not in terms of a continuous evolution, but as a series of convulsions, destructions, upheavals, explosions and catastrophes. Anticipating insights by Thomas Kuhn, he writes that "the history of science is a permanent revolution (*permanentnaia revoliutsiia*)."[22] Despite this insight, Florensky remarks,

17. Lintsbakh, *Printsipy filosofskogo iazyka.*
18. Florensky, "Antinomiia iazyka," 173–74.
19. Florensky, "Dialektika," 118.
20. Florensky, "Dialektika," 118.
21. Florensky, "Nauka kak simvolicheskoe opisanie," 112.
22. Florensky, "Dialektika," 120 (my translation).

the sciences still pursue the ideal of an unambiguous method, and demand permanence and immutability. But it is the dynamism and flux of *time* that unmasks this ideal as an illusion, and that relativizes the significance of the schematic constructions by means of which we seek to achieve epistemically reliable knowledge about the world. Once the reductive character of science is recognized, it becomes clear that *time* and *life* must become a "method." For Florensky, it is the task of philosophy and (Platonic) dialectic to develop such a method.[23] The dependence of meaning on time and context is an important aspect of the *pragmatic* dimension of linguistic meaning, which is the focus of the next section.

It follows from this that it is not possible to evaluate rival scientific theories in a fully rational way by checking them against, neutral, uncontested observational facts or sensory data. If a description and an explanation are not qualitatively different kinds of discourse, verification can no longer serve as a criterion to distinguish between meaningful and meaningless statements. As Florensky notices, every explanation is (also) a description, and every description is (also) an explanation. Otto Neurath, a founding member of the Vienna Circle and logical positivism, came to the same conclusion and challenged the radical empiricism of his colleagues. He questioned the belief that there is a clear-cut distinction between *protocol sentences* that do not need to be verified because they record immediate or atomic experiences, and *interpretations* of protocol sentences that do require verification. Neurath argued that it is problematic to regard protocol sentences as the manifestation of private sense experience because language is always inter-subjective.[24] Even protocol sentences are accepted by a particular scientific community and at a particular time and are therefore—like the hypotheses inferred from these sentences—subject to revision and change. When we evaluate the scientific character of a sentence, he argued, we compare it to the entire system accepted by the scientific community, and not to a pre-linguistic, empirical reality. If the sentence contradicts the system, we discard it as false, or we accept it as true and change the system in order to maintain consistency.[25] Accordingly, Neurath concluded, the theory of meaning as reference—as conceived of by the logical positivists—is no longer plausible.

23. Florensky, "Dialektika," 121.
24. Neurath, "Protocol Sentences," 205.
25. Neurath, "Protocol Sentences," 203.

Meaning as Use: Ordinary Language Philosophy

In the first half of the twentieth century, philosophy of language was mainly concerned with sentence meaning. It considered sentences independent of their use and did not pay attention to the actions speakers or writers perform in using them. The transition from ideal language philosophy to ordinary language philosophy was largely motivated by the discovery of the *pragmatic* dimension of meaning. In the wake of the later Wittgenstein's insight that very often "the meaning of a word is its use in the language,"[26] philosophers such as J. L. Austin, J. Searle, and H. P. Grice significantly widened the scope of philosophy of language. It now became clear that not all sentences describe states of affairs and state facts that are either true or false. The meticulous analysis of the different properties of *utterances*, of *language in use*, brought to the fore a wide range of additional linguistic features that had hitherto escaped scrutiny. If the pragmatic aspect of linguistic meaning is taken seriously, the focus is no longer exclusively on reference, truth, syntax and grammar, but on the *users* and the *context* of language use. Whereas semantics deals with stable and conventional rules of meaning, pragmatics seeks to explain how one and the same sentence can express different meanings in different contexts, and studies features such as ambiguity, indexicality, and conversational implicature.[27] Moreover, speech act theorists distinguish between the propositional content of a speech act (locutionary act), the *action* we perform *in* saying something (illocutionary act), and the *effects* we bring about *by* saying something (perlocutionary act).[28]

Whereas ideal language philosophy has an empiricist, scientistic and anti-metaphysical orientation, ordinary language philosophy is anti-scientistic, and tends to be less hostile to metaphysical questions. Proponents of the latter movement hold that the technical terms of scientific language would be incomprehensible without reference to words with ordinary meanings.[29] Human life and culture, including the sciences, are based on a pre-theoretical understanding of the world. This view brings ordinary language philosophy into proximity to certain strands of Continental

26. Wittgenstein, "Philosophische Untersuchungen" §43 (my translation).

27. Bach, "Pragmatics"; Fotion, "Pragmatics."

28. Austin, *How to Do Things with Words*, 94–108.

29. Martinich, *Ordinary Language Philosophy*.

philosophy.[30] In Phenomenology, key ideas such as *lifeworld* (*Lebenswelt*) and *Dasein* are used to articulate our primordial, non-cognitive and non-epistemic engagement with the world that precedes any reflection on the correspondence, or non-correspondence, of propositions with determinate states of affairs.

Florensky's and Bulgakov's philosophies of language are (in some respects) close to the tradition of ordinary language philosophy and its Continental equivalents. On Florensky's view, scientific discourse and its rigid methods tend to disregard temporality and the inexhaustible semantic depth of reality. Through everyday thinking (*zhiteiskaia mysl'*), everything is always already explained. However, the explanations are generated on an *ad hoc* basis: they occur in an unsystematic and unorderly way, are characterized by ceaseless, arbitrary shifts from object to object, and from one perspective to the next.[31] This lack of method is no problem for philosophy, which strives to achieve a comprehensive and integral understanding of reality. Although philosophy is more abstract than the everyday thinking of people, it springs from the folk soul and not from school philosophy.[32] According to Florensky, philosophy is not the kind of discourse that merely *reminds* us of the primordiality of the contingent, temporal, and pre-cognitive dimension of human existence, while itself remaining an abstract and detached meta-perspective on the world. Philosophy is *itself* a living discourse that models its method on time. *Dialogue* and (Platonic) *dialectic* are the linguistic manifestations of a dynamical, apophatic, Christian philosophy that seeks to penetrate deeper and deeper into the layers of reality, without ever equating its symbolizations with reality itself.[33] Language, which is intrinsically dialectical, entails the "explanation of being."[34] (*ob"iasnenie bytiia*)

The dialectic method embraces the pragmatic dimension of meaning and pays attention to the fact that human discourse is context-dependent. There are no *absolute* formulas that are meaningful outside of any context, Florensky explains; there are no *absolute* judgements, and utterances cannot express *absolute* truth. In order to understand the meaning of an utterance, we must pay attention to the addressee, to the location *where* the

---

30. See, e.g., Braver, *Groundless Grounds*.

31. Florensky, "Dialektika," 119.

32. Florensky, "Obshchechelovecheskie korni idealizma," 147.

33. Florensky, "Dialektika," 123–24.

34. Florensky, "Dialektika," 140 (my translation).

utterance occurs, to the time *when* it occurs, as well as to the purpose of the utterance.[35] Drawing on the work of Aleksandr Potebnia, Florensky distinguishes between the "inner" and the "outer form" of the word, but inverses the meaning of this terminology. For Potebnia, the inner form, the true soul of the word, is the objective, stable, enduring and transpersonal semantic core of a word that can be retrieved by means of etymological analysis. For Florensky, by contrast, this aspect of the word is only its *outer form*, its body, consisting of the phoneme and the morpheme. The *telos* and purpose of the outer form, however, is the inner form of the word, the sememe, which Florensky also calls the soul of the word. The sememe of a word is always determined by the individual speaker and by the particular context in which the utterance occurs as a unique and unrepeatable event.[36]

Florensky and Bulgakov are both *metaxological* thinkers, who philosophize about the *boundary* between immanence and transcendence. The transcendent is grasped in and through the contingencies of the immanent sphere, which means that the flux of time as well as spatial difference and movement are not opposed to the transcendent, but positively *mediate* it. Finitude is viewed as the vehicle of infinitude. The multiplicity of co-existence in the sense of alterity, and the multiplicity of succession in the sense of temporal change and development are *loci* of divine presence and Truth.[37]

Having highlighted some affinities between ordinary language philosophy and Florensky's theory of language, I will now discuss some of the theologically more controversial and problematic aspects of ordinary language philosophy (and its Continental equivalents).

Post-Metaphysical Finitism

In twentieth-century philosophy of language, the (re-)discovery of pragmatics as a central aspect of meaning often turned out to be a continuation, or even radicalization, of a restrictive, *post-metaphysical finitism* that is incompatible with Florensky's and Bulgakov's metaxology. Pragmatics investigates the relationship between the sign and the sign users as well as the finite, spatio-temporal conditions under which the act of interpretation is carried out. And if this aspect of meaning is overemphasized, pragmatics

35. Florensky, "Dialektika," 141.

36. Florensky, "Stroenie slova," 212–20.

37. Florensky, *Stolp i utverzhdenie istiny*, 46.

becomes a linguistic tool to justify and reinforce the post-Kantian opacity of the thing-in-itself. There is, in many cases, a close connection between (a particular interpretation of) pragmatics and post-metaphysical philosophy. I will elucidate this in more detail by giving, first, a brief account of some of the characteristic features of post-metaphysical epistemology. Second, I will explain how post-metaphysical epistemology is (or can be) intertwined with pragmatics by looking at Günter Abel's philosophy of interpretation (*Interpretationsphilosophie*).

According to Quentin Meillassoux, the dominant trend in twentieth-century Continental and (post-)analytic philosophy can be described as *correlationsim*.[38] In the wake of Kant, it is believed that we can only have access to the correlation between thinking and being, but never to either of them taken in isolation. We are told that it is impossible for the human mind to take an external perspective on the act of cognition and to compare the world as it is "in itself" to the world as it is "for us"; to distinguish what results from our relationship with the world from that which only belongs to the world. Truth is no longer conceivable in terms of *adaequatio intellectus ad rem*—for a mind-independent object is epistemically unavailable—but as *intersubjectivity*, as the consensus of a community. In analytic philosophy, the correlation is mediated by language, and in phenomenology—by consciousness. As Meillassoux explains: "Consciousness and its language certainly transcend themselves towards the world, but there is a world only insofar as a consciousness transcends itself towards it."[39] We are always conscious *of something*, and we speak *about something*. It is not denied that there is exteriority, but this exteriority is always already "domesticated," for we must be able to be *conscious* of it, and we must be able to *say* it. On the one hand, language and consciousness disclose reality because they are *world*-constitutive; on the other hand, insofar as they are world-*constitutive*, language and consciousness imprison us, for the outside turns out to be entirely relative, relative to us.

According to Meillassoux, there is an increase of opacity of the thing-in-itself from Kant to the two main representatives of analytic philosophy and phenomenology: Wittgenstein and Heidegger. In Kant, we do not only know that the thing-in-itself exists, but also that it is non-contradictory. Although the thing-in-itself is unknowable, it is at least *thinkable*. Wittgenstein and Heidegger go a step further and claim that the thing-in-itself

38. Meillassoux, *Après la finitude*, 16–24.
39. Meillassoux, *Après la finitude*, 21 (my translation).

is also *unthinkable*. As logicality is metaphysically groundless and thus lacks absolute necessity, it can only serve as a criterion for that which is thinkable for us, but not for that which is possible in the absolute sense. The finitism advocated by Heidegger and Wittgenstein inevitably generates the quasi-religious idea of the "wholly-other." That is, the notion of the "wholly-other" is the inevitable obverse of this finitism. It is the outcome of reason's discovery of its own ability to access the absolute: *the stricter the finitism, the stronger the agnosticism about the absolute.*[40]

In Wittgenstein's *Tractatus*, it is the logical form of the world, the very fact that the world is sayable, that cannot be expressed by logical discourse.[41] Likewise, Heidegger states that "among all beings, only the human being, called upon by the voice of being, experiences the wonder of all wonders: *that* beings *are*."[42] In both Heidegger and Wittgenstein, what eludes metaphysical reason is the fact "that beings are." This facticity, the fact that there is a world, can only be grasped by negative implication. We cannot think the unthinkable, but—as both philosophers seem to presume—we can somehow "know" the internal limits of our world, and we can "think that it is not impossible for the impossible to be."[43] Meillassoux strongly emphasizes the sceptico-fideist character of this understanding of reality. Both Wittgenstein and Heidegger are thus viewed as thinkers, who (re-) discovered our *originary finitude*, and who demolished our misguided, metaphysical illusions.[44] Finitude "*is our fundamental way of being*,"[45] as Heidegger remarks.

Post-Metaphysical Finitism and Pragmatics

Before I return to Florensky and Bulgakov, I will examine how the above outlined notion of human finitude is (in some thinkers) related to pragmatics. On the most basic level, "correlationism" can be interpreted in the sense that our perception and understanding of the world is always already

40. Meillassoux, *Après la finitude*, 68.

41. Wittgenstein, "Tractatus Logico-Philosophicus" 6.44, 522.

42. Heidegger, "Nachwort," 307 (my translation). The original quotation reads as follows: "Einzig der Mensch unter allem Seienden erfährt, angerufen von der Stimme des Seins, das Wunder aller Wunder: *dass* Seiendes *ist*."

43. Meillassoux, *Après la finitude*, 70 (my translation).

44. Braver, *Groundless Grounds*, 223–39.

45. Heidegger, *Fundamental Concepts of Metaphysics*, 6.

mediated by language—a view that merely excludes a naïve realism, but not *any* kind of realism. This leaves the question open as to how precisely semiosis is conceived of. On the one hand, it can be understood within the framework of a linguistic idealism that transforms correlationism into some form of *constructivism*.[46] On the other hand, correlationism can be developed in the direction of more complex and more subtle *realism* (that goes beyond traditional idealism and realism).

In what follows, I will examine Günter Abel's *philosophy of interpretation (Interpretationsphilosophie)*.[47] I will argue that in his approach, pragmatics (or what he calls human interpretive practices) override(s) all other aspects of meaning. And it is an idealist position, because it is based on the principle that "whatever the mind knows the mind itself constitutes or makes,"[48] in the sense that "what the mind knows" is determined by language.

According to Abel, we are always already located in a particular world of interpretation and involved in the interpretative practice of a life-world that discloses reality to us. Distinguishing between different levels of interpretation, he points out that on the most basic level, our language usage fulfils a categorizing and individuating function. On this plane we find the logical concepts of "existence" and "object," spatio-temporal localization, as well as individuation. These components are always already presupposed in every organization of experience. On the highest level, interpretation occurs when we establish theories and hypotheses, or engage in literary exegesis.

The shift from intension to extension must be thought of in pragmatic terms, so that the question of how our words and signs refer to the world becomes obsolete. Abel points out that if our use of signs and our discourses are successful, guided by and imbedded in a well-attuned practice of interpretation, reference to the world is always already ensured. In successful and effective processes of sign-use, world and reality are experienced as immediately present, so that it would be nonsensical to raise the question of how we can reach the world.[49] Meaning is not an occult quality that a sign possesses intrinsically (as in magic), nor is it the result of a merely subjective

---

46. Boghossian, *Fear of Knowledge*.

47. Abel, *Sprache, Zeichen, Interpretation*.

48. Deely, *Four Ages of Understanding*, 691.

49. Abel, *Sprache, Zeichen, Interpretation*, 49.

and arbitrary interpretation on the part of the sign-user or interpreter (as in relativism).[50]

Abel acknowledge that the statement "everything is interpretation" implies that this statement is itself (only) an interpretation. Abel's defense against this possible critique brings to light that his approach is indeed a "linguistification" of Kant's transcendentalism. Abel emphatically points out that philosophy of interpretation is not another absolute or dogmatic philosophy that claims to have a perspective of totality on the world. Rather, as a philosophy of *radical finitude*, it opens up the possibility of a *critique* of any totality.[51] As finite minds, we are not in a position to make definitive, essentialist and universal statements about what exists, and what that which exits essentially is. Thus, the word "everything" in the statement "everything is interpretation" is not to be taken in the metaphysical sense, but has a transcendental meaning. It means that everything that is spatio-temporally located, individuated and identified, is inevitably a product of interpretation—even if, on the most basic level, human consciousness is not aware of the interpretative conditionedness of its perception and knowledge. Consequently, when we say that "everything that is, is interpretation," we are not making a statement about the thing-in-itself, but only about *appearances*.[52]

On the one hand, our interpretive practices delimit what can be regarded as *being* and as *non-being*.[53] On the other hand, that which signs pragmatically "show" to the sign-user—and which cannot be rendered in propositional terms, due to the unsurpassable evidence of this "showing" that renders any further interpretative mediation superfluous—is not based on a "*metaphysical isomorphy*."[54] Rather, that which self-evidently shows itself remains *ontologically neutral*, for the showing results from the interplay between different levels of interpretations and is not rooted in external reality.[55]

Abel's philosophy of interpretation centers on *negative finitude* and is thus closer to a linguistic idealism than to a semiotic realism or meliorism in the sense of C. S. Peirce. A negative finitism sees our finite condition as a

50. Abel, *Sprache, Zeichen, Interpretation*, 176.

51. Abel, *Sprache, Zeichen, Interpretation*, 62.

52. Abel, *Sprache, Zeichen, Interpretation*, 63.

53. Abel, *Sprache, Zeichen, Interpretation*, 182.

54. Abel, *Sprache, Zeichen, Interpretation*, 174 (my translation).

55. Abel, *Sprache, Zeichen, Interpretation*, 184.

hindrance to knowledge, and as a separation from Being.[56] This quasi-sceptical position may appear to be an expression of epistemic modesty, but in fact posits the human being as the center of the world. Peirce's semiotics is more sophisticated and breaks with nominalism that has dominated Western philosophy (of language) from the late middle ages up to the present. Although our perception and understanding of the world is always already mediated by linguistic and non-linguistic signs, this is not to say that our acts of interpretation are merely immanent clarifications of concepts that have no foundation in reality. The view that signs always only refer to other signs, is at once true and false: it is true because we never have immediate, i.e., *un*mediated access to the world-in-itself; but it is false insofar as a "true interpretation" can only possess a truth-value because it has a foundation *in re* that is irreducible to a sign function.[57]

Peirce differentiates between the *immediate* and the *dynamic object*. Whereas the immediate object is the object as represented or cognized in the sign, the dynamic object is that which brings about the representation. In semiosis, the dynamic object fades away and gives way to the immediate object, i.e., to the ensuing interpretations (of the dynamic object). The dynamic object is the *raison d'être* of the concatenation of signs, but is only "present in the mode of absence."[58] Put differently, the dynamic object is gradually replaced by the immediate object, although the former remains present in the latter, thus enabling the interpreter to acquire ever more accurate knowledge. The possibility of this dynamic process is based on the cosmological-metaphysical axiom that there is an affinity between the human mind and the world. Florensky and Bulgakov share this presupposition.

Meaning as Sense: Semantic Realism

According to Bulgakov, genuine cognition is possible in the sense that the abyss between noumenon and phenomenon that dominates a great deal of post-Kantian philosophy can be bridged. In fact, for the Russian thinker, the abyss is always already bridged by everyday language through our acts of *predicating* and *naming* (*imenovanie*). In the act of naming, the copula connects the transcendent *hypokeimenon* or *ousia*, the thing-in-itself, with an immanent predicate, with a word-idea expressing a cosmic mode

56. Gilson, *Metaphysical Presuppositions*, 95.
57. Oehler, "Über Grenzen der Interpretation," 63–66.
58. Oehler, "Über Grenzen der Interpretation," 62 (my translation).

of being. The transcendent-actual (first hypostasis) contemplates itself in immanent being, in the realm of language and ideas (second hypostasis). The first hypostasis manifests itself energetically, by affirming itself through the act of naming, and the copula "is" brings about the unity between the transcendent and the immanent (third hypostasis). The noun (*imia sushchestvitel'noe*) establishes the primordial realism of human language and thinking that is at the same time also an idealism. For the noun and the copula achieve an agglutination of a *res* with an *idea*.[59]

The noun thus stands not only for a quality, a general idea, but also for the general idea's realization in a concrete object.[60] In Bulgakov's sophiolog-ical philosophy of language, words as pure senses and ideas have a general signification and exist independently of any particular being. They consti-tute cosmic potentialities that need to be realized. In a predication, when something is named, the concrete is expressed through the general. Every name, Bulgakov explains, is the concrete use of a general idea. Every name is first an idea and only becomes a name when attributed to a person. Names can thus be characterized as proper-common (*sobstvenno-naritsatel'nye*), or concrete-universal (*konkretno-vseobshchie*).[61] Every being can receive different namings (A, B, C, D . . .), all of which are mediated by the copula "is," and all of which are manifestations of an object's energy. These differ-ent energetic manifestations can be of different intensity, i.e., some of them are more proper than others. The "is" is never absolute. Different ideas can be predicated of one and the same substance, and inversely, one and the same idea can "clothe" different substances.

According to Bulgakov, these infinite possibilities of linguistically mediated interrelationships have an ontological foundation, and are not merely culturally conditioned. The copula expresses the "*world connection of everything with everything*, the cosmic communism of being and the al-truism of each of its elements, i.e., the capacity to express itself through an other."[62] In and through our words, the world itself is speaking, and the human mind is the place of the universe's auto-ideation.[63]

Florensky, too, argues that language is capable of manifesting the cos-mic order, the *logos*, and words or symbols are the *loci* of the encounter

59. Bulgakov, *Filosofiia imeni*, 70.
60. Bulgakov, *Filosofiia imeni*, 48.
61. Bulgakov, *Filosofiia imeni*, 62.
62. Bulgakov, *Filosofiia imeni*, 71 (my translation).
63. Bulgakov, *Filosofiia imeni*, 23.

between the cognizing subject and the cognized object. As mentioned above, Florensky is critical of an overemphasis on language as *ergon* (thingness), as determinate, objective, eternal and trans-temporal *logos*. He seeks to do justice to the pragmatic aspect of meaning, to the insight that language is also *energeia* (activity). Linguistic meaning, he points out, is also indeterminate, dependent on the spontaneous, creative activity of the human mind as well as on contextual factors. But this is not to say that the *logos*-aspect of language can be disregarded. Language is "monumental," the milieu in which we move, the space which we always already indwell as linguistic beings, without which communication would not be possible. For Florensky, there is an *antinomy* between language as *ergon* and language as *energeia*, between language as something pre-given and language as a human activity.[64]

Bulgakov argues along similar lines that theologically, the relationship between language and human beings should neither be thought of in terms of *anthropomorphism*, nor in terms of *conventionalism*. In the former case, it is believed that words, or an entire language, were passively received by human beings from God. In the latter case, only the linguistic capacity is given by God, whereas the words are invented by human beings. Language is thus reduced to a human invention that is only of utilitarian, instrumental and grammatical value.[65] Both these extreme views are implausible according to Bulgakov. Rather, the antinomy of language as *energeia* and language as *ergon* corresponds to the antinomy of freedom and necessity. On the one hand, predicating and naming always involve an act of human will and freedom. Things can be named in different ways, because we can ask different questions about them, but without being able to invent the answers. Bulgakov describes the complex, reciprocal interplay between object and subject as follows: The thing looks at me, and—as it were—asks about itself; but this dialogical encounter cannot take place without my consent and requires an act of free will. Language does never merely passively mirror the world, but must be understood as a living, creative, and ongoing process. Naming is thus in some sense the result of a thing's self-revelation, that is, the thing names itself—although the naming always involves the human being as microcosm.[66]

---

64. Florensky, "Antinomiia iazyka," 144, 53.

65. Bulgakov, *Filosofiia imeni*, 33–34.

66. Bulgakov, *Filosofiia imeni*, 68–69.

The human being's creative work (*tvorchestvo*) is *anthroposophic* (*antroposofiino*): the human being is actively and freely involved in the process of naming, but human creativity is constraint by the regularity (*zakonomernost'*) of the world's sophianicity.[67] Bulgakov's philosophy of language is firmly embedded in his sophiological world view that distinguishes between the Divine and creaturely Sophia.[68] Like Florensky, Bulgakov seeks to think together the contingent, historical, diachronic change and synchronic difference with the eternal and absolute. Words only exist because of the one Word, and idea-senses are rooted in the one Idea-Sense (*Ideia-Smysl*). On the one hand, there is Sophia: the World soul; the Wisdom of the world; the intelligible, ideal foundation of the world; the cosmos. On the other hand, there is our spatio-temporal world, which is the same cosmos, but in a state of becoming (*stanovlenie*) and dissolution in non-being (*nebytie*). Due to the extra-sophianic and even anti-sophianic character of the fallen world, the ideas are never accessible in their purity, but form the ideational foundation of the world.[69] As predicates and ideas, words are rays of the intelligible world that become manifest in the epistemic fogginess of our empirical world. It is the predicative energy, the copula, which serves as the connecting ladder between the two worlds. We name things according to their intelligible image.

For Bulgakov, one noumenal *logos* underlies the diachronic, historical development of one and the same language as well as the synchronic differences between the wide varieties of different languages. It is what he calls the inner word (*vnutrennee slovo*), the sense (*smysl*) that constitutes the inner unity and linguisticality (*iazychnost'*) of the different languages.[70] This sense-aspect was not affected by the Babylonian confusion of languages (Gen 11), which only made it impossible to *understand* the different idioms of language that already existed before. But no new languages were created through this divine intervention. There was already a *plurality* of languages before the Babylonian confusion, but these languages were *one*, in the sense that they were transparent for the underlying *logos*. Bulgakov views Pentecost as the healing of nature, as a (re-)manifestation of the world's primordial, true essence as well as its elevation to a higher level. Pentecost restores the *unity*-in-difference and re-establishes the comprehensibility of the

67. Bulgakov, *Filosofiia imeni*, 69.
68. Bulgakov, *Nevesta agntsa*, 7–88.
69. Bulgakov, *Filosofiia imeni*, 74–75.
70. Bulgakov, *Filosofiia imeni*, 34.

ORTHODOXY AND PHILOSOPHY OF LANGUAGE

phenomenologically, historically, sociologically diverse languages. There is therefore an equivalence between the different languages: they all constitute, though in different ways, the voice of the world and of thought.[71]

Bulgakov's and Florensky's semantic realism flies in the face of the dominant trends in twentieth-century philosophy of language, whose roots can be traced back to the rise of nominalism in the late middle ages, especially to the work of Ockham. The major philosophical movements that came to dominate modernity, rationalism, empiricism, and Kantianism, are all based on nominalist presuppositions. Although empiricism favored sensory impression, rationalism assigned primacy to reason, and Kantianism sought to synthesize the two traditions, all three movements hold that ideas, understood as mental representations, constructed in the interiority of the human mind "wholly constitute the direct and immediate object of human experience."[72] There is a dichotomy between the external world, which remains inaccessible and unknowable, and internal, mental representations, by means of which the human mind depicts this external world. This bifurcation between mind-independent being and mind-dependent knowledge results in a division of ontology and epistemology.

Yet Bulgakov and Florensky by no means stand alone in their quest for a realist philosophy of language. In the twentieth century, it was primarily linguists and semioticians influenced by Charles Sanders Peirce, such as Roman Jakobson or John Deely, who questioned the all-pervasive influence of nominalism in modern Western philosophy of language. Peirce's pragmaticism radically questions the nominalist *Weltanschauung*, which denies the reality of relations, laws and universals outside the sphere of thought, in the realm of mind-independent being.[73] However, he does not propose a naïve realism, where an unmediated encounter with the world in itself is considered possible. Peirce acknowledges that our grasp of the world is always already semiotically and linguistically mediated. But his triadic understanding of the sign achieves a reconciliation of philosophy of being with philosophy of knowledge and renders a clear-cut division between nature and culture implausible. Concomitantly, signification is no longer solely based on conventionally and culturally established codes.

Anthroposemiosis cannot be reduced to language, but comprises all sign processes human beings are involved in. The species-specific linguistic

71. Bulgakov, *Filosofiia imeni*, 38.
72. Deely, *Descartes & Poinsot*, v.
73. Forster, *Peirce and the Threat of Nominalism*.

semiosis of human beings is intricately interwoven with more basic types of perceptual semioses that can also be found in other biological species.[74] In fact, for the human being as *microcosmos*, the semiotic web not only extends to other "animals," but also to the entire physical environment that is replete with virtual signs.[75] But what marks off cultural linguistic activity from these more basic levels of semiosis is the fact that, in mind-dependent being, relations can be formed that are only based on other relations. Linguistic communication is open to infinity insofar as it enables human beings to form relations that are based on other relations that are based on yet other relations, *ad infinitum*.[76] Günter Abel's focus is exclusively on this aspect of anthroposemiosis, which gives his theory of language and interpretation a one-sided and reductive character.

Concluding Remarks

Florensky and Bulgakov take into consideration all three dimensions of linguistic meaning discussed in this chapter: *meaning as reference, meaning as use*, and *meaning as sense*. First, language has the capacity to refer to an extra-linguistic reality. Second, linguistic meaning is to a large extent dependent on temporal and spatio-contextual factors and involves the sign-user or interlocutors. However, these finite and contingent communicative conditions can be viewed as a *vehicle of infinitude* and are not intrinsically tied to metaphysical finitism. Third, naming and predicating are creative human activities, and in the interaction between the object and the interpreter an infinite number of attributes can be predicated of the object. But predicating and naming cannot be reduced to a perspectival and merely culturally conditioned way of talking about the world. Rather, they have an ontological foundation in creation.

Semiotically speaking, Florensky and Bulgakov embrace a *triadic* understanding of semiosis. The linguistic sign stands for an object (reference), and represents this object to somebody, to the sign-user (use). Furthermore, the sign represents the object in some respect, i.e., the object, say A, is interpreted as either B, C, or D . . . (sense). This triadic semiosis has an explicitly trinitarian character: the first hypostasis manifests itself in an act of self-revelation, in the Word, the second hypostasis; and the

74. Deely, *Basics of Semiotics*, 28.

75. Deely, *Basics of Semiotics*, 28, 83–104.

76. Deely, *Purely Objective Reality*, 44.

third hypostasis brings about the unity between the transcendent first and the immanent second hypostases. This triadic, trinitarian understanding of language corresponds to Peirce's differentiation between the object, the representamen, and the interpretant.[77]

However, there is a difference between the two triadic notions of semiosis. In the above-cited passage from Bulgakov's *Philosophy of the Name*, the third hypostasis mediates between the first and the second hypostases. Semiotically speaking, this means that the third hypostasis stands for the relation between the sign and the object that it represents. Theologically speaking, the third hypostasis, the Holy Spirit, is conceived as the *"copula, the living bridge of love between the Father and the Son, the hypostatic Between."*[78] Yet for Peirce, the interpretant is the effect the sign (i.e., the representamen) has on the interpreter. This means that the focus is on pragmatics, on the relation between the sign and the sign-user. Evidently, both the inner-trinitarian relationship between the Father and the Son (semiotically, the relation between the sign and the object it represents), and the relationship between the Son and the spiritually inspired believer[79] (semiotically, the relationship between sign/word and the sign-user) is the fruit of the work of the Holy Spirit.

Florensky's and Bulgakov's approaches transcend the traditional division between realism and idealism. Perception and understanding of the world are always already mediated by signs and language. We can know the world as it is in itself, but due to the apophatic nature of reality, knowledge ensues only in the course of an infinite semiotic process. Predication goes beyond the dichotomy between freedom and necessity, as every act of interpretation involves at once the experience of the world's resistance *and* an act of creativity. In other words, "the sign stands neither in the world of nature nor in the world of culture exclusively, but in the interweaving and the intersection of these together in the world of human experience."[80]

Bibliography

Abel, Günter. *Sprache, Zeichen, Interpretation*. Frankfurt am Main: Suhrkamp, 1999.

77. Peirce, *Collected Papers*, 2:228; *New Elements of Mathematics*, 4:54.

78. Bulgakov, *Comforter*, 181.

79. Bulgakov, *Comforter*, 219–358.

80. Deely, *Purely Objective Reality*, 172. Yet it is possible to distinguish between different kinds of discourses: some are (almost) purely natural while others are (almost) purely cultural.

Austin, J. L. *How to Do Things with Words*. 2nd ed. Oxford: Clarendon, 1975.

Ayer, Alfred J. *Language, Truth, and Logic*. 2nd ed. London: V. Gollancz, 1946.

Bach, Kent. "Pragmatics and the Philosophy of Language." In *The Handbook of Pragmatics*, edited by Laurence R. Horn, et al., 463–87. Malden, MA: Blackwell, 2006.

Boghossian, Paul Artin. *Fear of Knowledge: Against Relativism and Constructivism*. Oxford: Clarendon, 2007.

Braver, Lee. *Groundless Grounds: A Study of Wittgenstein and Heidegger*. Cambridge, Massachusetts: MIT Press, 2012.

Bulgakov, Sergii. *The Comforter*. Grand Rapids: Eerdmans, 2004.

———. *Filosofiia imeni*. Paris: YMCA, 1953.

———. *Nevesta agntsa. O bogochelovechestve*. Vol. 3. Paris: YMCA, 1945.

Carnap, Rudolf. "The Elimination of Metaphysics through Logical Analysis of Language." In *Logical Positivism*, edited by A. J. Ayer, 60–81. New York: Free Press, 1959.

Chapman, Siobhan. *Language and Empiricism: After the Vienna Circle*. Basingstoke: Palgrave Macmillan, 2008.

Coseriu, Eugenio. *Die Geschichte der Sprachphilosophie von der Antike bis zur Gegenwart. Eine Übersicht. Teil I: Von der Antike bis Leibniz*. Tübingen: Gunter Narr, 1969.

Deely, John N. *Basics of Semiotics*. Bloomington, IN: Indiana University Press, 1990.

———. *Descartes & Poinsot: the Crossroad of Signs and Ideas*. Scranton, PA: University of Scranton Press, 2008.

———. *Four Ages of Understanding: the First Postmodern Survey of Philosophy from Ancient Times to the Turn of the Twenty-First Century*. Toronto: University of Toronto Press, 2001.

———. *Purely Objective Reality*. Berlin: Mouton de Gruyter, 2009.

Florensky, Pavel. "Antinomiia iazyka." In *Sochineniia v chetyrekh tomakh*, edited by Andronik Trubachev, et al., 141–84. Vol. 3.1. Moscow: Mysl', 2000.

———. "Dialektika." In *Sochineniia v chetyrekh tomakh*, edited by Andronik Trubachev, et al., 118–41. Vol. 3.1. Moscow: Mysl', 2000.

———. "Nauka kak simvolicheskoe opisanie." In *Sochineniia v chetyrekh tomakh*, edited by Andronik Trubachev, et al., 104–118. Vol. 3.1. Moscow: Mysl', 2000.

———. "Obshchechelovecheskie korni idealizma (filosofiia narodov)." In *Sochineniia v chetyrekh tomakh*, edited by Andronik Trubachev, et al., 145–68. Vol. 3.2. Moscow: Mysl', 2000.

———. *Stolp i utverzhdenie istiny. Opyt pravoslavnoi teoditsei v dvenadtsati pis'makh*. Moscow: Pravda, 1990.

———. "Stroenie slova." In *Sochineniia v chetyrekh tomakh*, edited by Andronik Trubachev, et al., 212–30. Vol. 3.1. Moscow: Mysl', 2000.

Forster, Paul. *Peirce and the Threat of Nominalism*. Cambridge: Cambridge University Press, 2011.

Fotion, Nick. "Pragmatics." In *The Oxford Companion to Philosophy*, edited by Ted Honderich, 23–43. Oxford: Oxford University Press, 1995.

Frege, Gottlob. "Begriffsschrift, a Formula Language, Modeled upon that of Arithmetic, for Pure Thought (1879)." In *Frege and Gödel: Two Fundamental Texts in Mathematical Logic*, edited by Jean Van Heijenoort, 1–82. Cambridge, MA: Harvard University Press, 1970.

Graeser, Andreas. "Aristoteles." In *Klassiker der Sprachphilosophie. Von Platon bis Noam Chomsky*, edited by Tilman Borsche, 33–47. München: C. H. Beck, 1996.

Heidegger, Martin. *The Fundamental Concepts of Metaphysics: World, Finitude, Solitude.* Translated by William McNeill, et al. Bloomington, IN: Indiana University Press, 1995.

———. "Nachwort zu: 'Was ist Metaphysik?'" In *Wegmarken.* edited by Friedrich-Wilhelm von Herrmann, 303–312. GA 9. Frankfurt am Main: Klostermann, 1976.

Hempel, Carl Gustav. "Empiricist Criteria of Cognitive Significance: Problems and Changes." In *Aspects of Scientific Explanation and other Essays in the Philosophy of Science,* edited by Carl Gustav Hempel, 101–119. New York: Free Press, 1965.

Leffler, Oliver. *Wilhelm von Ockham. Die sprachphilosophischen Grundlagen seines Denkens.* Werl: Dietrich-Coelde, 1995.

Leiss, Elisabeth. *Sprachphilosophie.* 2nd ed. Berlin: De Gruyter, 2012.

Lintsbakh, Iakov. *Printsipy filosofskogo iazyka. Opyt tochnogo iazykoznaniia.* Petrograd: Novoe Vremia, 1916.

Martinich, A. P. "Ordinary Language Philosophy." *Routledge Encyclopedia of Philosophy.* Online. 1998. https://www.rep.routledge.com/articles/thematic/ordinary-language-philosophy/v-1/sections/paradigm-case-arguments.

McGee, Vann. "Truth." In *The Blackwell Guide to the Philosophy of Language,* edited by Michael Devitt, et al., 392–410. Malden, MA: Blackwell, 2006.

Meillassoux, Quentin. *Après la finitude. Essai sur la nécessité de la contingence.* Paris: Seuil, 2006.

Neurath, Otto. "Protocol Sentences." In *Logical Positivism,* edited by A. J. Ayer, 199–208. New York: Free Press, 1959.

Nöth, Winfried. *Handbook of Semiotics. Advances in Semiotics.* Bloomington, IN: Indiana University Press, 1995.

Oehler, Klaus. "Über Grenzen der Interpretation aus der Sicht des semiotischen Pragmatismus." In *Zeichen und Interpretation,* edited by Josef Simon, 57–72. Frankfurt am Main: Suhrkamp, 1994.

Peirce, Charles S. *The Collected Papers of Charles Sanders Peirce.* Edited by Charles Hartshorne, et al. Vol. 2. Cambridge, MA: Harvard University Press, 1932.

———. *The New Elements of Mathematics.* Edited by Carolyn Eisele. 4 vols in 5. The Hague: Mouton & Co., 1976.

Rorty, Richard. "Introduction: Metaphilosophical Difficulties of Linguistic Philosophy." In *The Linguistic Turn: Recent Essays in Philosophical Method. With Two Retrospective Essays,* edited by Richard Rorty, 1–39. Chicago: University of Chicago Press, 1992.

———. "Twenty-Five Years After." In *The Linguistic Turn: Recent Essays in Philosophical Method. With Two Retrospective Essays,* edited by Richard Rorty, 371–74. Chicago: University of Chicago Press, 1992.

Smith Gilson, Caitlin. *The Metaphysical Presuppositions of Being-in-the-World: A Confrontation between St. Thomas Aquinas and Martin Heidegger.* New York: Continuum, 2010.

Wittgenstein, Ludwig. "Philosophische Untersuchungen." In *Tractatus Logico-Philosophicus. Tagebücher 1914-16. Philosophische Untersuchungen,* by Ludwig Wittgenstein, 225–580. Frankfurt am Main: Suhrkamp, 1995.

———. "Tractatus Logico-Philosophicus." In *Tractatus Logico-Philosophicus. Tagebücher 1914-16. Philosophische Untersuchungen,* by Ludwig Wittgenstein, 7–85. Frankfurt am Main: Suhrkamp, 1995.